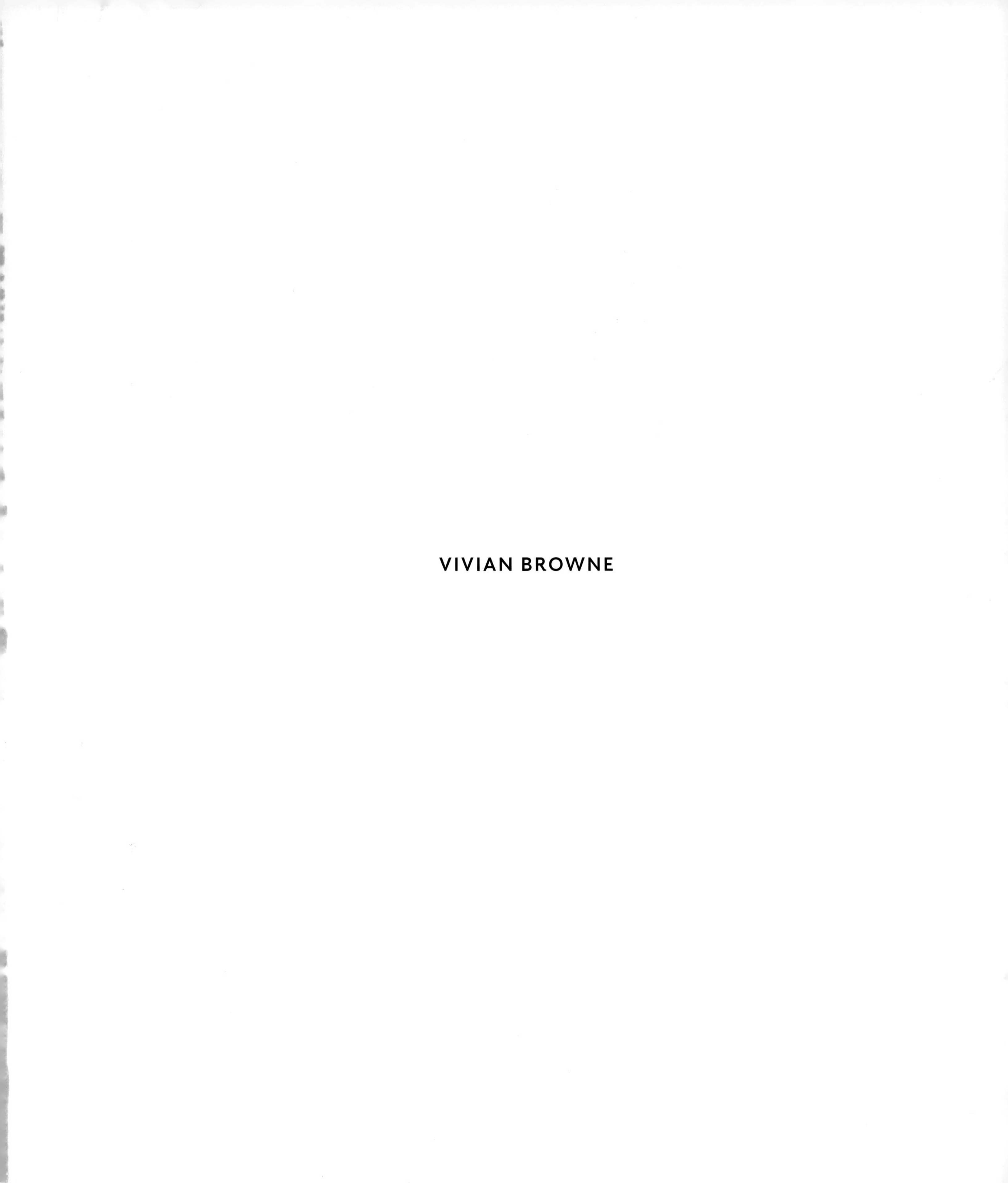

VIVIAN BROWNE

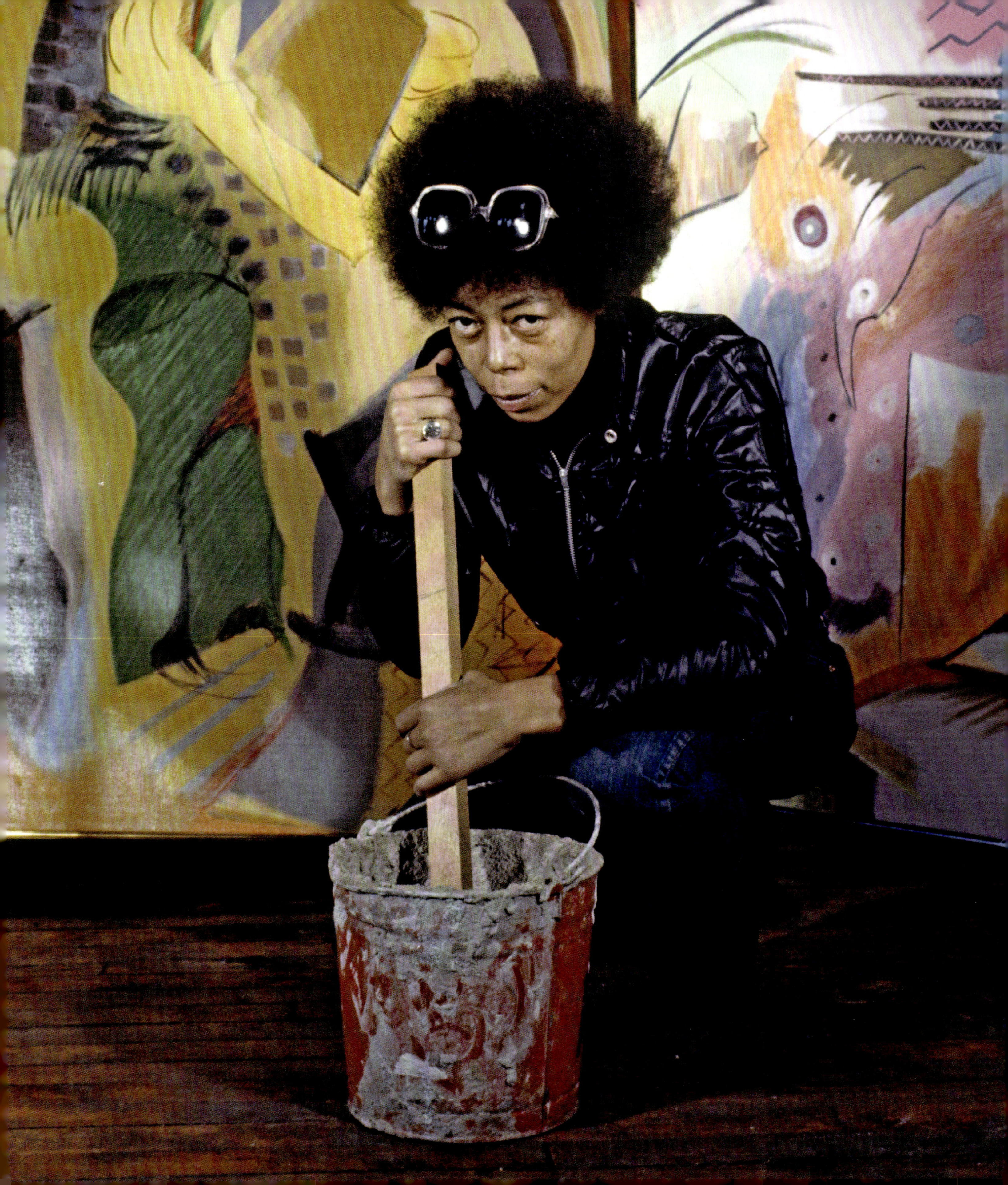

VIVIAN BROWNE
My Kind of Protest

Edited by Amara Antilla and Adrienne L. Childs

Contributions by Amara Antilla, Adrienne L. Childs,
Darby English, Ethel Renia, and Lowery S. Sims.
With Forewords by Christina Vassallo, Alice & Harris
Weston Director of Contemporary Arts Center,
and Jonathan P. Binstock, Vradenburg Director
& CEO of The Phillips Collection

The Phillips Collection, Washington, DC
In association with D Giles Limited

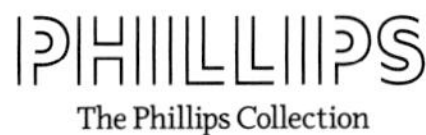

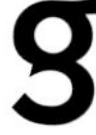

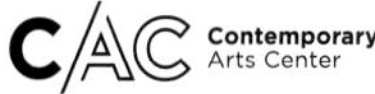

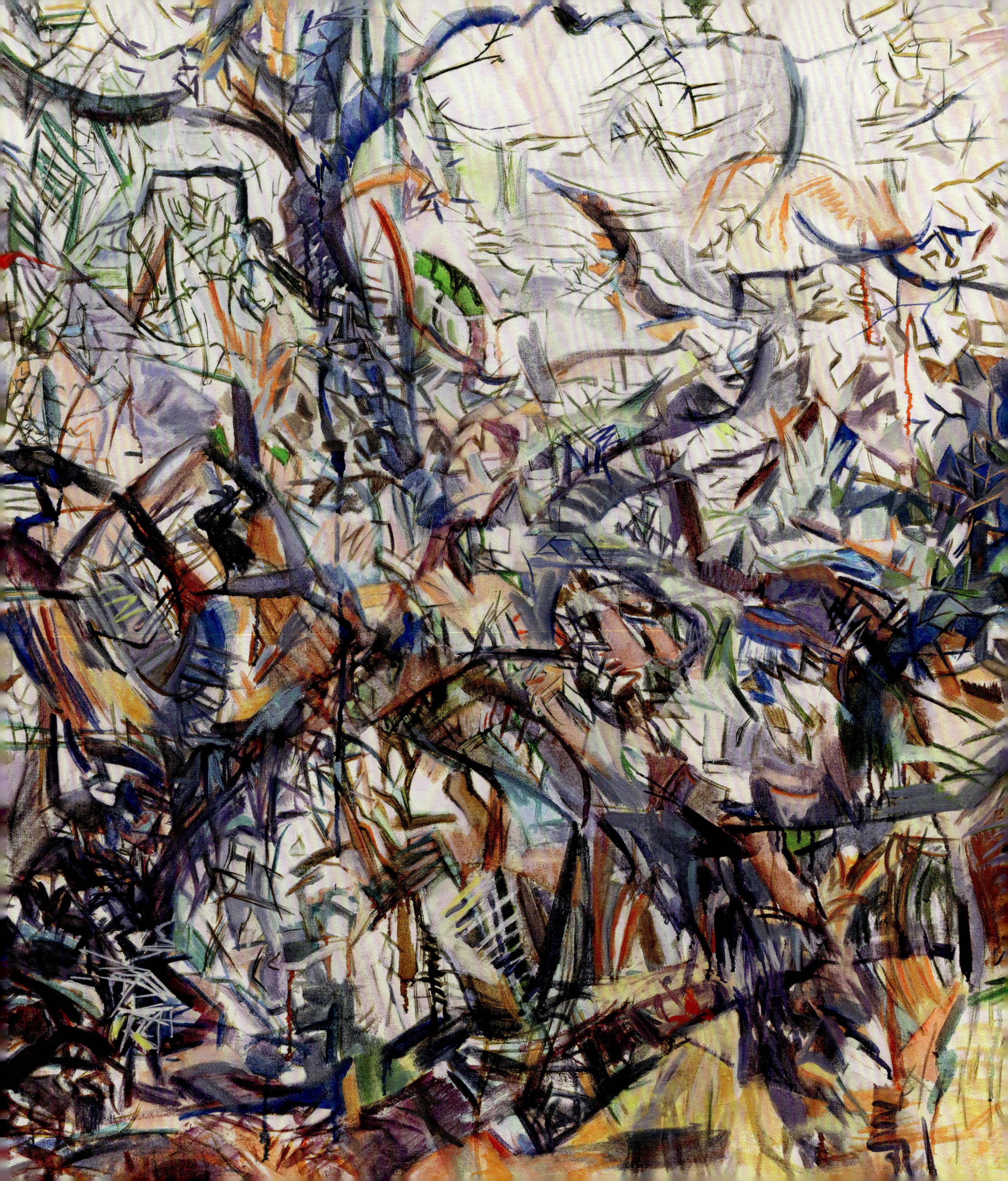

Contents

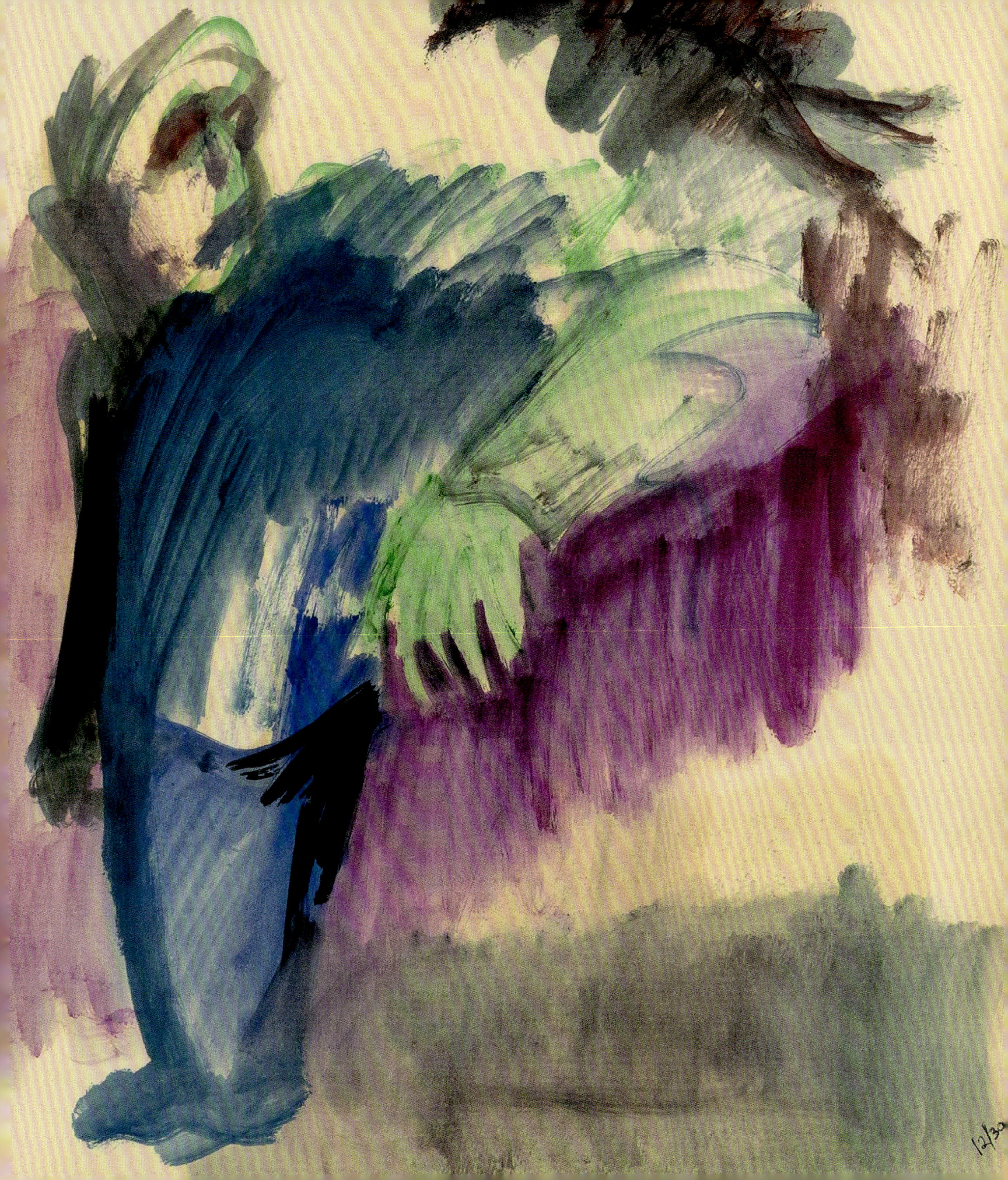
12/30

Director's Foreword

Christina Vassallo, Alice & Harris Weston Director
Contemporary Arts Center, Cincinnati, OH

The Contemporary Arts Center (CAC) is a lab for understanding ourselves, others, and the world around us through the experience and creation of all contemporary art forms. Why, then, would the CAC initiate the planning of an exhibition, in 2021, of the work of Vivian Browne—an understudied American artist and activist who died in 1993?

The themes present in Browne's work continue to resonate today and inform current conversations about power, political systems, and the importance of intersectional feminism. *Vivian Browne: My Kind of Protest* is the first comprehensive museum retrospective to examine how the artist engaged a multitude of cultural and social issues. Through her practice and her activism, Browne provided critical portrayals of whiteness, examined the ways in which the Black Power movement reinforced patterns of patriarchy, and called for alternatives to mainstream feminist discourse which centered the white middle class.

As I write this foreword, we are only months away from a U.S. presidential election and I find it impossible to cleave the exhibition from this context. Browne's quote from a 1968 interview with curator and art critic Henri Ghent is a prescient warning about the current political climate: "When you consider the office of president, you know, the first thing I can say is, 'How can anybody want to do that? …' And after considering that question there must be something in that man … that's a little bit Napoleonic or hypo-egocentric searching and needing power to want to do that. So how can you believe them?"[1] This interview was conducted as the artist created her *Little Men* series of paintings, between 1966 and 1969, comprising satirical portraits of infantilized men, some of which are included in *Vivian Browne: My Kind of Protest*. One can hear the echoes of Browne's frustrations in the late 1960s pervade today's political discourse of seemingly unresolvable differences between our two dominant political parties and the men within them. In August, Kamala Harris clinched the Democratic presidential nomination, making her the first woman of color to lead a major party ticket. Despite this momentous achievement, she was only granted this opportunity after Joe Biden belatedly withdrew from the race. Though Harris's nomination may mark the beginning of the dismantling of our patriarchal political system, it is also representative of how US politics continues to be in the hands of men unwilling to give up their power.

For her consideration of the powers at play, I am grateful for the opportunity to present a cross-section of Vivian Browne's work to the distinct audiences of the CAC and those of our exhibition co-organizer, The Phillips Collection.

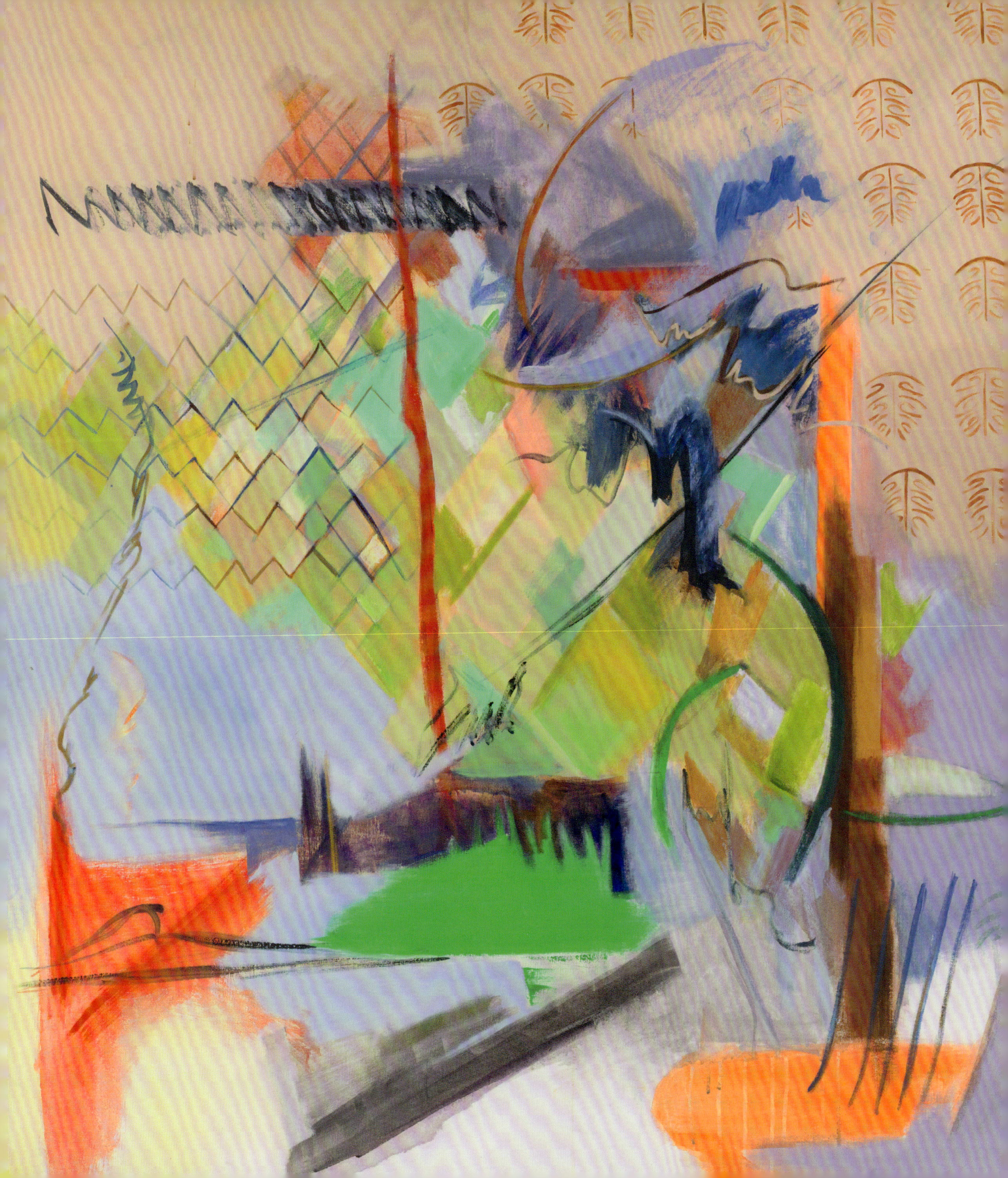

Director's Foreword

Jonathan P. Binstock, Vradenburg Director & CEO
The Phillips Collection, Washington, DC

The Phillips Collection has long been an incubator for American artists like Vivian Browne who innovate, motivate, and challenge the status quo. Browne, an under-recognized painter working from the 1960s through the early 1990s, defies categorization and challenges us to reconsider what it meant to be a Black female activist artist in an era of dynamic change in the American art world. We are proud to present the landmark exhibition *Vivian Browne: My Kind of Protest* in partnership with the Contemporary Arts Center in Cincinnati, Ohio. The exhibition brings together for the very first time the breadth and depth of Browne's work across the expanse of her four-decade-long career. As her practice developed, Browne worked in distinct series that reflected her social, political, personal, and aesthetic concerns. The exhibition features expressionistic character studies from her *New Yorkers* and *Little Men* series, and deeply considered aesthetic meditations on form and color from her *Africa Series* and *China Series*. We also present a body of work executed toward the end of Browne's career when she became immersed in the majesty of the California landscape, its cultural histories, and its tense relationship with technology.

While many of her colleagues and associates such as Faith Ringgold, Benny Andrews, Emma Amos, and Howardena Pindell have been recognized for their important activism and artistry by histories of American art—particularly Black art—Browne has gone virtually unrecognized in this story. Recent exhibitions of the *Little Men* series (2019) and the *Africa Series* (2022) at RYAN LEE Gallery in New York have garnered Browne renewed attention. Exhibition co-curators Amara Antilla and Adrienne L. Childs came together with the Contemporary Arts Center in Cincinnati, RYAN LEE Gallery, and the Adobe Krow Archives, administered by Browne's extended family, to embark on an exhibition project to revisit, explore, and amplify Browne's singular creative vision. We at The Phillips Collection felt strongly about supporting this important project as co-organizers. *Vivian Browne: My Kind of Protest* features previously unknown paintings, prints, drawings, and archival materials meticulously preserved by the artist's estate. We are excited to introduce Vivian Browne's dynamic body of work to our visitors and to explore how it enhances our understanding of the complexity of American art and its diverse histories. We hope it will connect to today's audiences interested in issues of feminism, power and politics, race, gender, and the spirit of the natural environment.

Acknowledgments

Christina Vassallo, Alice & Harris Weston Director,
Contemporary Arts Center, Cincinnati, OH

Jonathan P. Binstock, Vradenburg Director & CEO,
The Phillips Collection, Washington, DC

We would like to first extend our deepest gratitude to the collectors, directors, curators, and scholars who have so generously facilitated the loans of the works and shared the knowledge and research that have made this exciting presentation of Vivian Browne's artistic career possible. In particular we would like to thank the artist's family, including Vickiy Strutt-Hackman, Jon Hackman, and Ken Hackman. We add our deepest appreciation to Mary Ryan, Daisy Fornengo, Mikhail Mishin, Luke Austin, Lisette Fischer, and Jeffrey Lee of RYAN LEE Gallery, for partnering with us to support the evolution of this exhibition and catalogue. We thank Adobe Krow Archives and Hatch-Billops Archives for their generous sharing of precious archival material in support of this project. In preparing artworks for this exhibition, we owe a debt of thanks to Ashton Allen for assessing the works in Los Angeles, and Joe Protheroe and Thomas Baldwin for coordinating the conservation and shipment of the works. For their deep understanding of how salient Browne's concerns are for contemporary art audiences, we thank the exhibition's co-curators, Amara Antilla and Adrienne L. Childs.

The Contemporary Arts Center would like to thank all staff and board members, for their long-standing devotion to the art and ideas of our time, especially Board Officers Jeff Ahrnsen, Amy Goodwin, Rick Michelman, Kyle Pohlman, and Gale Beckett, who worked alongside members of the exhibitions department, Rebecca Roman-Sutton, Director of Exhibitions; Theresa Bembnister, Curator; David Dillon, Head of Media Arts; former Curatorial Assistant Erin Adelman; and Tyler Hamilton, Director of Installations & Facilities, who leads our team of Art Handlers, Clay Brown, Kara Daniel, Hannah Parrett, Cody Schriever, and Sara Torgison. We also wish to recognize our education department, including Shawnee Turner, Chief of Interpretation and Experience;

Elizabeth Hardin-Klink, Creativity Center Director; Nytaya Babbitt, Community & Adult Programs Manager; Shawn Braley, Teen Programs Manager; Krista King-Oaks, School Program & Tours Manager; and L.D. Nehls, Creative Learning Educator. Additional thanks go to Carolyn Hefner, Chief of External Affairs; Shannon Morris, Director of Donor Experience; Autumn R. Stiles, former Assistant Director of Development; Chloe Cecil, Development Manager; Marcus Margerum, former Deputy Director & Chief Business Officer; Aly Laughlin, former Human Resources Director; Chevonne Childs, Rentals & Events Manager; Aspen Stein, former Visitor Experience Associate & Education Assistant; Kelsey Robinson, Visitor Experience & Store Manager; as well as our Visitor Experience Associates, Docents, Facility Technician and Custodians, and Security Specialists and Security Staff.

At The Phillips Collection, we wish to thank our Board of Trustees, led by John Despres, for their enthusiastic support of this exhibition. We would also like to thank all the museum's staff for their tireless work in support of this project. Our deepest gratitude to Grace McCormick, Curatorial Assistant, for her careful, dedicated oversight of the catalogue's production. Special thanks to Elsa Smithgall, Chief Curator; Bradley Freedman, Chief Operating Officer; Cheryl Nichols, Chief Financial Officer; Angela Gillespie, Director of Human Resources; Yuma I. Tomes, Horning Chair for Diversity, Equity, Access, and Inclusion; Nehemiah Dixon III, Director of Phillips@THEARC; the entire education team, including Ashley Whitfield, Director of Public Programs and Anne Taylor Brittingham, former Deputy Director for Education and Responsive Learning Spaces; Elizabeth Steele, Head of Conservation; Patricia Favero, Conservator; Alexandra Schuman, Manager of Exhibitions and Curatorial Projects; Kathryn S. Rogge, former Manager of Exhibitions; Sarah Perdue, Associate Registrar for Exhibitions; Michele De Shazo, Senior Registrar for Collections; Renée Littleton, Chief Communications Officer and Director of Marketing; Vivian Djen, Head of Editorial and Design Services; Emily Ames, Marketing Manager; Lauryn Cantrell, Publicist; Collin Warren, Head of Digital Experience; Elizabeth Racheva, Chief Advancement Officer, and the entire Advancement staff, including Bridget Zangueneh, Director of Foundation, Government, and Corporate Affairs; Maglyn Bertrand, Grants Manager; Sarah Hyde, Director of Major and Planned Giving; Lauren Sharrock, Director of Membership; Victoria Potucek, Director of Advancement Operations; and Jessica Teaford, Director of Advancement Events; Pete Bernal, Head of Retail Operations and Guest Services; Steve Bernal, Security Operations Manager and his dedicated security team; Caitlin Hoerr, Chief of Staff and Board Liaison; Meredith Magnuson, Executive Assistant to the Director; Huy Huynh, Chief Engineer; Alec MacKaye, Chief Preparator; Carson Garhart, Preparator; Matthew Harmon, Associate Preparator; and dRi Guillen, Assistant Preparator.

We are also deeply grateful to the scholars who have contributed such engaging essays to the catalogue: Darby English, Carl Darling Buck Professor of Art History, University of Chicago; and Lowery S. Sims, independent curator and art historian; and to Ethel Renia, former Assistant Director of Research and Communications at RYAN LEE Gallery and current art history graduate student at the Courtauld Institute of Art, for her informative comprehensive artist chronology. We are grateful to Dan Giles, Allison McCormick, and Louise Ramsay of D Giles Limited, for producing this beautiful publication and for guiding it smoothly through design and production. A special thanks to Jenny Wilson for her diligent copy editing; and to Ocky Murray for his creative design.

A venture like this could not have been realized without generous sponsors, who for this exhibition include the Mellon Foundation, the National Endowment for the Arts, Terra Foundation for American Art, the Emily Hall Tremaine Foundation, Reid Walker, and the Andy Warhol Foundation for the Visual Arts. Their commitment to this project has enabled and encouraged our explorations into art of the recent past that continues to resonate today.

Illustrated Timeline

Ethel Renia

1929

Vivian Elaine Browne is born on April 26 in Laurel, Florida. Two months later, she and her family relocate to Jamaica, Queens.

1950

Browne graduates with a Bachelor of Arts in Fine Arts from Hunter College in New York, and plans to be an art teacher.

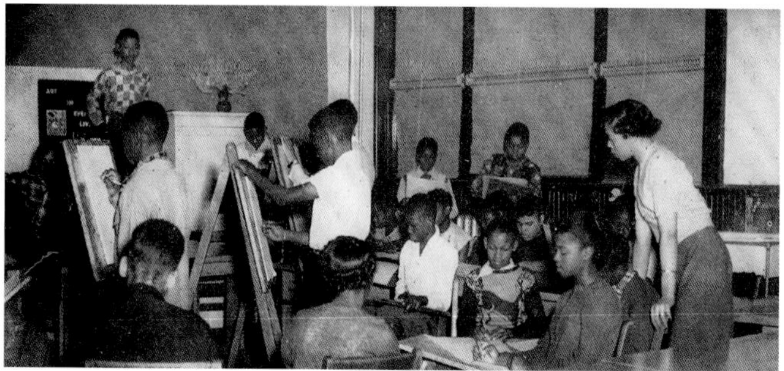

Vivian Browne teaching art at the Booker T. Washington High School, 1952

1951–53

Browne moves to Columbia, South Carolina, to teach at the segregated Booker T. Washington High School, where she works for two years.

1953

Browne quits her job as a teacher in South Carolina and moves back to New York, where she works as a secretary for women ministers.

1950s

Browne receives a scholarship from the New School for Social Research in New York, which enables her to attend a painting workshop in the Berkshires for two summers.

"In the mid-1950s," she crosses paths with renowned artists Romare Bearden, Jacob Lawrence, and Norman Lewis.[2] The latter two become good friends and mentors of hers.

1955

Browne travels to England, France, and Italy. This is her first time leaving the United States and marks the first of many important experiences abroad.

"Negroes didn't at that time travel much. And I know one of the reasons, you just couldn't get accommodations and couldn't be comfortable…. But after being in England for a while I began to come out a little bit, and I found that in Europe you are not a Negro. You're a person. And that was, oh, that was just a wonderful, wonderful experience. I didn't want to come home."[3]

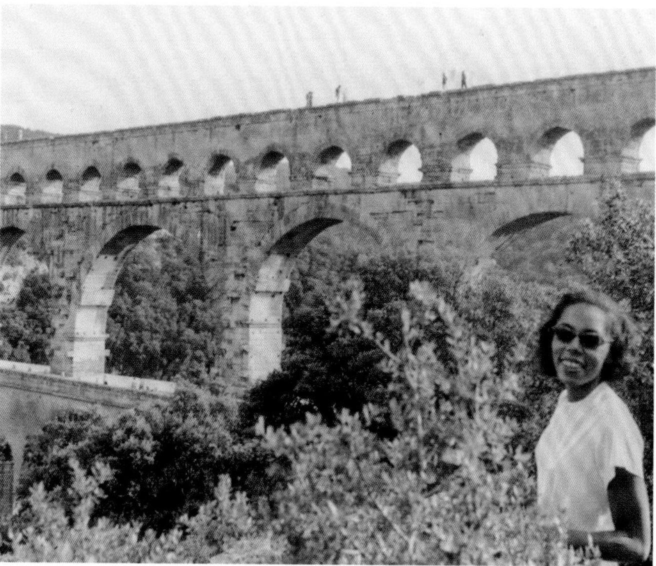

Vivian Browne in front of the Pont du Gard in the south of France, 1955

c. 1955

Browne moves into her own apartment in Greenwich Village.

1955–64

Browne returns to teaching in Bayside, Queens. In total, she teaches in public schools across New York and South Carolina for eleven years. She loves to teach, but hates the restrictive administrative trappings of the profession.

1959

Browne completes her Master of Fine Arts degree from Hunter College.

1964

Browne is awarded a six-month fellowship at the Huntington Hartford Foundation in southern California. She considers this experience life-changing. Here, she meets the artist Camille Billops.

"I knew what it meant to spend every day all day on painting from that experience. I knew that, and when I came back to the high school situation … I also knew that I couldn't do that. So, I quit."[4]

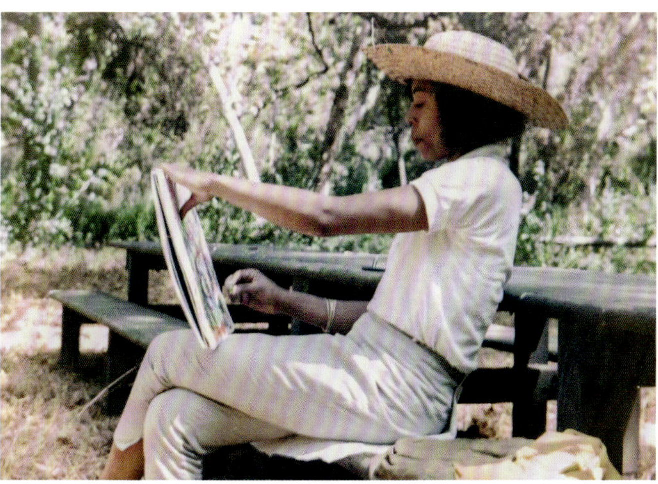

Vivian Browne sketching at the Huntington Hartford Foundation, 1964

1965

Browne exhibits with the important Black artists collective Spiral at the Sixth Annual Arts Festival at Temple Emanu-El in Yonkers, New York. Browne and the artist Emma Amos are the only two women included in the exhibition.

1966–71

Browne accepts an art supervisor position at New York's Board of Education, thinking it will only last six months. She stays there for five years. Her experiences prove fertile ground for her *Little Men* series.

"I was art supervising, I continued to paint these little men. Because the people I ran into were superintendents, and principals, and coordinators, and people of that ilk who were busily trying to preserve some small, teenie weenie little place in their lives where they were important. And not putting in for that importance. They were just important people—they thought. And it was like little men playing games all the time. That's not how I started painting those little men but that's how it ended up."[5]

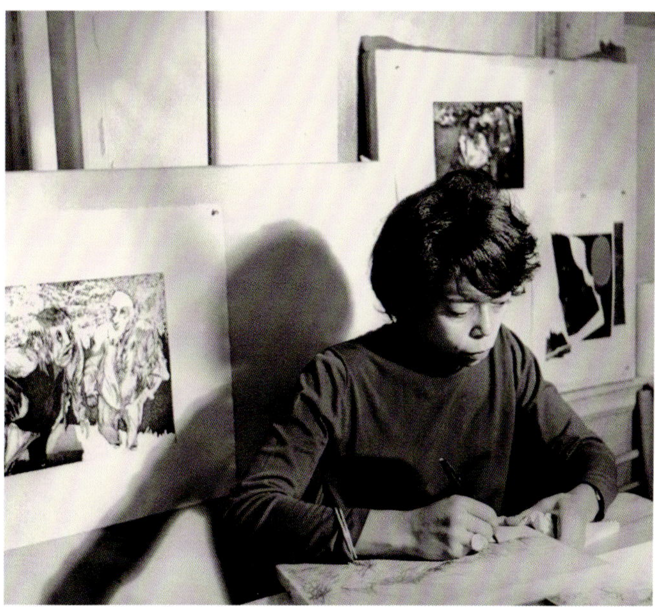

Vivian Browne in her studio, c. 1970

Browne's *Little Men* series includes over 200 works on paper and oil paintings on canvas. She paints furiously, digging into her subject, creating hundreds of sketches in just four months. This is her first major series.

Browne begins to experiment with etchings. Finding that she has little time to paint while working a full-time job, she takes a printmaking class. "I … relate to this medium very well. It has a certain strength in and of itself…. And etching has helped me see so much in my painting."[6]

1968

Browne, along with Henri Ghent and Faith Ringgold, protests the Whitney Museum of American Art's exhibition *The 1930's: Painting & Sculpture in America* for its omission of Black artists. They are joined by Benny Andrews, and other important members of what would become the Black Emergency Cultural Coalition (BECC). Following the protest, Browne co-curates a counter-exhibition entitled *Invisible Americans: Black Artists of the '30s* at the Studio Museum in Harlem.

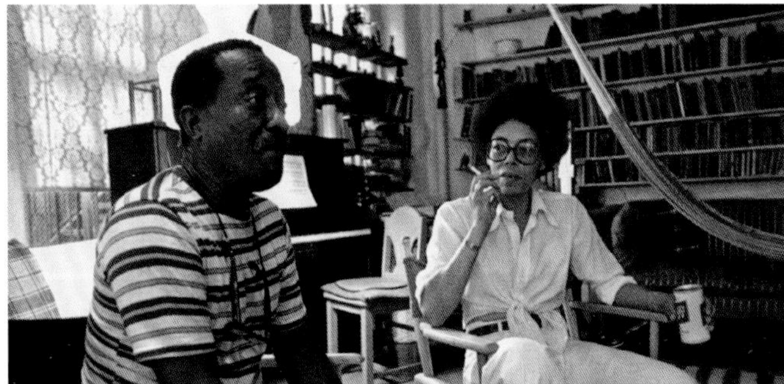

Vivian Browne interviewing Norman Lewis as part of the Hatch-Billops Oral History of Black Culture series, 1972

That same year, Martin Luther King, Jr. is assassinated, and Browne is deeply impacted. She is included in the exhibition *In Honor of Dr. Martin Luther King* at the Museum of Modern Art, New York.

That summer, Browne travels to Portugal, Spain, Italy, and France.

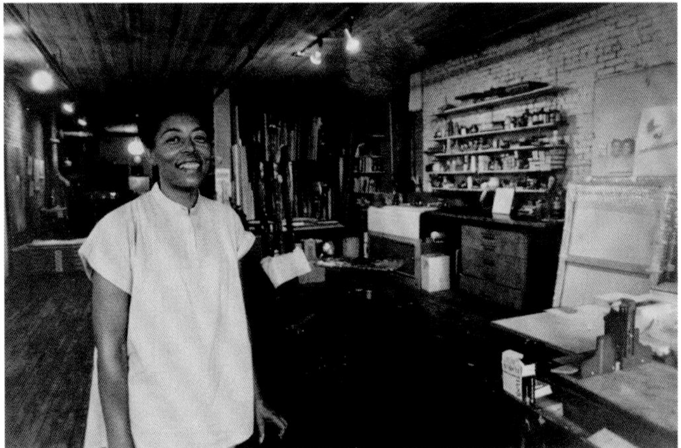

Vivian Browne in her loft at 451 West Broadway, 1981

Browne acquires her loft at 451 West Broadway with the help of her friend and mentor, Norman Lewis. She will maintain this address for the rest of her life.

1969

Browne is a founding member of the BECC. This organization posits to fight anti-Black discrimination within the art world. A statement from the group declares: "The Black Emergency Cultural Coalition came into being in January 1969 in response to what its founders deemed a travesty of the cultural ethics of the Metropolitan Museum of Art, an institution invested with the guardianship of society's cultural integrity."[7]

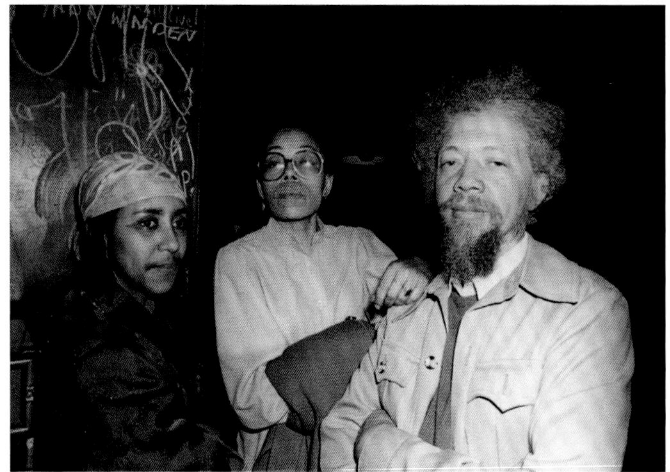

Camille Billops, Vivian Browne, and Benny Andrews at the Broome Street Bar in New York's SoHo, 1976

1971

1971 is a landmark year for Browne. She makes her first trip to Africa: she and the painter and scholar Floyd Coleman travel to Ibadan, Nigeria, where Browne studies at the University of Ibadan for six weeks. They make excursions to Lagos and Ghana. Following this trip, Browne begins her *Africa Series*, a body of work that reflects the vigor and emotion she felt upon her return to the U.S. This series marks a shift toward abstraction in her work. She switches to acrylics to accommodate the speed at which she is working.

The backdrop of this artistic breakthrough includes several professional accomplishments and an ever-deepening engagement with her community. This is the year that she becomes involved in the National Conference of Artists—

today considered the oldest African American visual arts organization in continuous operation in the United States. She and other artists debate what defines so-called 'Black art.' Browne's take on the issue is as follows:

"I think that if an artist is Black, and that artist is honest and is concerned with integrity in his or her work, then he will paint his experience. Now, if he's Black, it's a Black experience. And that's sort of simplistic, but I think it's very, very true. It is something that has to be accounted for, though, and that is that the Black experience is not the same for everyone. It's not a universal."[8]

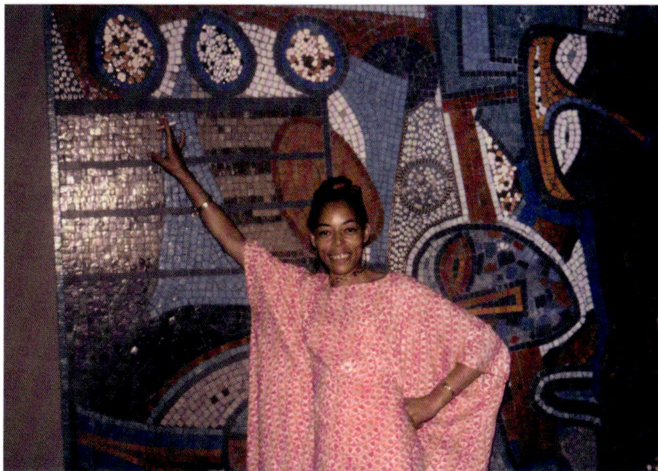

Vivian Browne in Nigeria, 1971

The Whitney mounts a controversial exhibition of contemporary Black artists following years of negotiation with the BECC. However, the BECC's demand for Black curatorial input is not met. As a result, Browne participates in the counter-exhibition at Acts of Art Gallery entitled *Rebuttal to the Whitney Museum Exhibition*.

She is also included in *Black Women Artists – 1971*, likewise at Acts of Art Gallery. This was the debut exhibition of Where We At, an important group of women artists led by founder Kay Brown, along with Dindga McCannon and Faith Ringgold.

Browne joins the art faculty at Rutgers University in Newark, New Jersey, as an Assistant Professor of fine art and art history. She is hired shortly after student uprisings, and teaches a newly established course about African American art history.

Following the prison rebellion at Attica, Browne paints *The Prisoner* for the artist book *Attica*, co-edited by Benny Andrews and the artist Rudolf Baranik, of the Artists and Writers Protest Against the War in Vietnam.

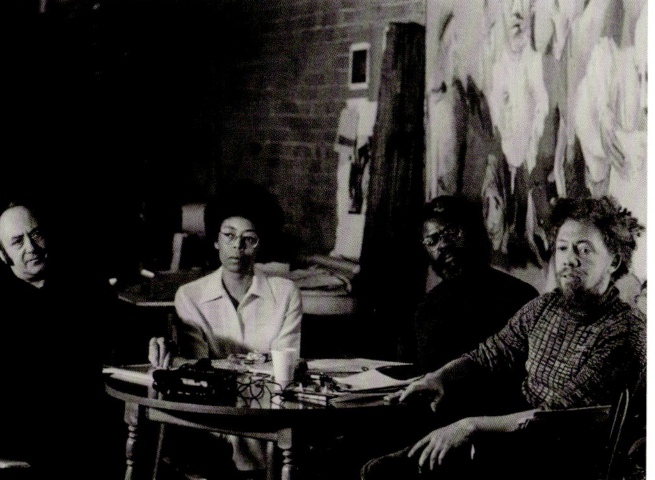

Rudolf Baranik, Vivian Browne, Cliff Joseph, and Benny Andrews working on the Attica publication at Browne's loft, 1972

The BECC begins a teaching program for prisoners and shifts its organizational focus to prison rights. Browne teaches at The Tombs, which is the colloquial name for the Manhattan Detention Complex, a municipal jail in lower Manhattan.

The same year, she and her BECC co-director Cliff Joseph exhibit in a two-person show, *1 to One: Beginnings of Unity*, at Countee Cullen Library, New York. The exhibition tackles gender disparity within the Black artistic community. "We were searching for a title describing getting together as Black males and females in this sexist society," Joseph explained. "Women are not given due recognition … we combined our talents … 'one to one.'"[9]

1973
Browne is the subject of her first solo exhibition, *African Memories*, organized by Rhode Island College.

In a bid to stage the exhibition he had urged the Whitney Museum to mount two years prior, Benny Andrews curates *BLACKS:USA:1973*. Browne is included in this exhibition of works by Black artists, curated by a Black artist.

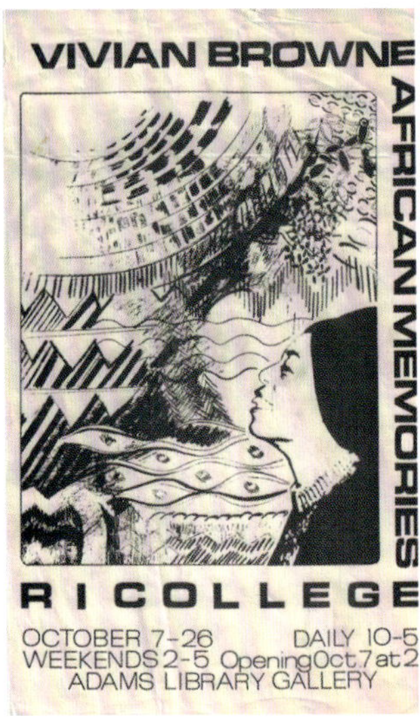

Exhibition poster for *Vivian Browne: African Memories*, Rhode Island College, 1973

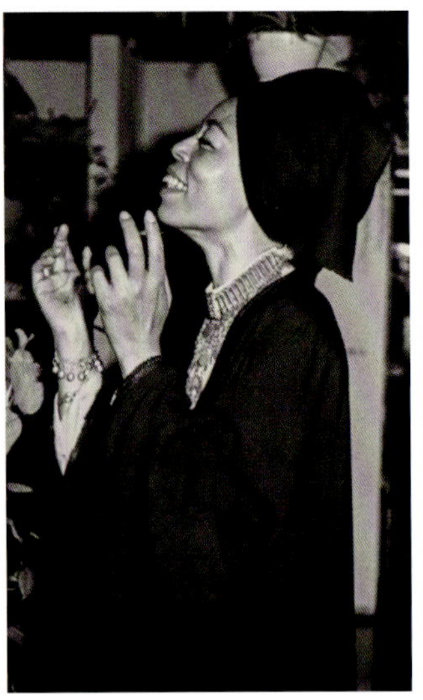

Vivian Browne, c. 1973

1974

Browne has her first solo exhibition in New York City, held at the famed jazz musician Ornette Coleman's Artist House—a multi-disciplinary arts and jazz loft in SoHo. Artist House was a pioneering site that served as a nucleus of interracial artistic activity throughout the 1960s and '70s.

Browne is included in *Synthesis*, the inaugural exhibition of Just Above Midtown—an art gallery led by Linda Goode Bryant—which foregrounded artists of color. Browne exhibits alongside Camille Billops, David Hammons, Norman Lewis, and Elizabeth Catlett, among others.

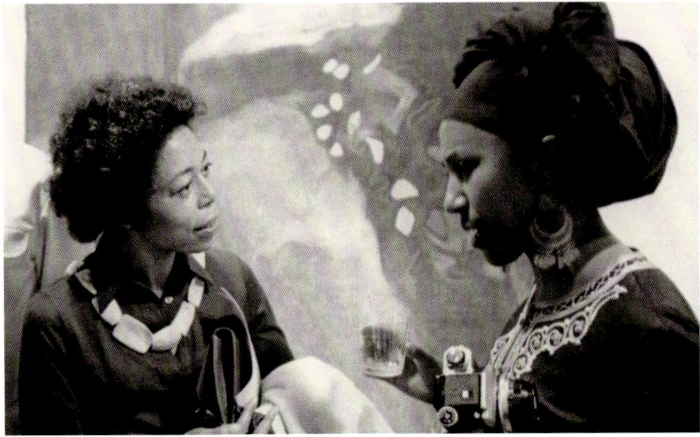

Vivian Browne and Camille Billops in front of *For You* (c. 1974) on the opening night of *Synthesis*, Just Above Midtown, 1974

1975

Browne is included in *Women I*, a traveling exhibition organized by the Robert Blackburn Printmaking Workshop.

Browne is promoted to Chairperson/Associate Professor of the Visual Arts Department at Rutgers University.

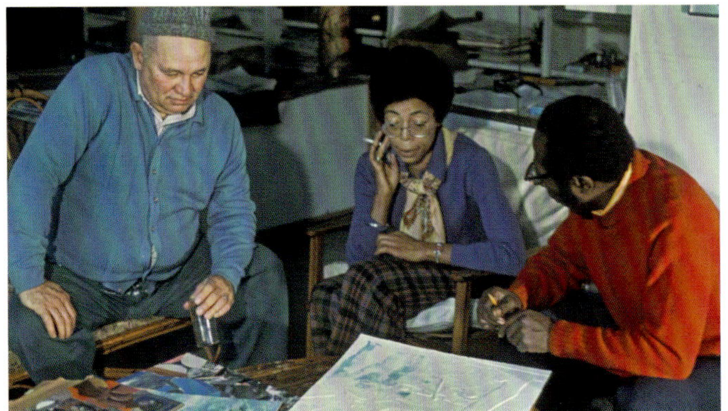

Romare Bearden, Vivian Browne, and Robert Blackburn reviewing a print, c. 1972

1976

The Whitney organizes an exhibition titled *Three Centuries of American Art*, which includes in its triple-centennial retrospective of American art the work of only one woman, and no Black artists. Browne and members of the BECC gather to picket the show.

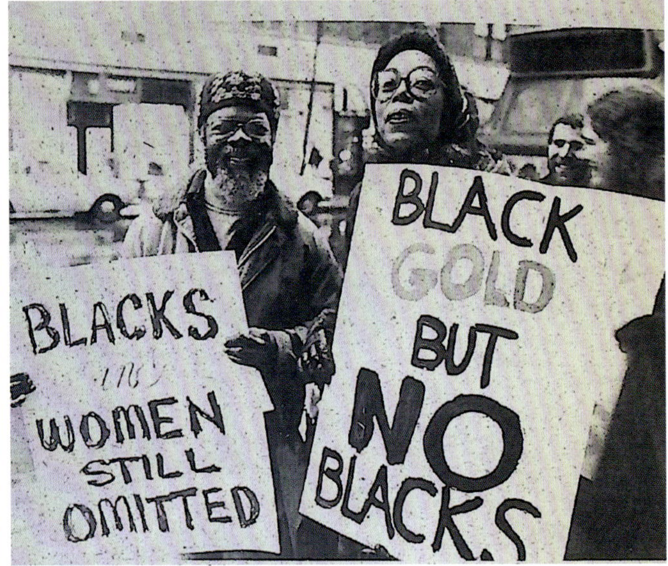

Cliff Joseph and Vivian Browne picketing the Whitney Museum, 1976

Browne is included in *6 Black American Woman Artists* at the
Black Student Union and The Art Guild in Bergen, New Jersey.
Local exhibitions such as these—frequently organized by
fellow women of color, or friends within feminist and Black
empowerment circles—constitute the bulk of exhibitions in
which artists such as Browne participate.

1977

Browne becomes the first African American woman to be
formally invited by the Chinese government to visit China
as part of a delegation of American artists and crafters.
Browne is selected to represent American "women and
Black artists."

This inspiring trip leads to Browne's *China Series*. The
work she produces upon returning to New York becomes
increasingly abstract, using a more restrained palette. Her
dark, shimmery compositions experiment with media and
line. She begins painting in layers and incorporates silk into
multidimensional installations.

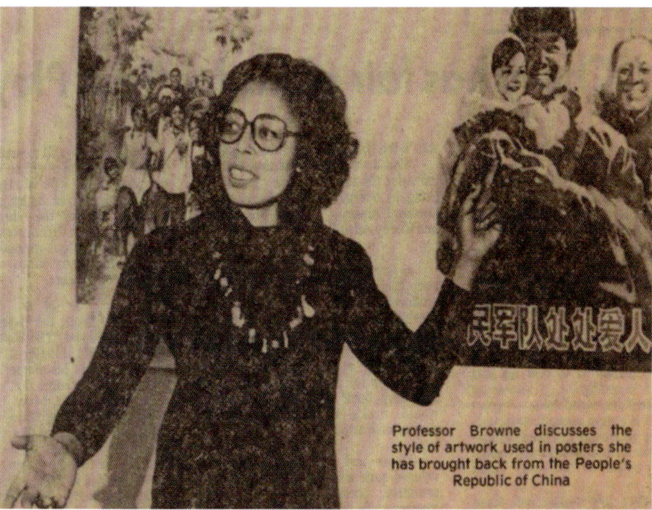

Vivian Browne discussing her experiences in China, as printed in the *Star Ledger*
on December 21, 1977

1978

Browne is a founding member of Black Artists Meeting, a
short-lived organization of artists tackling contemporary
issues facing Black artists. It includes Camille Billops, Emma
Amos, Adger Cowans, and Melvin Edwards, among others.
This group is disbanded by 1979.

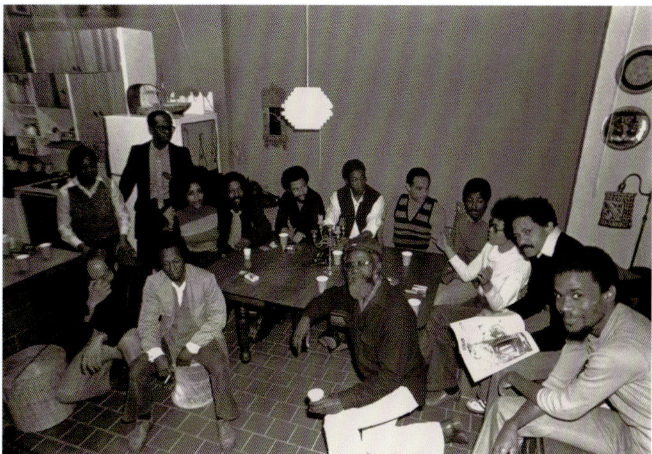

Black Artists Meeting at the Hatch-Billops loft, 1978

The cooperative gallery SOHO20 organizes an invitational
exhibition titled *Third World Women Artists*, which is
accompanied by an artist panel. The show and panel are
organized surrounding the release of the landmark publication
of the same name, published by the Heresies Collective.
Browne is on the editorial board of this issue and contributes
"A Photo Essay on the People's Republic of China."

1979-80

Browne is awarded a fellowship at the MacDowell Colony,
and officially joins SOHO20 as a member.

1981

Browne is invited to teach at UC Santa Cruz (UCSC) as
a visiting professor. This experience on the West Coast
accounts for the fourth and final major shift in creative
inspiration after her *Little Men* series, *Africa Series*, and *China
Series*. During this period, Browne re-discovers California and
her abiding love of nature. Her paintings progressively begin to
incorporate figuration again.

Browne meets the artist and educator Vida Hackman, who
also teaches at UCSC. Hackman will become a companion in
life for Browne.

1982

Browne travels to Cuba on a trip organized by Ana Mendieta
and the Círculo de Cultura Cubana. Her travel companions
include Carl Andre, May Stevens, and Rudolf Baranik.

Browne continues her work at Heresies by serving on the editorial board of edition #15 "Racism is the Issue," which illustrates contemporary concerns surrounding gender and racial equality.

Browne has her first solo exhibition at SOHO20, *Eastern Channels*, featuring her *China Series*. She is also included in *The Wild Art Show*, a group exhibition Faith Ringgold curates at MoMA PS1.

1983

Franklin & Marshall College in Lancaster, PA, organizes the fourth important solo exhibition of Browne's work, *Vivian Browne: Paintings and Pastels*, focusing on her *China Series*.

In August, Browne returns to China with Camille Billops and James V. Hatch as travel companions.

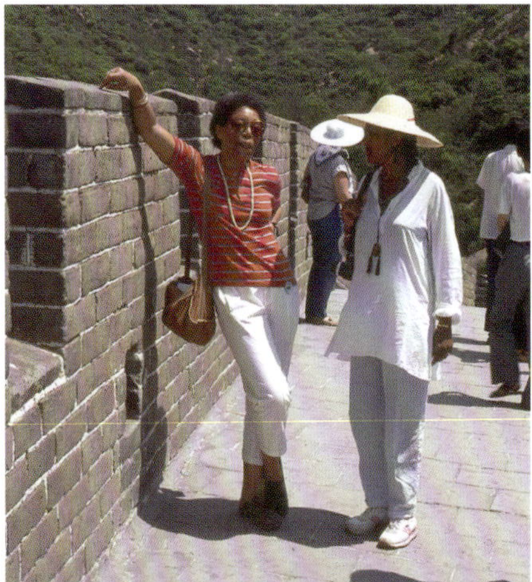

Vivian Browne and Camille Billops on the Great Wall of China, 1983

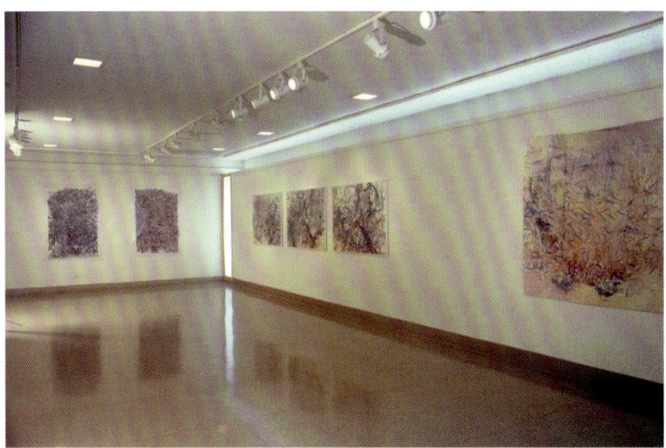

Installation view of *Vivian Browne: Recent Works* at the Bronx Museum of Art, 1985

1985

Browne is the subject of a mid-career retrospective at the Bronx Museum of Art. This is her first major solo exhibition at a museum, and the last during her lifetime.

1986

Browne is honored by Mayor Koch of New York City for her achievements in the arts.

The Studio Museum in Harlem organizes *Tradition and Conflict: Images of a Turbulent Decade 1963–1973*, an exhibition focused on Black activist artists.

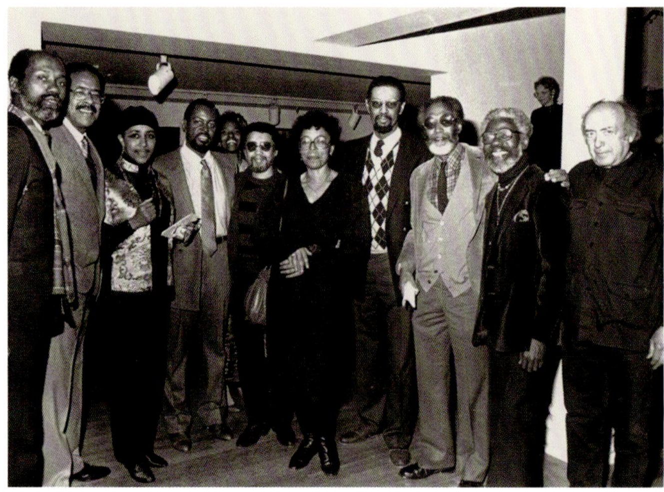

Group shot of the artists in *Tradition and Conflict* at the Studio Museum in Harlem, 1986

Other notable shows include the memorial exhibition for Ana Mendieta at Zeus Travia Gallery in New York; *Progressions: A Cultural Legacy* at the Clocktower, which she co-curates with Emma Amos and curator Julia Hotton; and *Over the Blockade (Por Encima del Bloqueo)*, an exhibition that inaugurated a gift of art to the people of Cuba.

1987

SOHO20 organizes Browne's tenth career solo exhibition, *The Trees Speak.* In her review of the exhibition, artist and friend May Stevens writes, "Vivian Browne's paintings have always been mysterious…. In the recent SOHO20 exhibition, paintings represent a more literal description of trees from differing vantage points…. The paintings, like the forest, are still until one goes into them." [10]

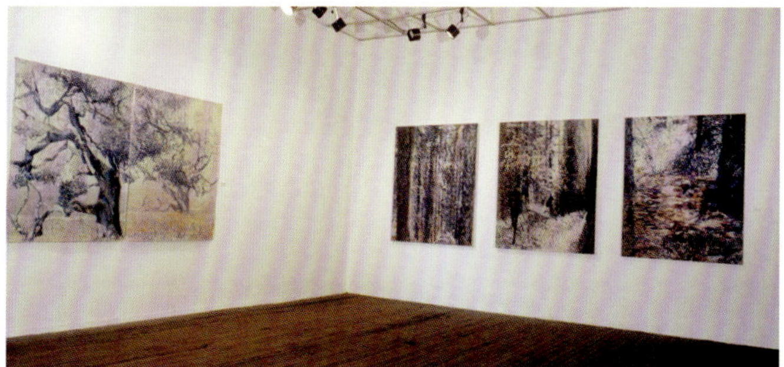

Installation view of *The Trees Speak,* SOHO20 Gallery, 1987

1988

Browne establishes a studio with Vida Hackman in Bakersfield, CA. She continues to maintain her loft in New York City.

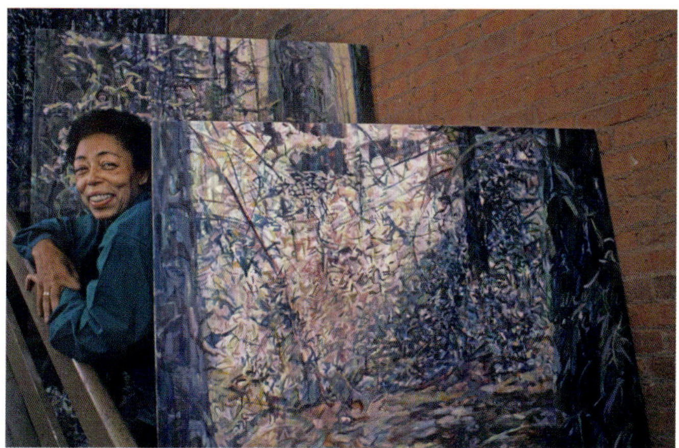

Browne in her California studio, c. 1991

1989

SOHO20 organizes *Sources,* a solo exhibition of Browne's *Trees.* This is her fourth solo show at the co-operative gallery.

1992

Browne, Vida Hackman, and Hackman's husband Ken Hackman establish the Adobe Krow Archives to help preserve and protect their separate and joint artistic endeavors, and to collect art.

1993

Browne dies on July 23. After her passing, SOHO20, June Kelly Gallery, and the Robeson Center Gallery at Rutgers University host memorial exhibitions in her honor.

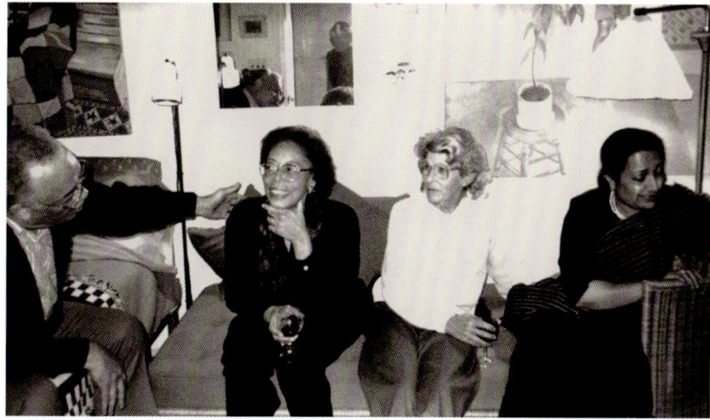

Vivian Browne, Vida Hackman, and Zarina Hashmi at Emma Amos's New Year's party, 1993

1995

Emma Amos pays tribute to Browne in an interview with feminist thinker bell hooks. She says: "I'm going to take Vivian Browne with me everywhere I go. I am not going to leave her behind."[11]

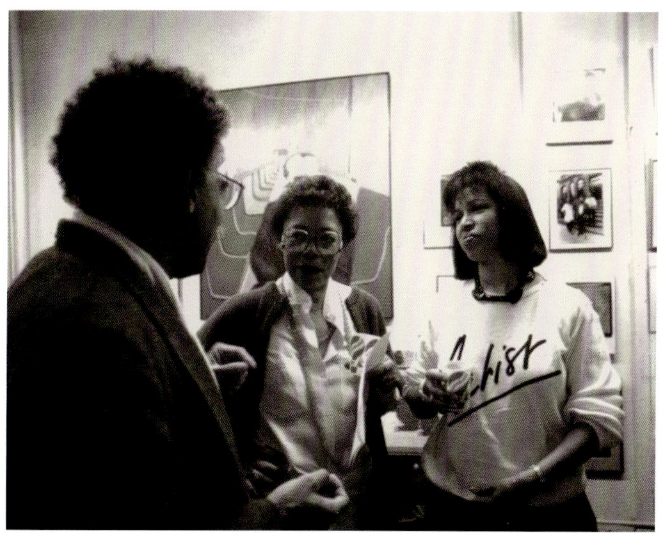

Vivian Browne and Emma Amos, 1986

2017

24 years after her death, Browne is included in the Brooklyn Museum's exhibition *We Wanted a Revolution: Black Radical Women 1965–85.*

2018

RYAN LEE becomes the representative for Browne's estate.

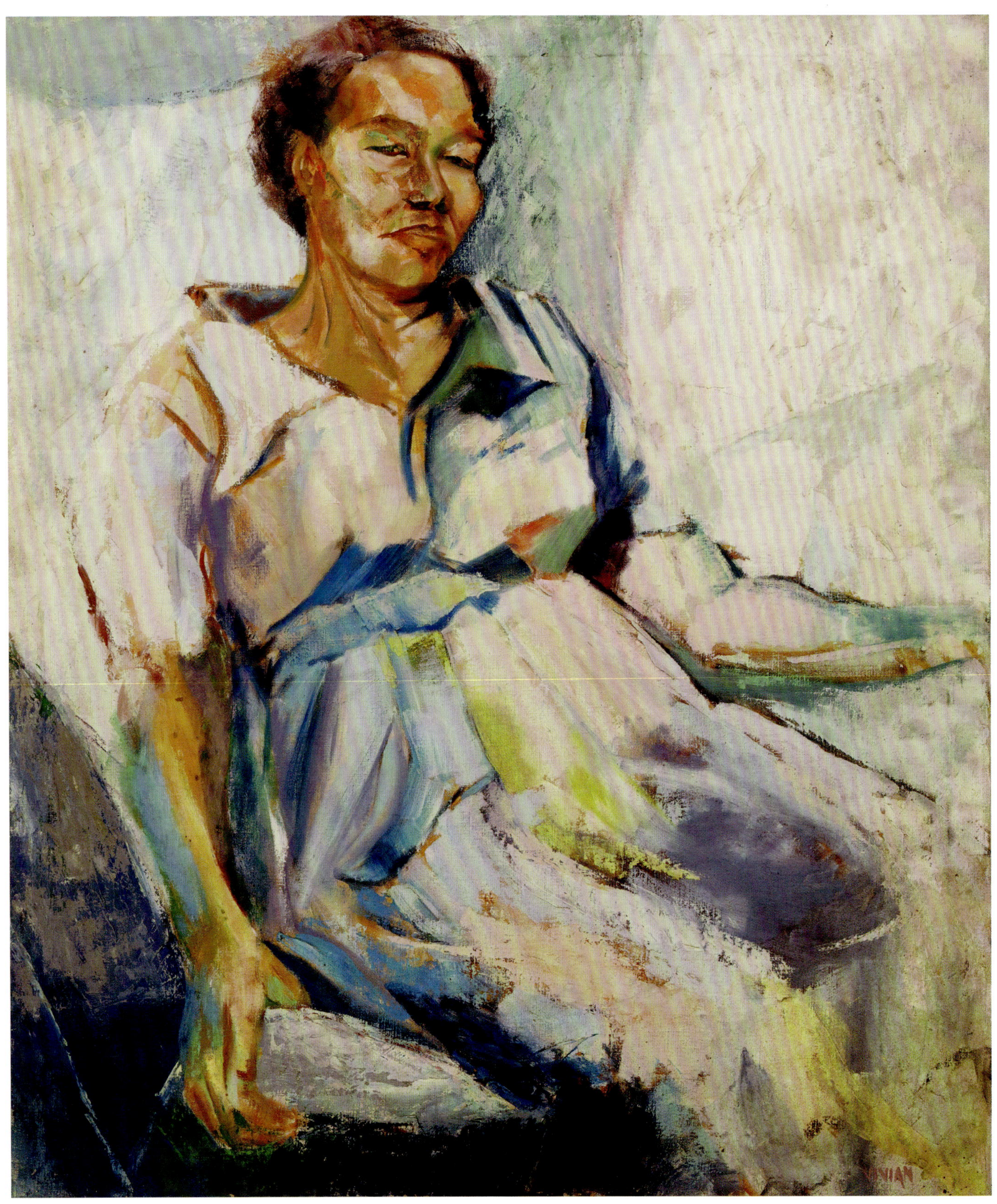

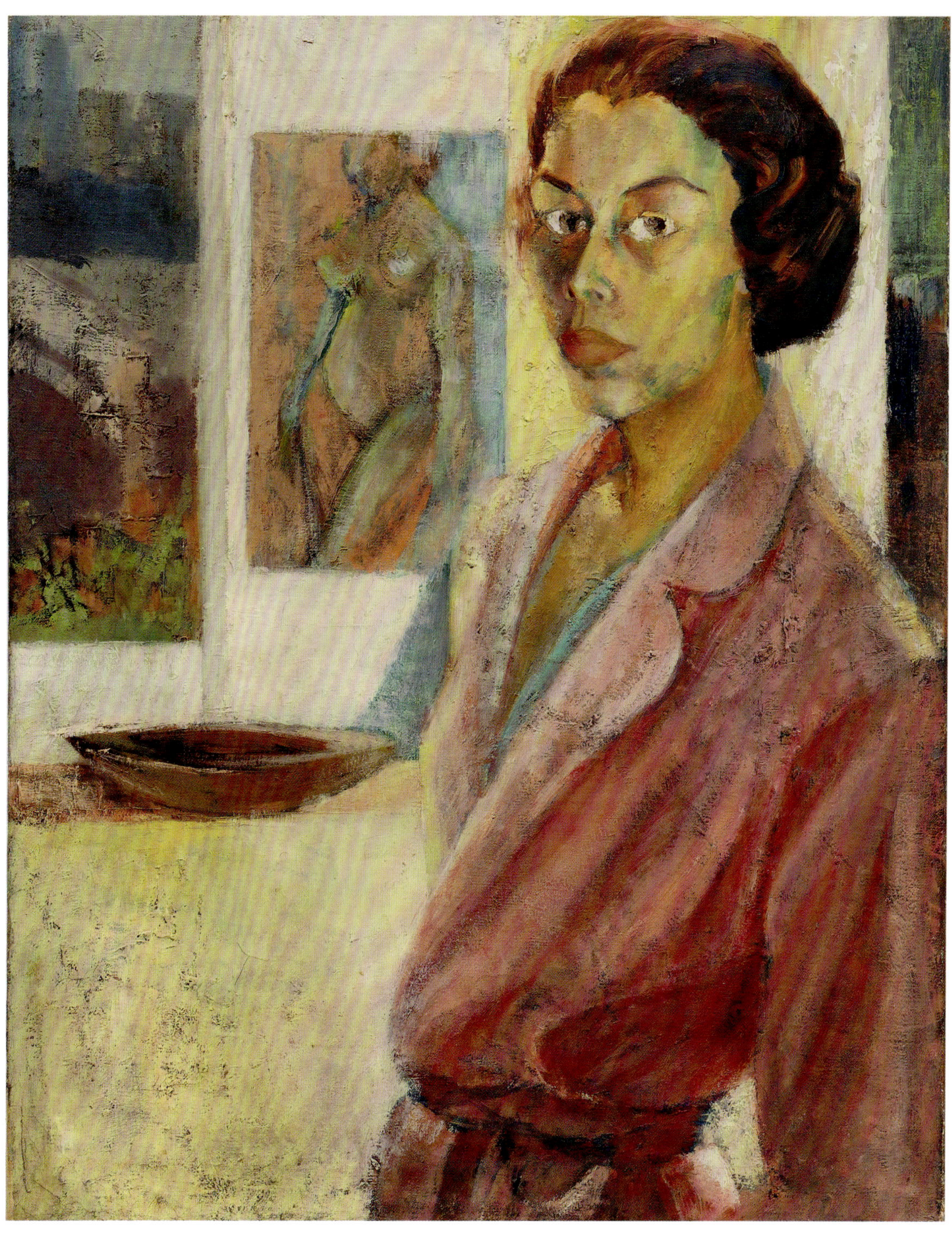

Plate 1
Mother, 1961
Oil on canvas
42 ½ × 36 ¾ inches
Adobe Krow Archives, CA
and RYAN LEE Gallery, NY

Plate 2
Vivian (Self-portrait), 1965
Oil on canvas
31 ½ × 25 3/8 × 1 ¾ inches
Private Collector, Delaware,
courtesy RYAN LEE Gallery

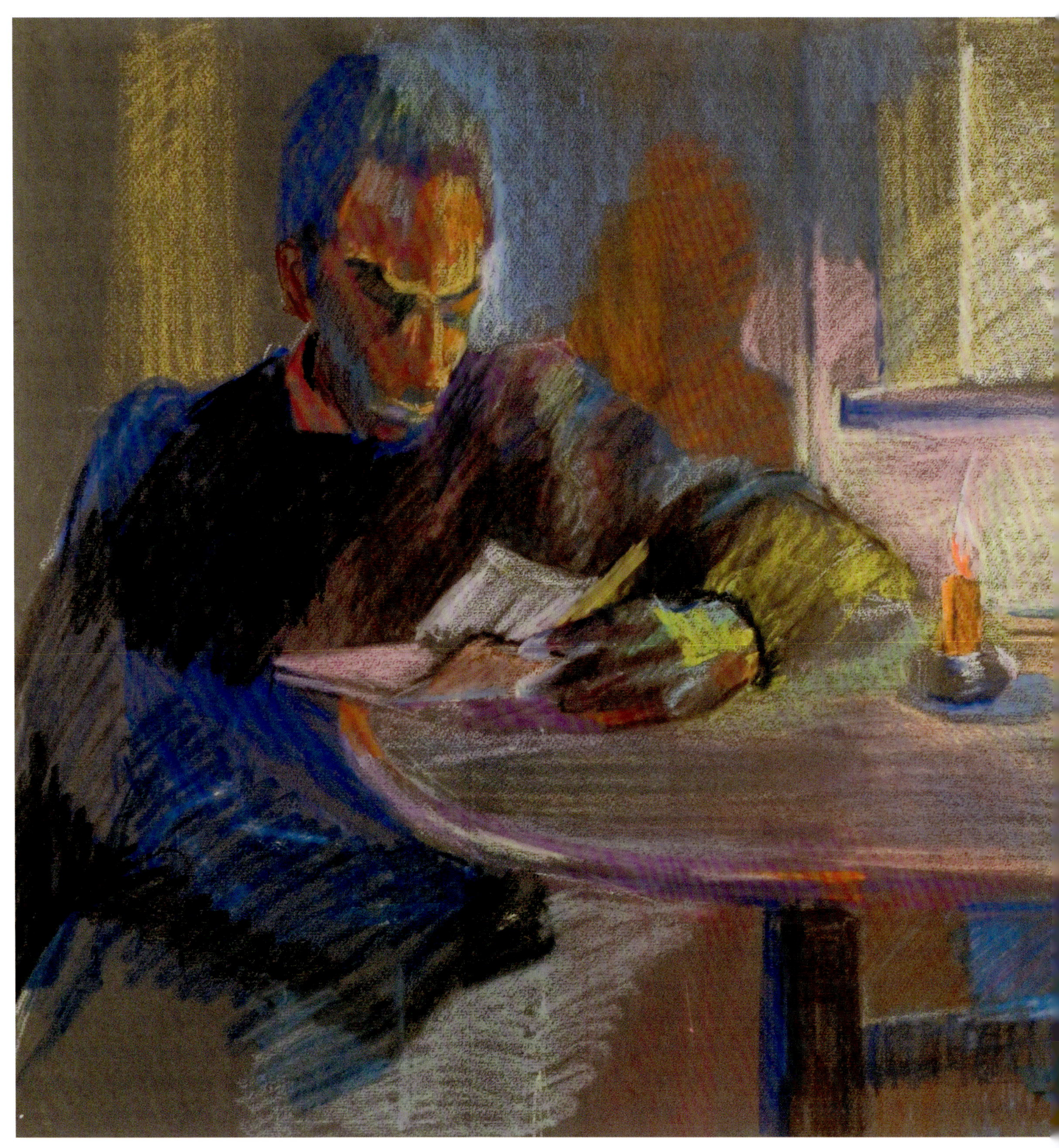

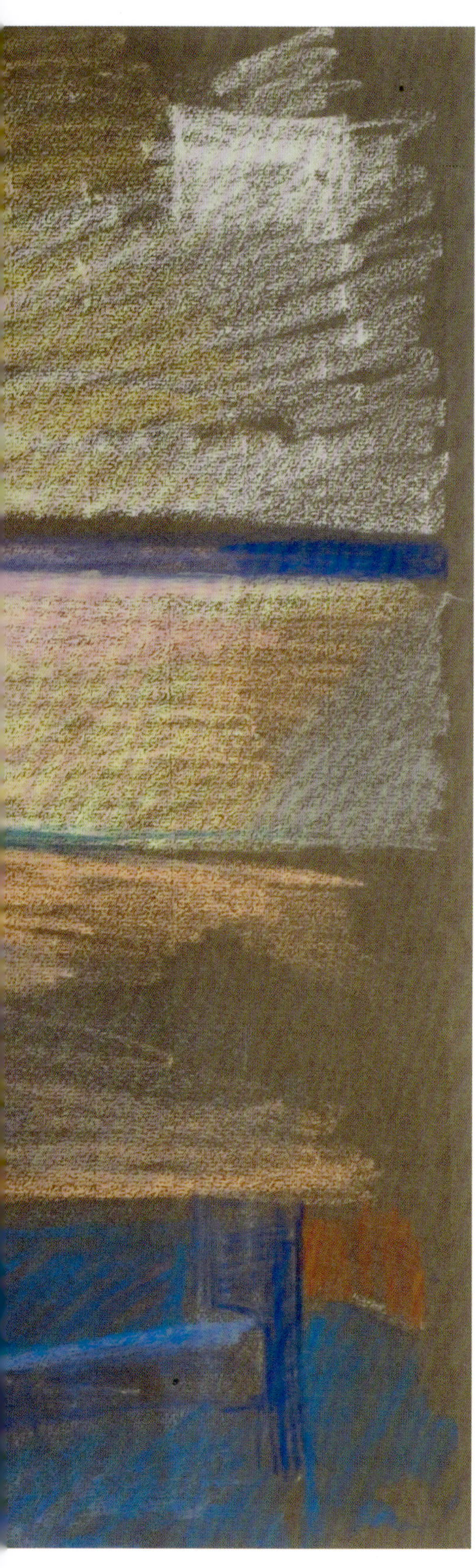

Plate 3
Nathan Barrett Playwright, c. 1960
Pastel on paper
20 × 26 ¾ inches
The Larry D. and Brenda A. Thompson Collection
of African American Art

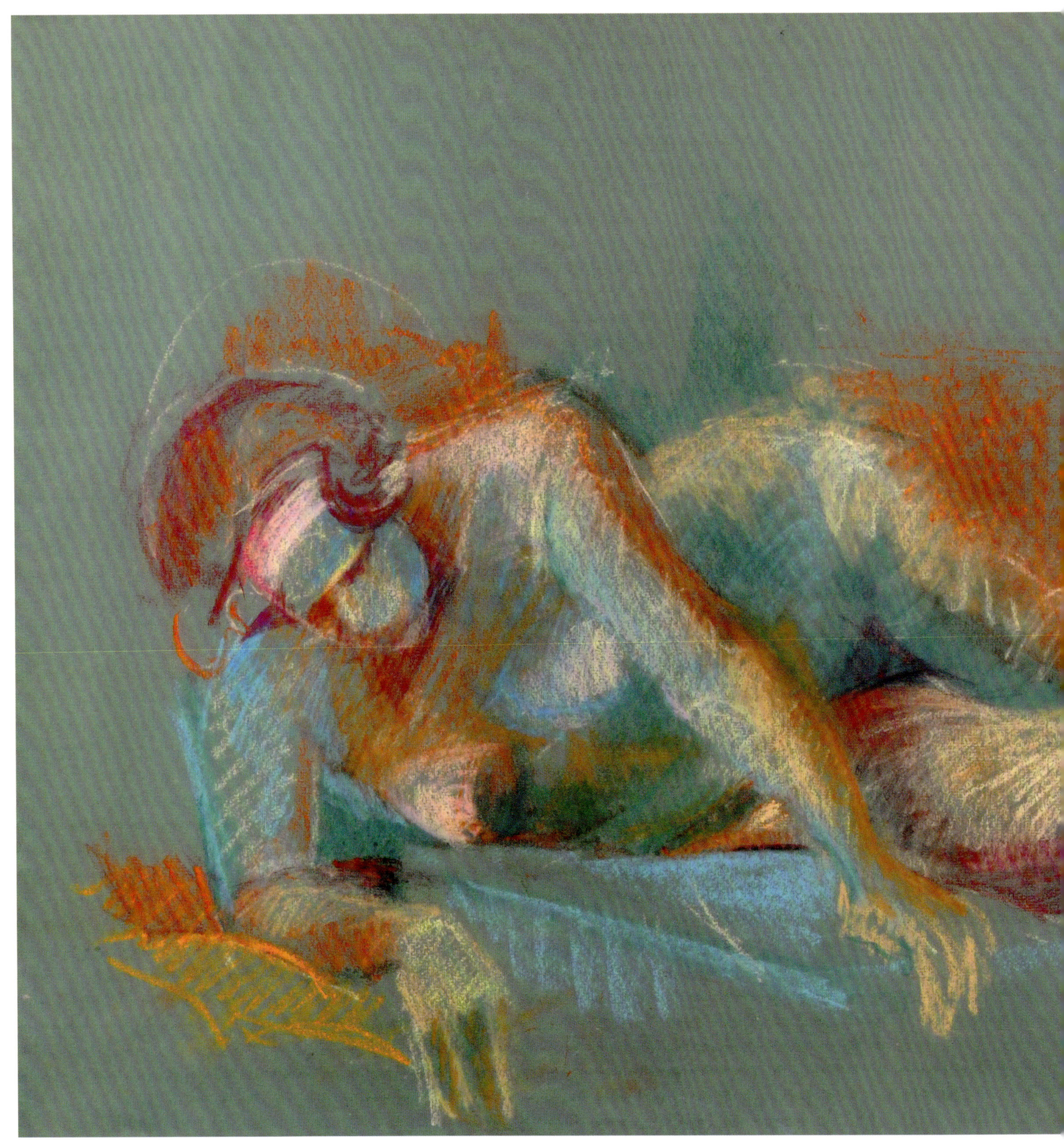

Plate 4
Nude, c. 1960
Pastel on paper
31 × 37 inches
The Larry D. and Brenda A. Thompson Collection
of African American Art

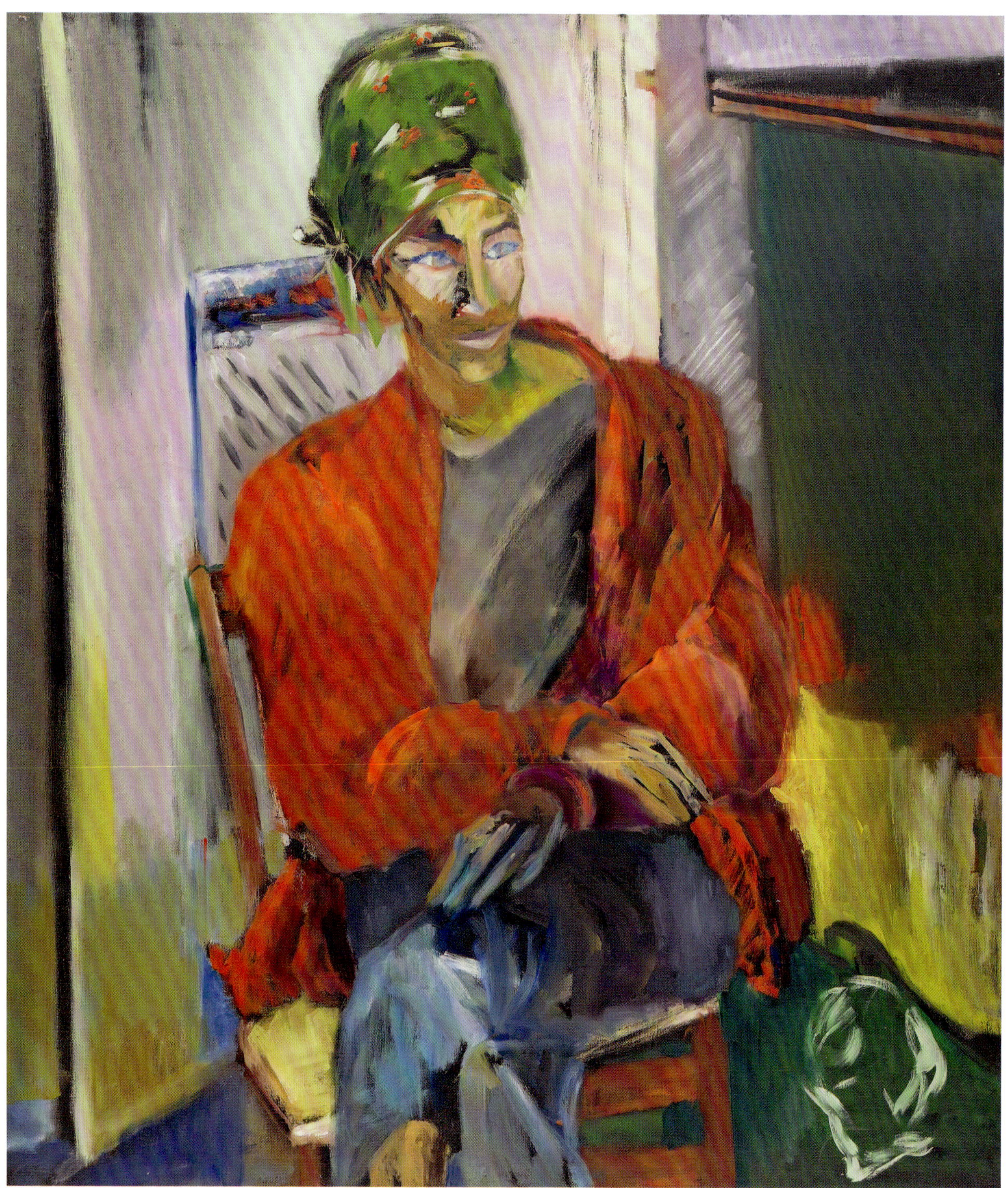

Plate 5
***Camille Billops*, 1965**
Oil on canvas
50 × 44 inches
Adobe Krow Archives, CA
and RYAN LEE Gallery, NY

Artist Statement, n.d.

Vivian Browne

Since I am Black and a woman and since I entered the labor force at the age of 14 and have remained there, I became involved with women's liberation on a very personal level long before it became fashionable.

In 1964, the receipt of a Huntington Hartford Painting Fellowship was a major turning point in my life and career. At the Hartford Foundation in California, I recognized my constant involvement with space and painted a number of landscapes in exploration of that theme. A year later, I resigned from teaching and began painting a series called 'Little Men,' adding to the spatial theme a personal commentary on some aspects of the human condition. Soon after that I began traveling and found that it directly and indirectly supplied me with many variations on spatial themes in addition to providing unique aspects of nature in various parts of the world thus emphasizing my concern for that which is real and universal.

My formal art training was based on the Cézanne aesthetic and included a large dose of Art History. As an artist, my development ranges from the generally figurative, i.e. portraiture, still life, landscape to the specific ('Little Men'). There is a short transition from this expressionistic response to American life to the abstractions which occurred as a visual response to life in Africa and which led to the 'African Series.' Currently, my work continues to deal with spatial themes, with rhythms and movements and with universal realities as seen in the light of my heightened awareness as a woman. In my work, there is great involvement with surfaces and translucencies, with color and the lack of color in an attempt to become more and more specific. Whether or not this is feminist art, I don't know but [it] comes close to my perceptions.

Courtesy of Adobe Krow Archives

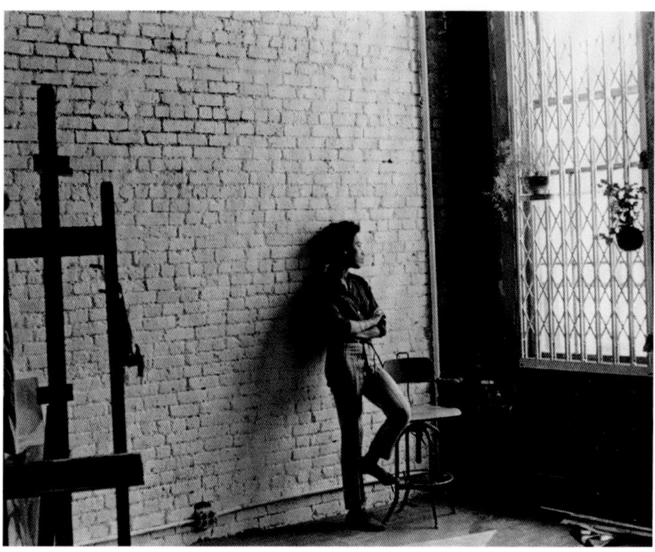

Vivian Browne in her studio, 1974

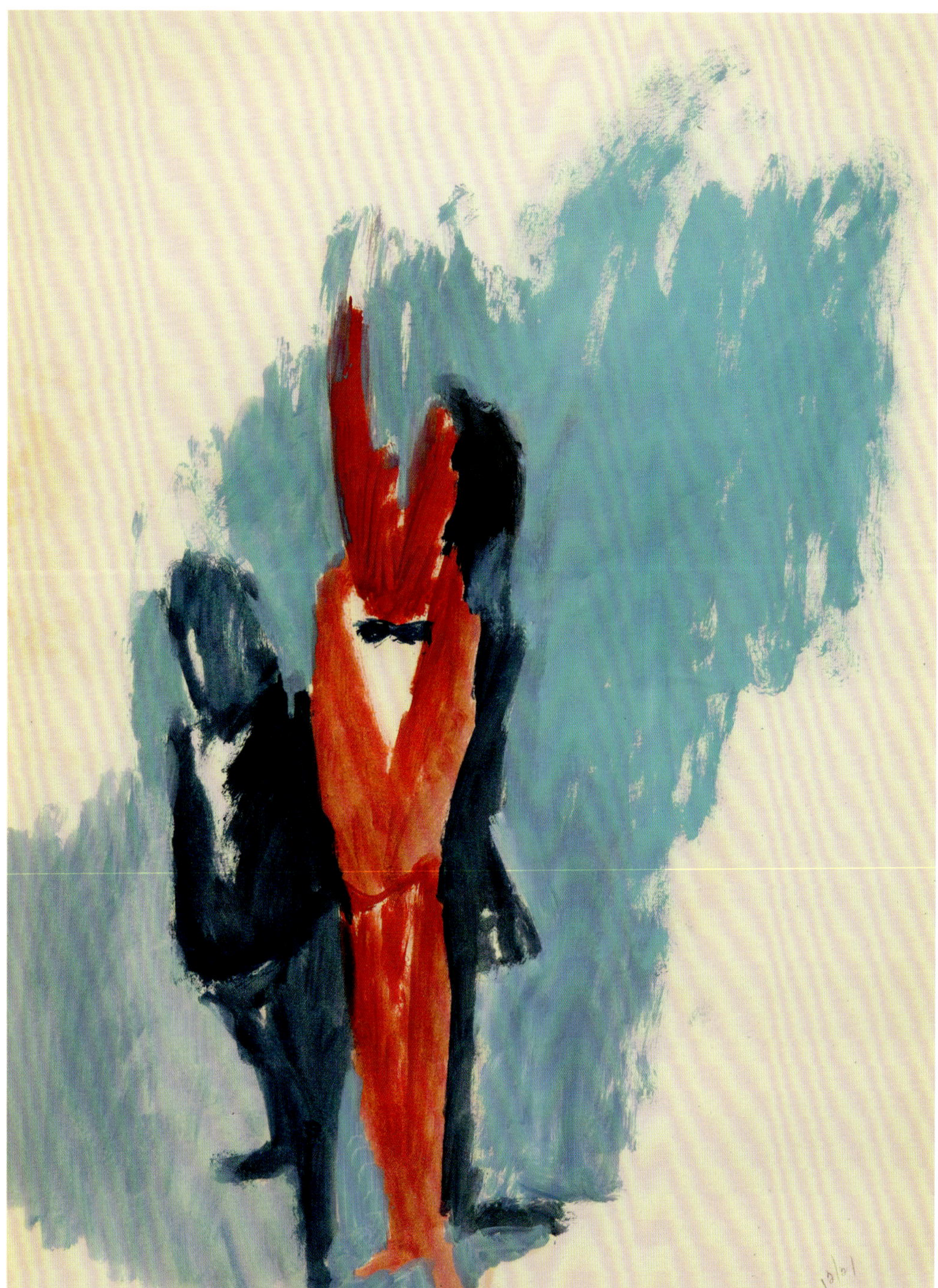

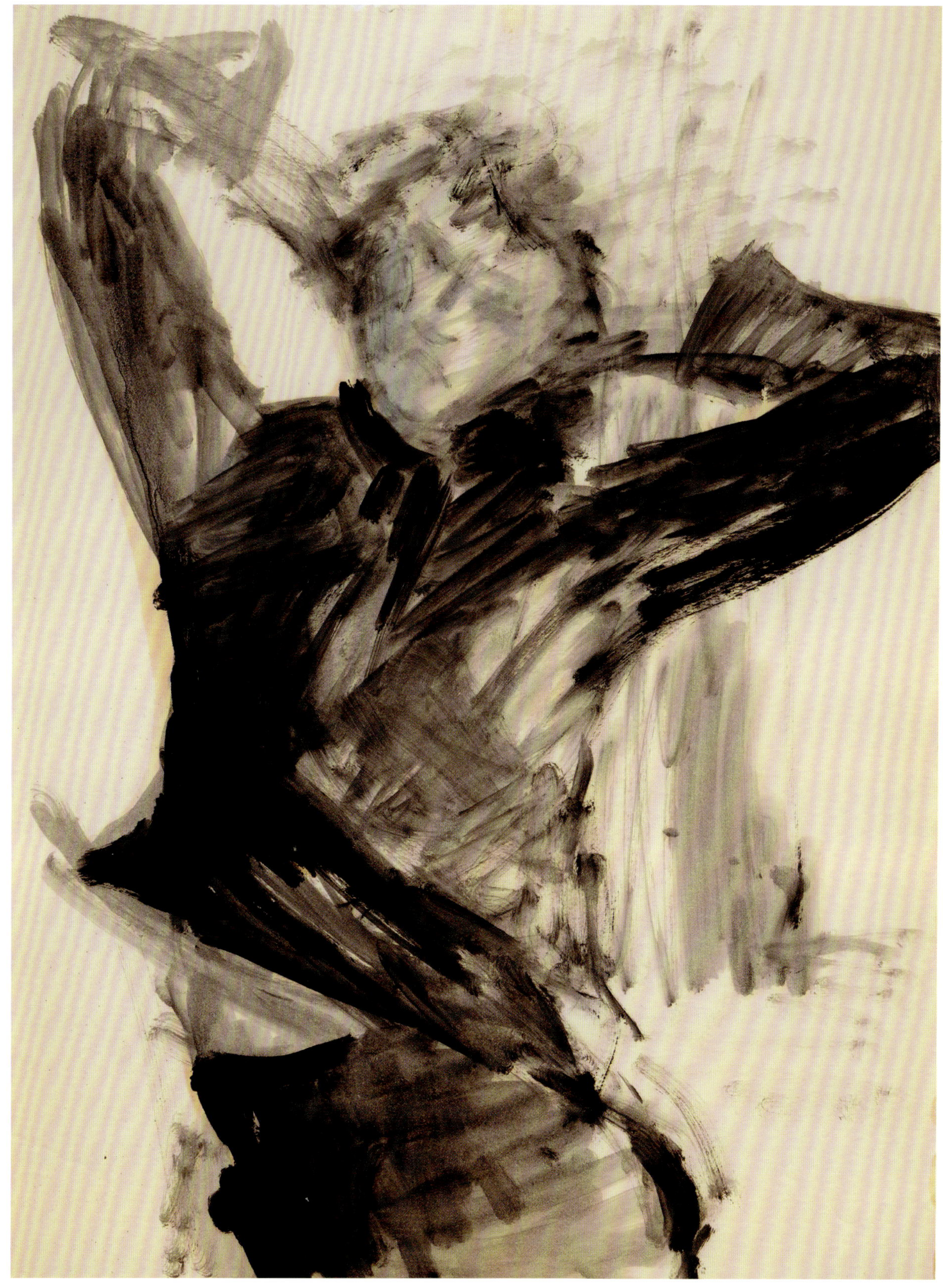

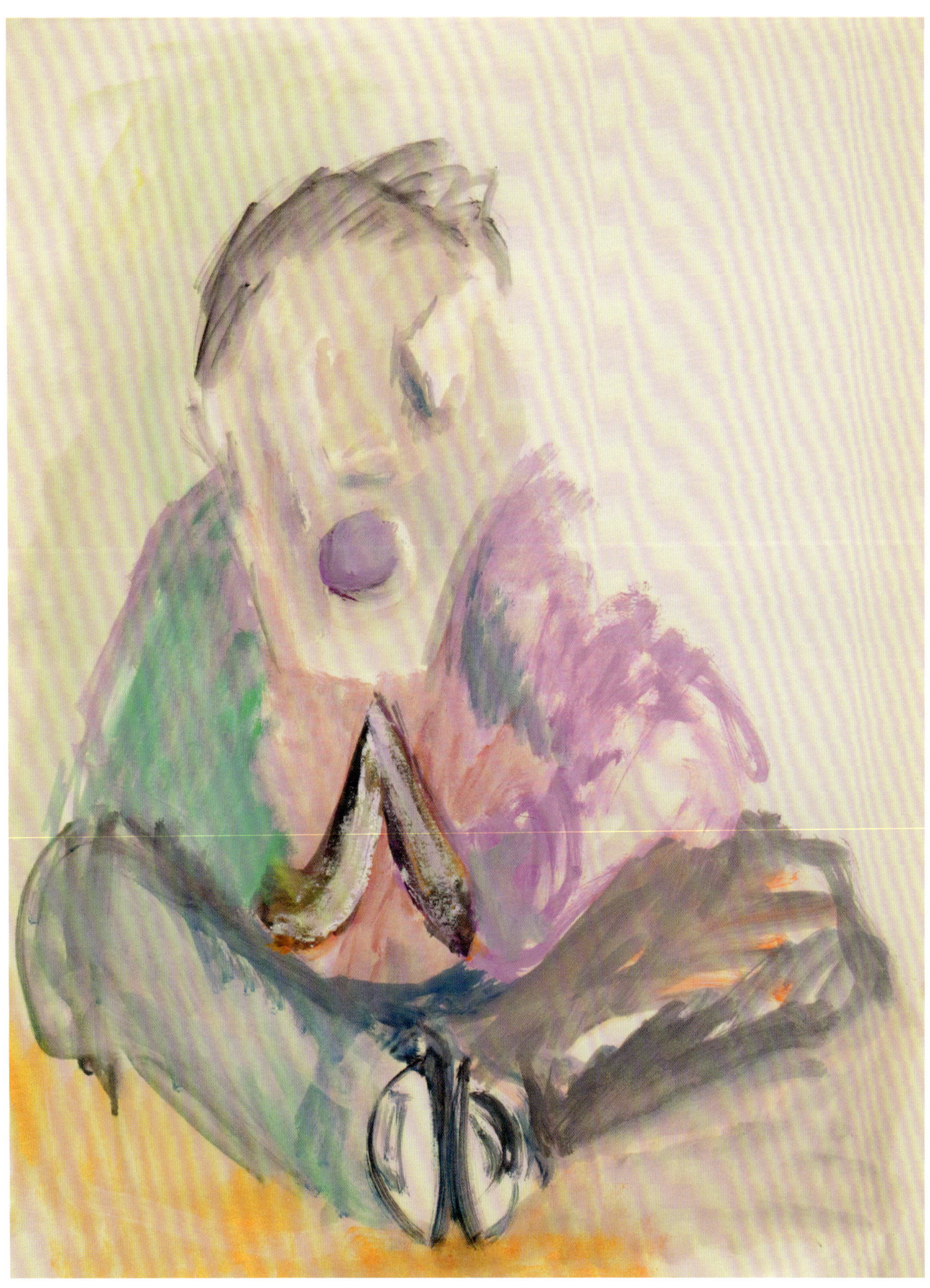

Plate 8
New Yorkers No. 34, c. 1965
Oil on paper
23 ¾ × 17 ½ inches
Adobe Krow Archives, CA
and RYAN LEE Gallery, NY

Plate 9
New Yorkers No. 14, c. 1966
Oil on paper
24 × 17 ¾ inches
Adobe Krow Archives, CA
and RYAN LEE Gallery, NY

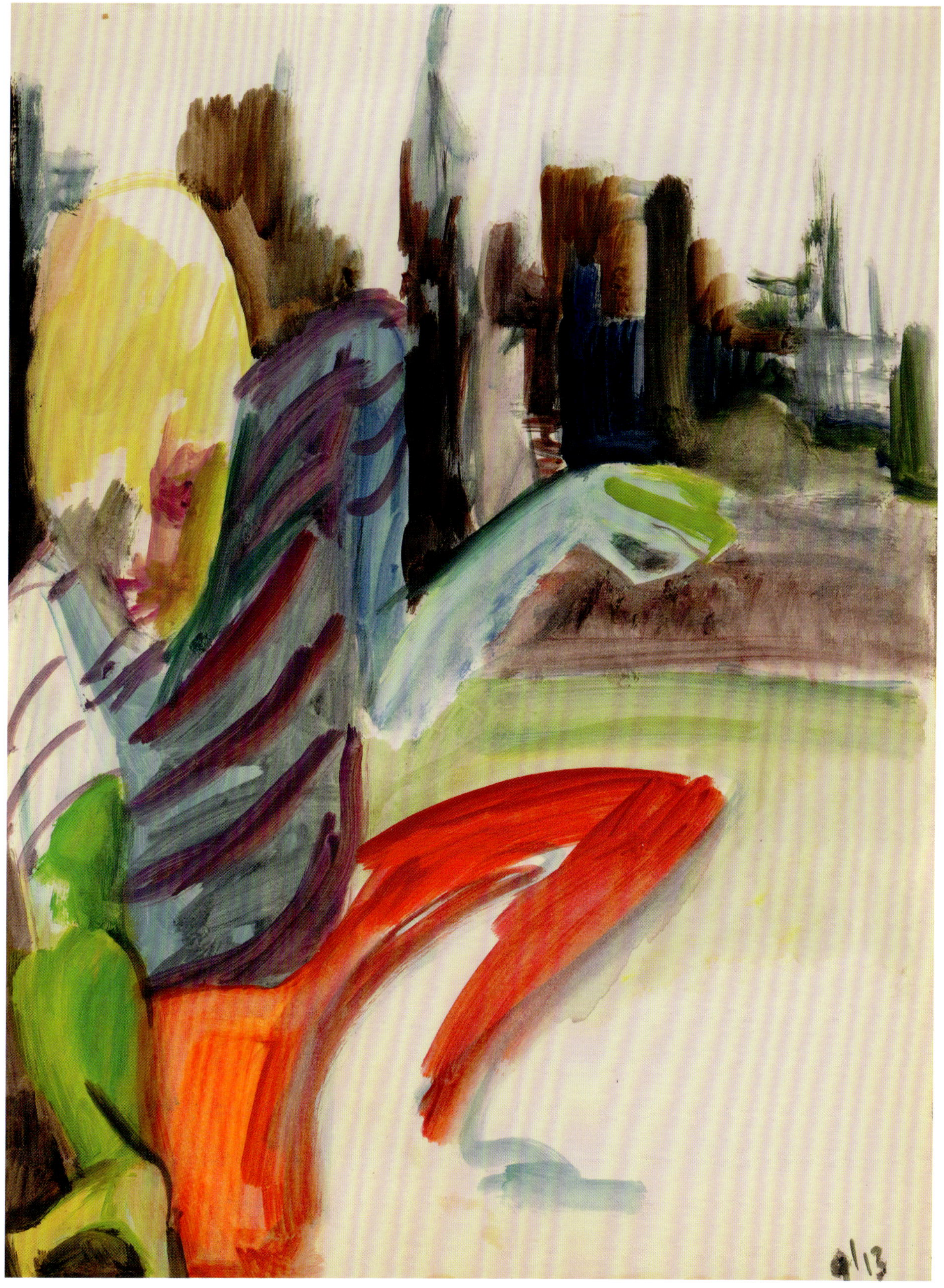

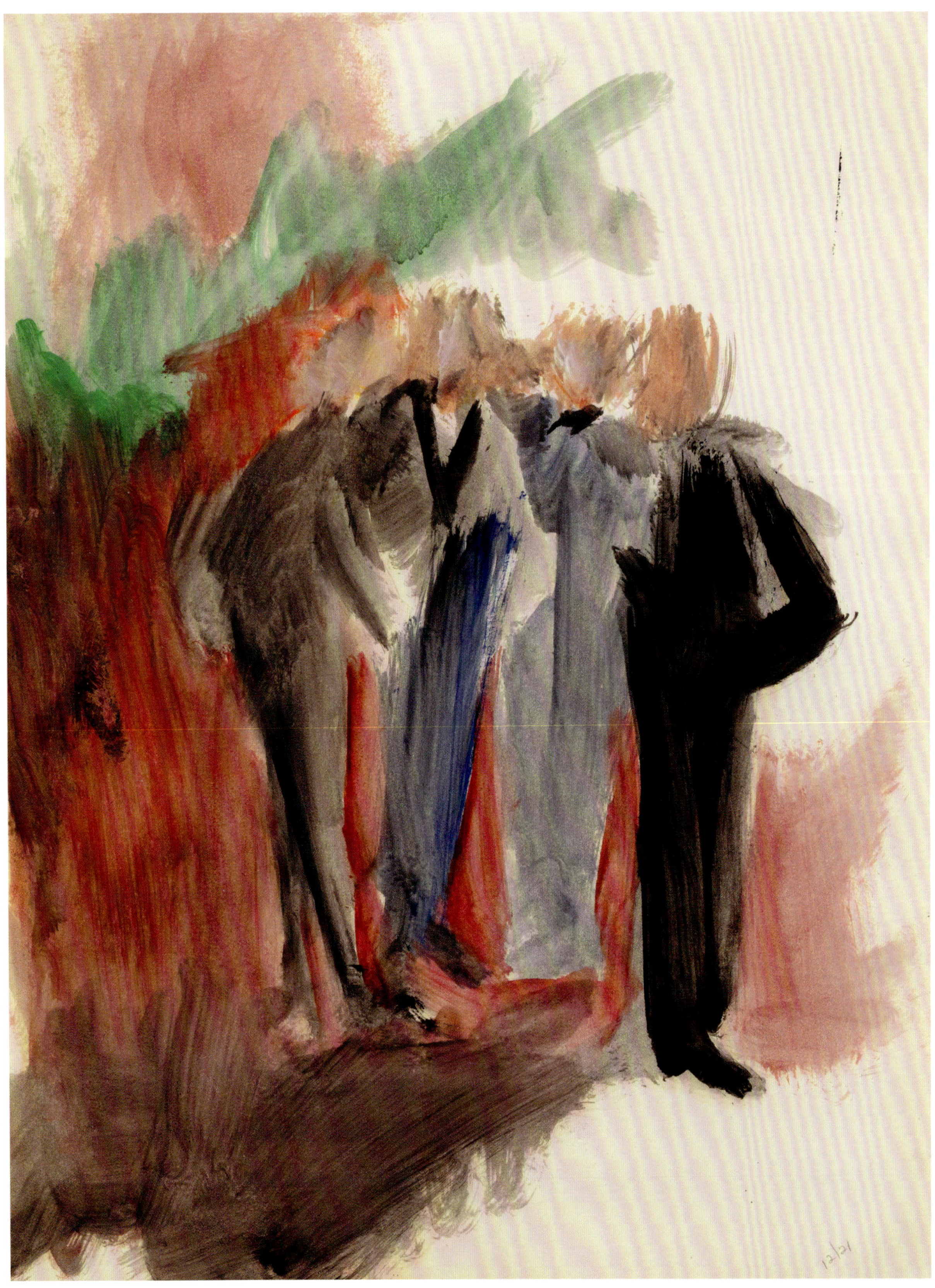

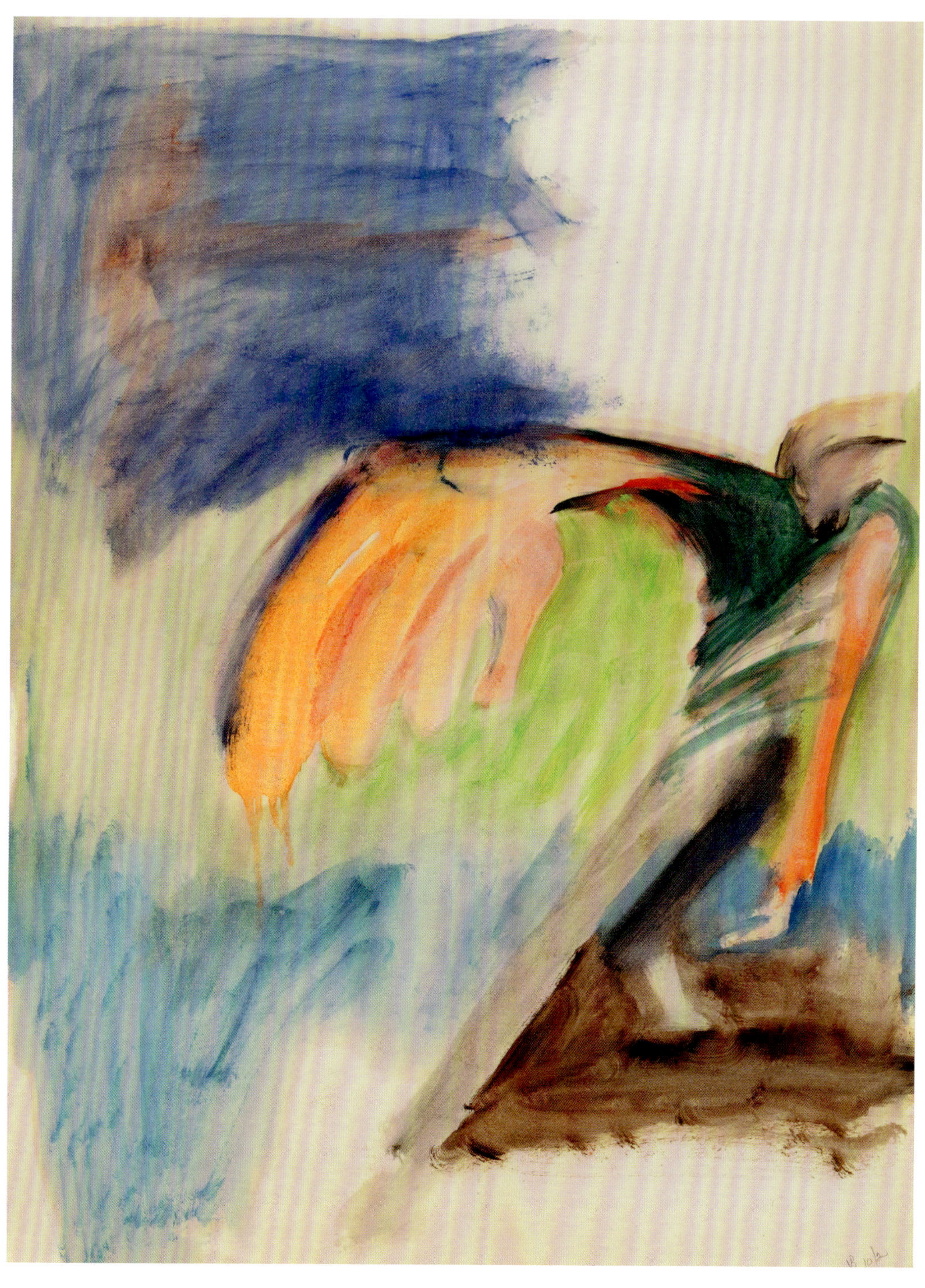

Plate 10
New Yorkers No. 11, 1966
Oil on paper
24 × 17 ¾ inches
Adobe Krow Archives, CA
and RYAN LEE Gallery, NY

Plate 11
New Yorkers No. 57, 1966
Oil on paper
24 × 17 5/8 inches
Adobe Krow Archives, CA
and RYAN LEE Gallery, NY

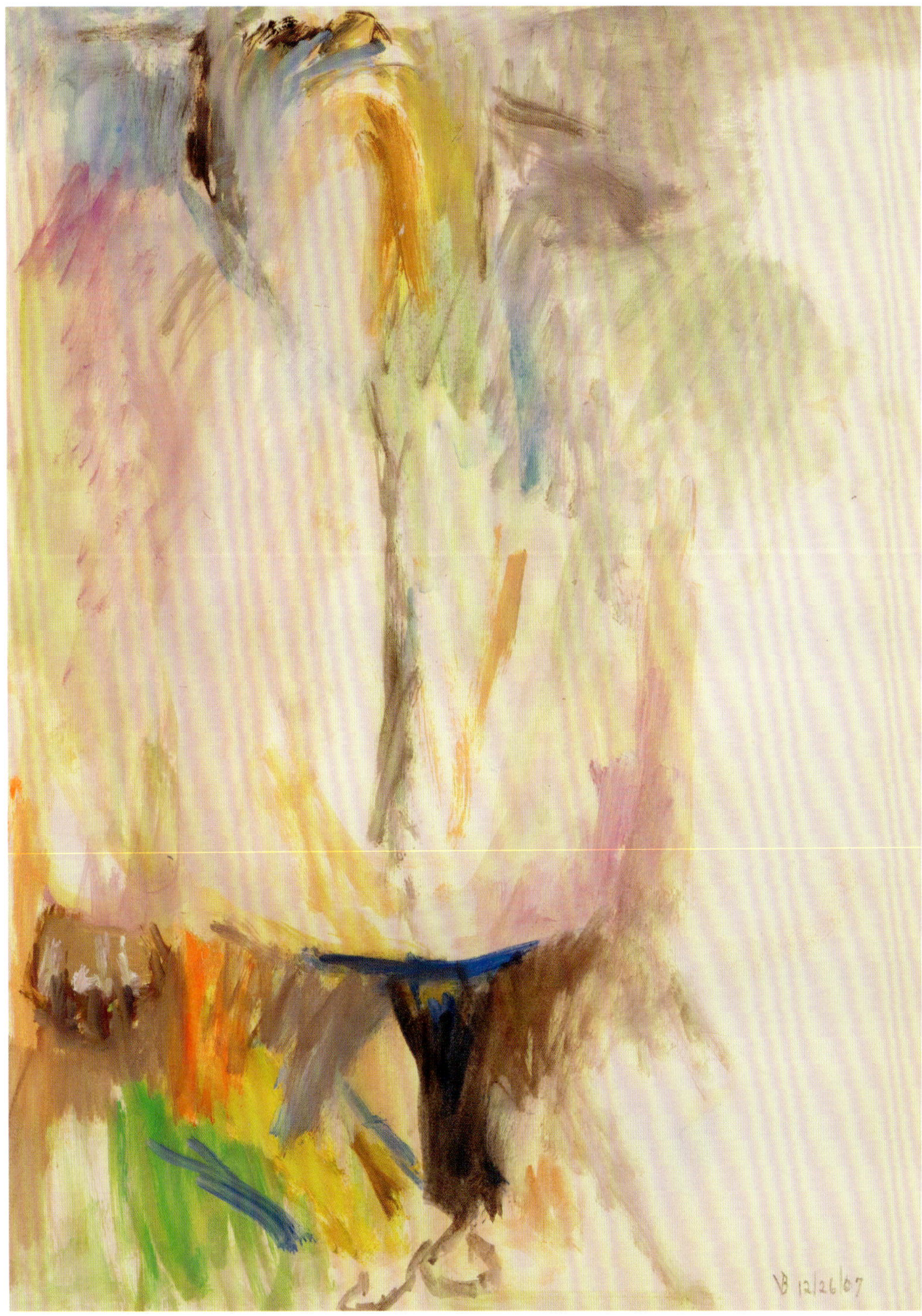

Plate 12
**New Yorkers No. 27, 1967
(12/26/1967)**
Oil on paper
23 ¾ × 17 1/8 inches
Adobe Krow Archives, CA
and RYAN LEE Gallery, NY

Plate 13
New Yorkers No. 22, c. 1967
Oil on paper
23 ¾ × 17 1/8 inches
Adobe Krow Archives, CA
and RYAN LEE Gallery, NY

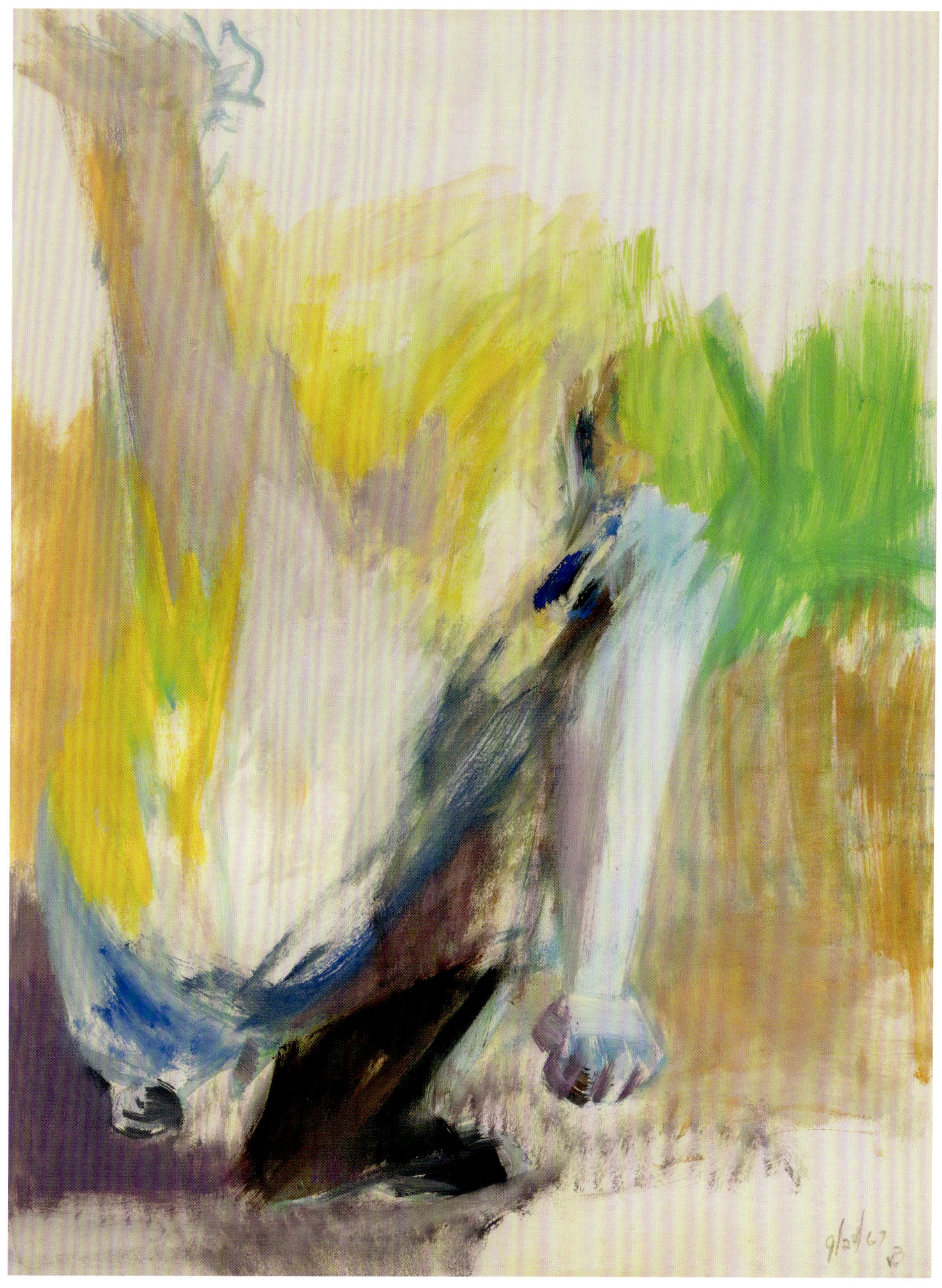

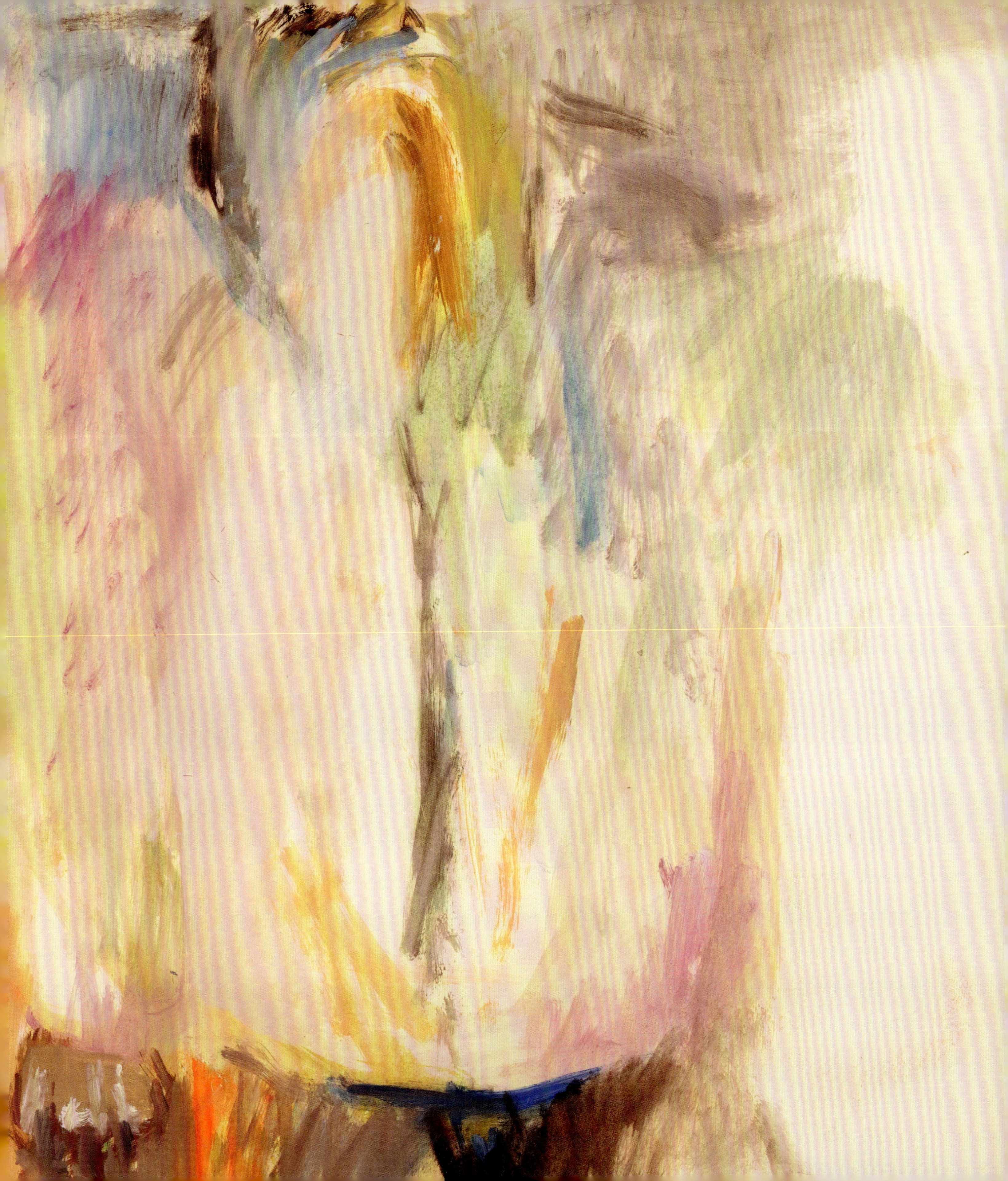

Highlights from Vivian Browne's Art and Activism

Amara Antilla

At Vivian Browne's memorial in 1994, longtime friend and fellow artist May Stevens described a memory of the artist speaking into a megaphone across the street from a museum to protest the exclusionary nature of the art world. "Elizabeth Catlett, Lois Mailou Jones, Edmonia Lewis, Emma Amos, Faith Ringgold, Howardena Pindell, Camille Billops, Dindga McCannon, Valerie Maynard, Alma Thomas, and on and on," Stevens related, "calmly, slow and clear, [Vivian] distinctly pronouncing each name, a long list of all the Black women artists who were not in the museum, including her own."[12] This wasn't the first time that Browne had picketed; she was among the organizers of protests that sought to reshape the art world towards the end of the Civil Rights movement and the height of the feminist art movement in the late 1960s and early 1970s. It is now impossible to separate Browne's art from her activism, although the connection was not always immediately clear.

Over an intense four-decade career, Browne produced work imbued with intimacy, expression, and covert social commentary. Raised in Jamaica, Queens, she created paintings, drawings, and prints, adopting a distinctive voice that reflected her concerns as a Black female artist practicing in the last decades of the twentieth century. Organized primarily into series, her practice may be grouped into four broad sets of concerns, and reflects aesthetic and chromatic choices explored across media. In the late 1950s and early 1960s, Browne focused primarily on landscapes and portraits, often creating tributes to close friends and allies. In the mid-1960s, her portraits became more gestural and expressive, also examining patriarchy and misogyny. In the 1970s and '80s, it revolved around reflections on her travels in Africa and Asia. And in the late 1980s and early 1990s, it meditated on ecology and the natural world. Browne's oeuvre is marked by an unwavering commitment to challenging the expectations and assumptions that were projected onto her, and to resisting the unequal treatment of women and Black people more broadly.

Browne was active in the Black Arts Movement (BAM) and the feminist art movement "before the rise."[13] She was one of the founding members of the Black Emergency Cultural Coalition (BECC), which grew out of protests against the Whitney Museum's exclusion of Black artists

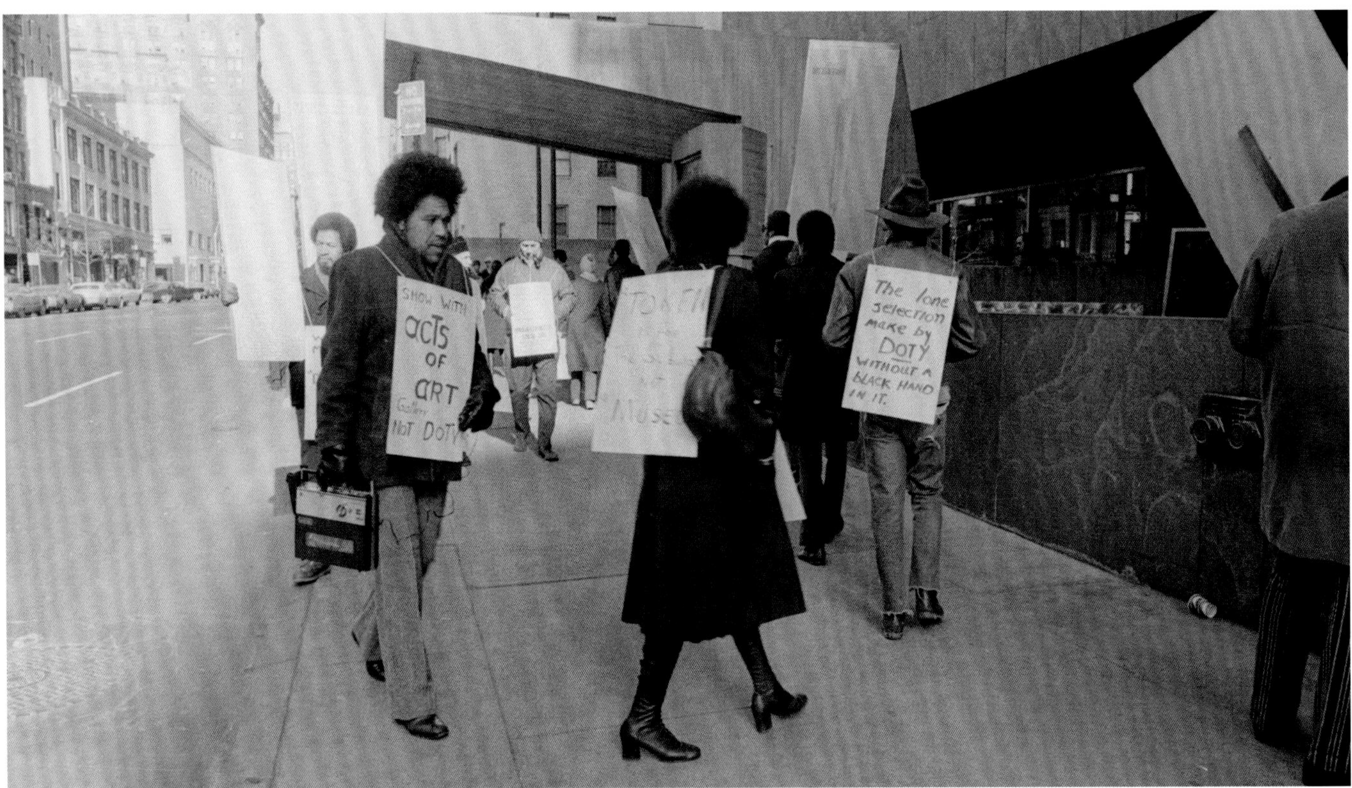

Fig.1
Cliff Joseph (left) and Vivian Browne (right) during
the Black Emergency Cultural Coalition protest at the
Whitney Museum on January 31, 1971

from *The 1930's: Painting and Sculpture in America* exhibition
(October 15-December 1, 1968) and the later *Harlem on
My Mind: Cultural Capital of Black America, 1900-1968*
exhibition at the Metropolitan Museum in January 1969.[14]
She was also a curatorial advisor to Henri Ghent, director
of the Brooklyn Museum's Community Gallery, and guest
curator of the response exhibition, *Invisible Americans: Black
Artists of the '30s* (November 19, 1968-January 5, 1969).
Hosted by the Studio Museum in Harlem, the exhibition
featured work by Romare Bearden, Ernest Crichlow, Jacob
Lawrence, Norman Lewis, and Hale Woodruff, among others,
thereby showcasing all the Whitney's omissions. Browne
also served on the Executive Committee of BECC alongside
Benny Andrews, Cliff Joseph, Reginald Gammon, and Russ

Thompson.[15] In that capacity, she led negotiations with
museum leadership about the BECC's demands for better
Black representation—conversations that came to a head in
the winter of 1971, when demonstrators, including Browne,
protested the museum's failure to honor its commitment
to mount a Black art exhibition during the prime season and
to include Black art experts (fig. 1 and fig. 2).[16] The planned
exhibition *Contemporary Black Artists in America* (April
6-May 16, 1971) would continue to enrage the community
until its opening, when several artists boycotted the show.[17]
Ultimately, this led to a celebrated rebuttal exhibition at Acts
of Art Gallery, of which Browne was a participant.[18]

Concurrently, Browne's studio practice had matured from
the figurative academic painting in which she was trained,

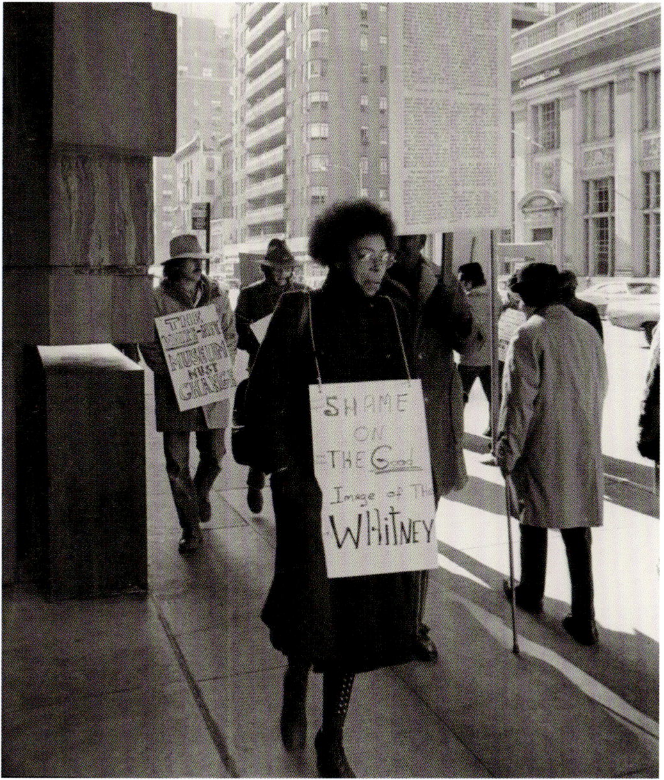

Fig. 2
Vivian Browne during the Black Emergency
Cultural Coalition protest at the Whitney
Museum on January 31, 1971

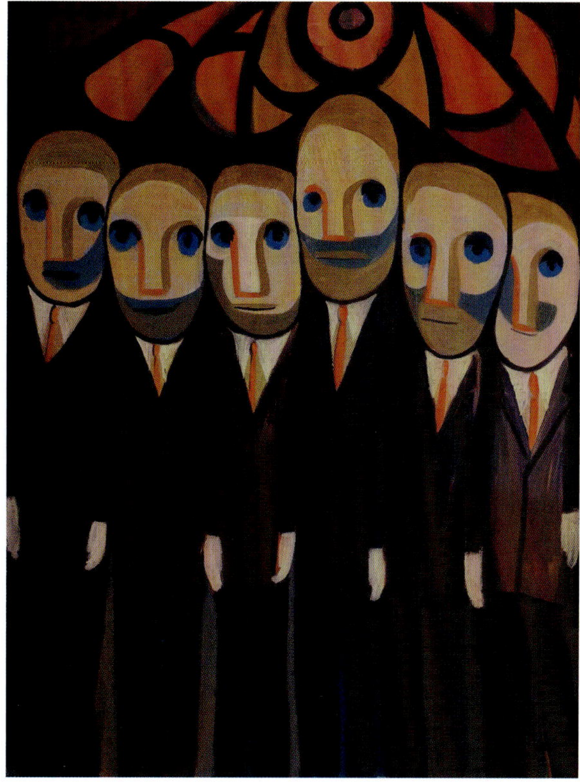

Fig. 3
Faith Ringgold
They Speak No Evil, 1962
Oil on canvas, 40 ¼ × 30 ¼ inches
ACA Galleries, New York

to more expressionistic "emotional landscapes"[19]. The *Little Men* series presents images of white businessmen in various states of dress, from suit-wearing to nude (see plates 14–28). The subjects often express exaggerated rage and terror, their mouths open, their eyes wide. They stamp their feet, pound their fists, and shake their heads. Their hands appear blurred, suggesting frantic movement; sometimes they are clenched or are shown thumb-in-mouth, like children attempting to self-soothe. And in the preceding series, others seem to dissolve into near complete abstraction. In *New Yorkers No. 27* (plate 12), bold brushwork in hues of blue and pink frame what appears to be the neck of a man looking upwards, anchored by the dark vertical hint of a tie. A purple-grey fist is held clenched at his side. The paintings reflect personal experiences

of sexism and racism as well as larger societal critiques. When referring to her series, she remarked, "yes, it's hard to look at. As you say, people are afraid of the reality. But I think that looking at that should not, perhaps, invoke fear so much as interest action [sic]."[20]

Browne was not the only female artist to paint white men in positions of power during this time. Faith Ringgold's *American People Series* (1962–67) features unsettling scenes of segregated spaces, apathy, and racial violence. From that series, *They Speak No Evil* (1962) is a chilling example (fig. 3). It pictures six besuited white men staring ominously out at the viewer, framed by red and orange shapes that suggest stained-glass windows. May Stevens's *Big Daddy* works (see fig. 4) similarly, depicting a white male figure with a smug expression that exudes passivity and entitlement. The figure, which was also inspired by her father, became an archetypal stand-in for her criticisms of abuses of power in the context of the Vietnam war, and other manifestations of American patriarchy. Comparing Browne to Faith Ringgold and Harmony Hammond for her use of "female-identified" techniques and materials that "merged fabrics and feminist politics in abstraction," Lucy Lippard acknowledges Browne's combination of core involvement with a paradoxically elusive approach. "Vivian Browne, too," she comments, "has been in the center of the maelstrom, though most of her work deals more quietly with the Black female experience. Her big, ambivalent, figurative oils from the late 1960s, such as *The Seven Deadly Sins* [plate 14], cast a jaundiced eye on the rich, the white, and the male, ironically rendered in soft focus as though their very real power were in fact an illusion."[21]

When asked, "Why are they all men?" Browne quipped, "It has come to my attention that men rule the country."[22] For Browne, the *Little Men* series might have been a response to Willem de Kooning's *Women* paintings (see fig. 5), as she cites the painter as an influence.[23] Her *Two Men* (plate 17) features a pair of figures, their swollen heads and thick necks twisted, presenting exaggerated features with mouth agape, and knees bent, as if crouching. The background demonstrates pastel hues of light blue, purple, green and off-white. "The *Little Men* series [has] become a commentary on the human condition," she stated. "[The works] grew out of my emotional upheaval in reaction to the world around me. If there was a message, it is about people and how they are reacting to each other and how we see them. Or how I see them."[24] Henri Ghent described the series as "social satire with uncanny perception" and "devastating in its accuracy."[25] When Whitney Museum curator Robert Doty visited Browne to see this body of work, he walked from one end of the studio to the other and exited, in a telling response to the painting's subject matter, without saying a word.[26] Browne's response: "I realized that the art community, that he represented, was not mine."[27]

Browne was acutely aware of the ways in which women artists were excluded from Black as well as white spaces. Although she participated in several exhibitions that focused on Black art in the 1960s and '70s, more telling are the exhibitions to which she was *not* invited.[28] As Browne's close friend and collaborator Faith Ringgold remarked, "Well, what happened is that when the opportunities increased for the black artist—it was really the black male artist—I thought I was included in that. But I found out later that they really meant men."[29] Browne was one of the founding members of Women Students and Artists for Black Art Liberation (WSABAL), which was organized by Ringgold and her daughter Michele Wallace. They demanded, among other things, that exhibitions be representative of

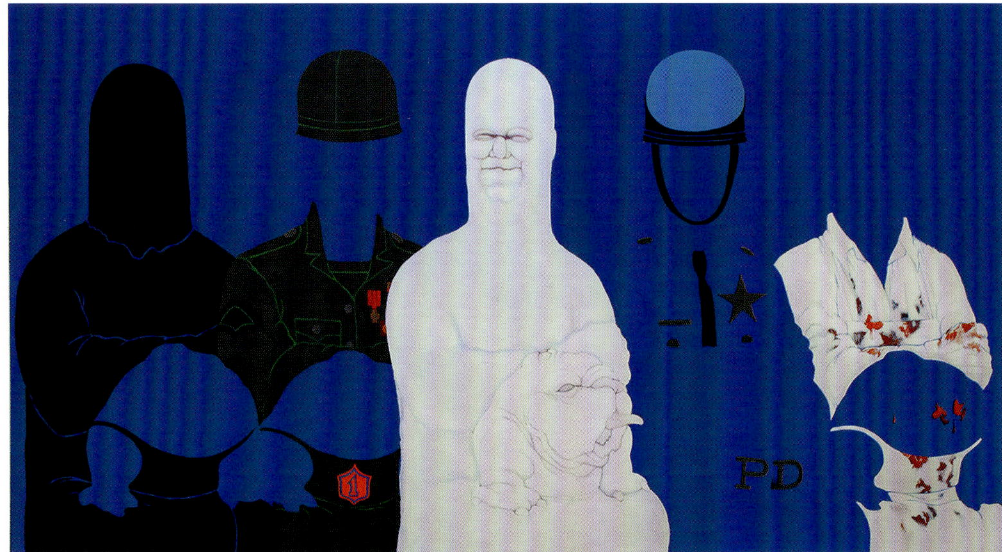

Fig. 4
May Stevens
Big Daddy Paper Doll, 1970
Acrylic on canvas
72 × 168 inches
Brooklyn Museum, gift of Mr. and Mrs. S. Zachary Swidler, 75.73

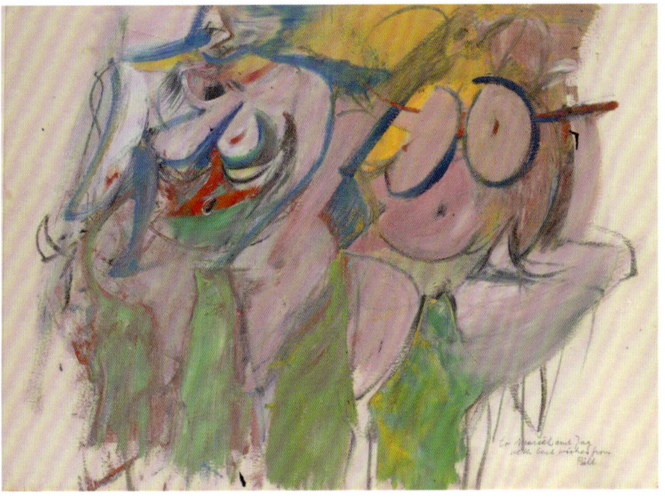

Fig.5
Willem de Kooning
Two Women, 1953
Oil, enamel and charcoal on paper
21 7/8 × 30 inches
Metropolitan Museum, New York, The Muriel
Kallis Steinberg Newman Collection, gift of Muriel
Kallis Newman, 2006.32.33

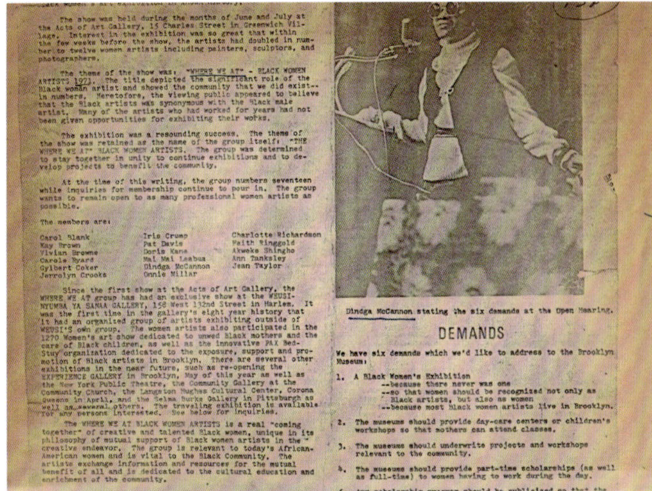

The show was held during the months of June and July at the Acts of Art Gallery, 15 Charles Street in Greenwich Village. Interest in the exhibition was so great that within the few weeks before the show, the artists had doubled in number to twelve women artists including painters, sculptors, and photographers.

The theme of the show was: "WHERE WE AT" – BLACK WOMEN ARTISTS 1971. The title depicted the significant role of the Black woman artist and showed the community that we did exist—in numbers. Heretofore, the viewing public appeared to believe that the Black artists was synonymous with the Black male artist. Many of the artists who had worked for years had not been given opportunities for exhibiting their works.

The exhibition was a resounding success. The theme of the show was retained as the name of the group itself: "THE WHERE WE AT" BLACK WOMEN ARTISTS. The group was determined to stay together in unity to continue exhibitions and to develop projects to benefit the community.

At the time of this writing, the group numbers seventeen while inquiries for membership continue to pour in. The group wants to remain open to as many professional women artists as possible.

The members are:

Carol Blank
Kay Brown
Vivian Browne
Carole Byard
Gylbert Coker
Jerrolyn Crooks

Iris Crump
Pat Davis
Doris Kane
Mai Mai Leabua
Dindga McCannon
Onnie Millar

Charlotte Richardson
Faith Ringgold
Akweke Shingho
Ann Tanksley
Jean Taylor

Since the first show at the Acts of Art Gallery, the WHERE WE AT group has had an exclusive show at the WEUSI-NYUMBA YA SAMAA GALLERY, 158 West 132nd Street in Harlem. It was the first time in the gallery's eight year history that it had an organized group of artists exhibiting outside of WEUSI'S own group. The women artists also participated in the 1270 Women's art show dedicated to unwed Black mothers and the care of Black children, as well as the innovative PAX Bed-Stuy organization dedicated to the exposure, support and promotion of Black artists in Brooklyn. There are several other exhibitions in the near future, such as re-opening the EXPERIENCE GALLERY in Brooklyn, May of this year as well as the New York Public Theatre, the Community Gallery at the Community Church, the Langston Hughes Cultural Center, Corona Queens in April, and the Selma Burke Gallery in Pittsburgh as well as several others. The traveling exhibition is available for any persons interested. See below for inquiries.

The WHERE WE AT BLACK WOMEN ARTISTS is a real "coming together" of creative and talented Black women, unique in its philosophy of mutual support of Black women artists in the creative endeavor. The group is relevant to today's African-American women and is vital to the Black Community. The artists exchange information and resources for the mutual benefit of all and is dedicated to the cultural education and enrichment of the community.

Dindga McCannon stating the six demands at the Open Hearing.

DEMANDS

We have six demands which we'd like to address to the Brooklyn Museum:

1. A Black Women's Exhibition
    --because there never was one
    --so that women should be recognized not only as Black artists, but also as women
    --because most Black women artists live in Brooklyn.

2. The museums should provide day-care centers or children's workshops so that mothers can attend classes.

3. The museums should underwrite projects and workshops relevant to the community.

4. The museums should provide part-time scholarships (as well as full-time) to women having to work during the day.

5. Any scholarship program should be publicized so that the

Fig.6
Where We At, 1977
Brochure

At Black Women Artists, Inc. (WWA) was established and included members Browne and Ringgold, alongside Carol Blank, Gylbert Coker, Dindga McCannon, Onnie Millar, Ann Tanksley, Jean Taylor, and others (fig. 6). The group described their purpose and activities as "a real 'coming together' of creative and talented Black women, unique in its philosophy of mutual support of Black women artists in the creative endeavor…. The artists exchange information and resources for the mutual benefit of all and [are] dedicated to the cultural education and enrichment of the community."[32]

Browne's feminist organizing continued, and she became involved with other women collectives and initiatives including the feminist publication *Heresies*, The Feminist Institute, the Women's Caucus for Art, and SOHO20. Although Browne never became an official member of the Heresies organization, she contributed to five issues, and participated in the activities of the group for over ten years. The Heresies Collective was founded in 1977 by an all-white cohort, including Joyce Kozloff, Lucy Lippard, and Harmony Hammond, with the goal of "examining art and politics from a feminist perspective."[33] Organized with the basic tenets of collectivism and exchange, each issue had an independent editorial collective to ensure different voices could contribute and the content could evolve to reflect diverse views. They wrote, "Our view of feminism is one of process and change, and we feel that in the process of this dialogue we can foster a change in the meaning of art."[34] And change it did, particularly after the lack of

the demographics of the local community, and that half of the participating artists be women. It was initiated after the exhibition *Afro-American Artists: New York and Boston* at the Museum of Fine Arts, Boston (May 19–June 23, 1970), included only nine women artists among a total of seventy invitees. "It was an intentional thing that me and Vivian Browne, you know, and Iris Crump and all of us had been left out again," Ringgold remarked. "So immediately WSABAL got together with the women artists supporting the students."[30]

In 1971, Browne participated in what has been deemed the first exhibition of all Black women artists in New York.[31] The exhibition *Where We At* took place at the Black-owned Greenwich Village gallery Acts of Art, which was run by Nigel Jackson. It galvanized the eponymous all-female Black artist collective that was founded by Kay Brown—the only female member of the Afrocentric Harlem-based collective Weusi. When her requests to invite more female artists were refused, she decided to start something new. Where We

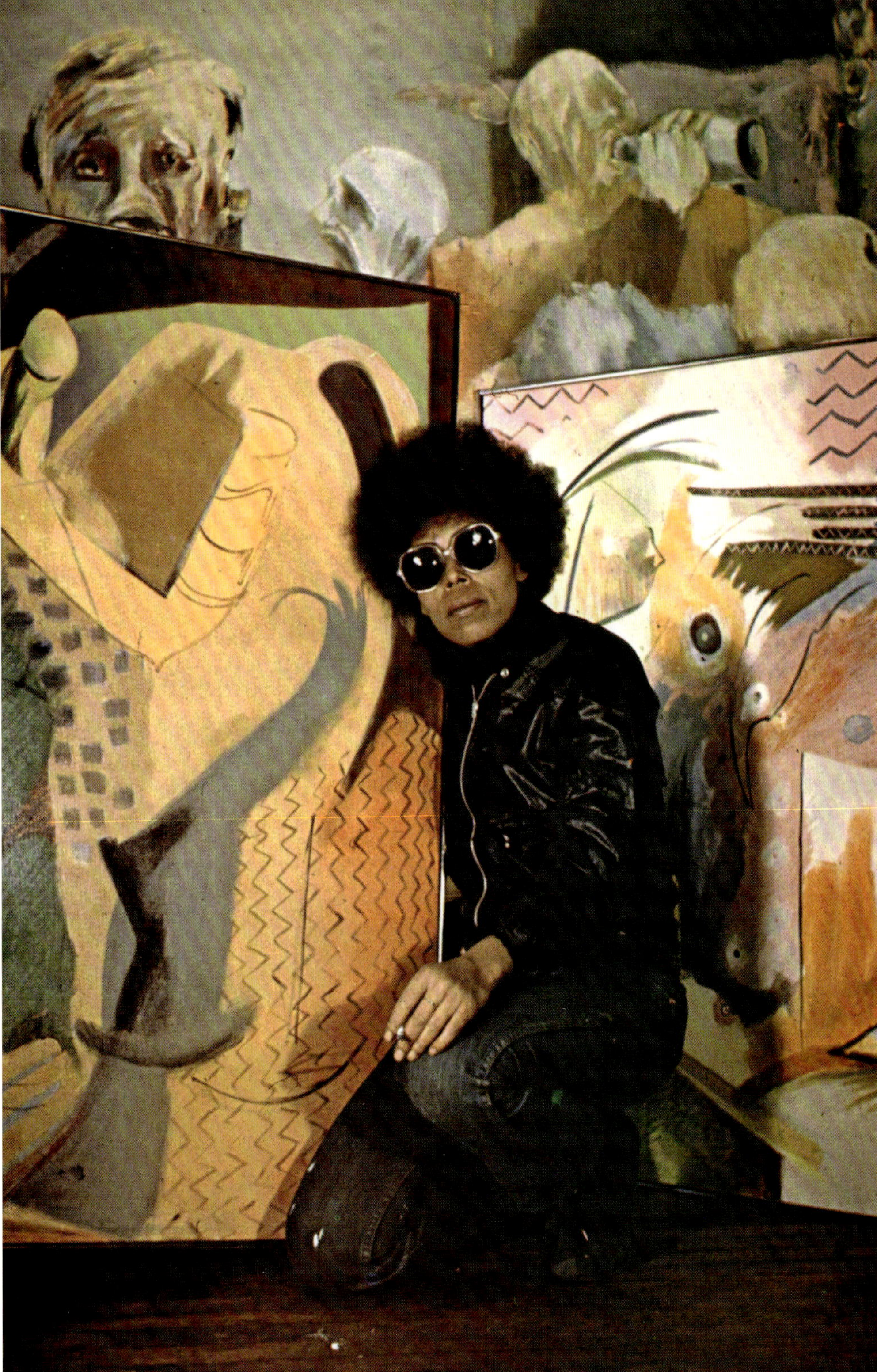

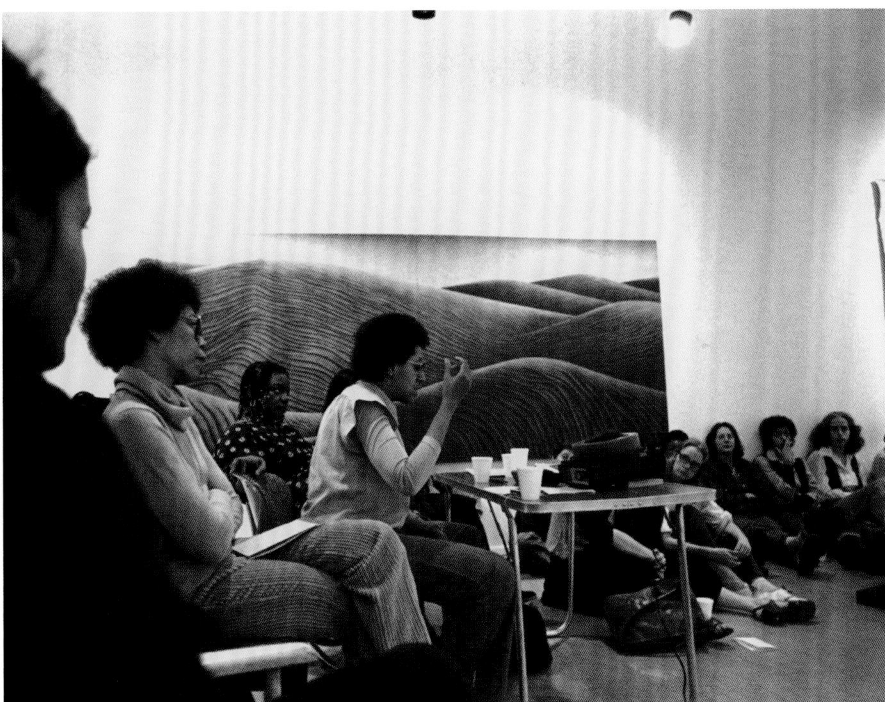

diversity was pointed out. The group responded by hosting several debates on race and inclusion, and by publishing several issues on these topics.

Browne contributed her first article to the eighth issue, "Third World Women," which was published two years after the journal's founding. Organized by an editorial collective that included no founding members, the issue displayed textual and visual contributions from over fifty writers and artists, including Howardena Pindell, Ana Mendieta, Betye Saar, Zarina Hashmi, Virginia Jaramillo, Audre Lorde, and Jaune Quick-to-See Smith. As a contributor, Browne attended an open meeting that was organized for the launch of the issue (fig. 8) and participated in discussions that led to 1982's "Racism is the Issue" edition, for which she served on the editorial collective.[35] Browne commented, "There was very great difficulty for the women of Heresies the major collective, in talking to the Third World. So we suggested that we just call it what it is and do an issue on racism."[36] Throughout the 1980s and until her death, Browne was involved as an advisor for Heresies, providing feedback and assistance as needed for various issues and events that were organized by the collective.[37]

Browne's investment in feminist circles and in tackling inequalities in the art world and beyond was a preoccupation that informed her life and art throughout her entire career. While eschewing the conventions of Black art or protest art, as well as the tenets of abstraction, she paved her own way, developing a singular voice that functioned alongside her activist and collective activities. Browne defiantly expressed what she was *not*, preferring not to be labeled "black," "woman," or "political." In a 1986 artist statement, she remarked: "I am not an issue-oriented painter, sometimes the questions interest me more … that keeps me at it."[38] The previous year, she had noted: "During the Civil Rights Era, one had to paint black themes, black people, black ideas. I didn't." She went on: "Now they're saying 'is there a women's art?' Then I was painting these little old white men."[39] Browne's work was radical in that it defied the expectations of what a Black woman artist should have been painting at the time. Her refusal to address overtly radicalized or sexualized subjects demonstrates an engagement with Black art and feminism in a more nuanced way that placed it outside of the neatly defined movements and styles—a testament to both her singular voice and her simultaneous commitment to collective action.

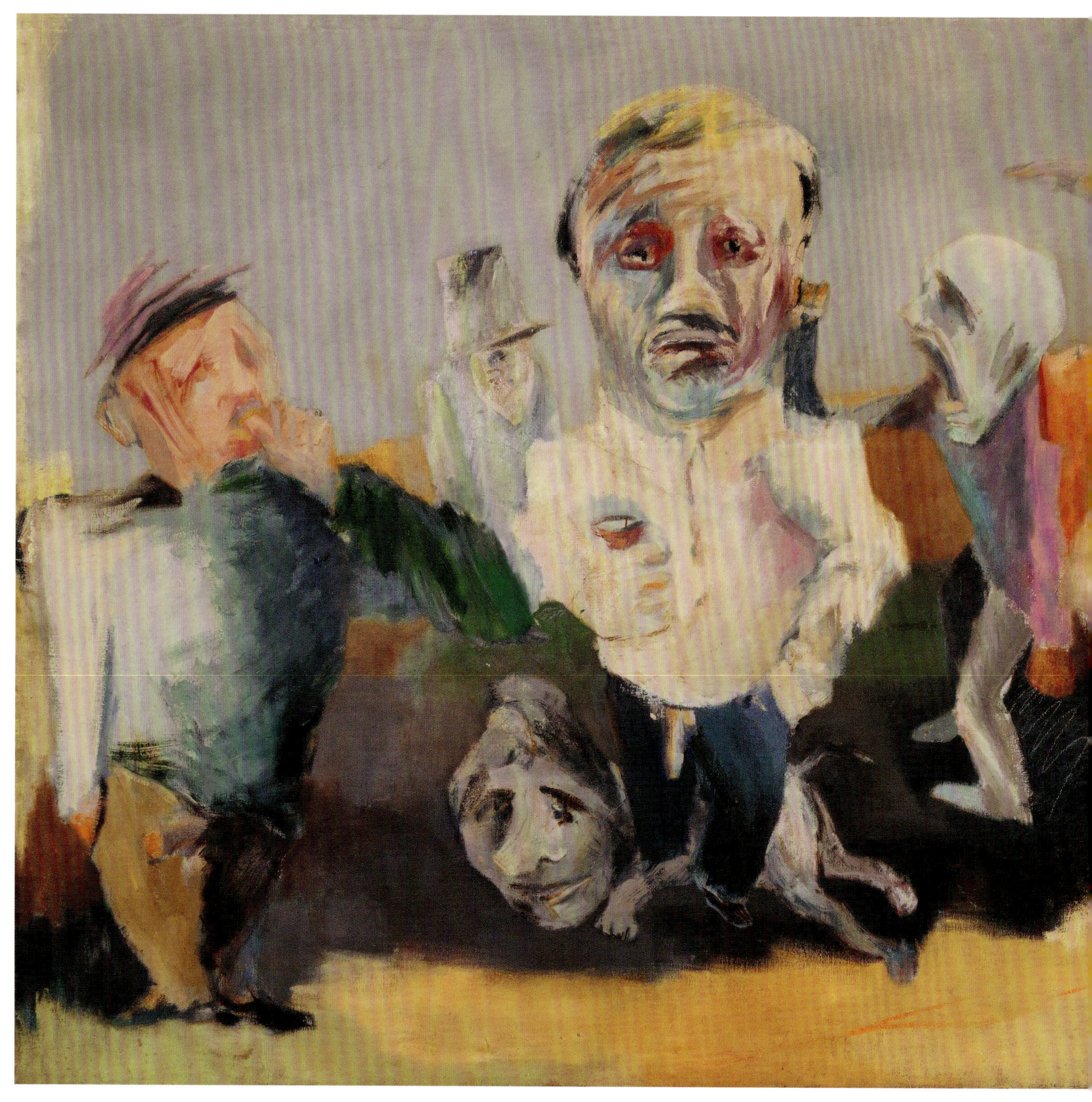

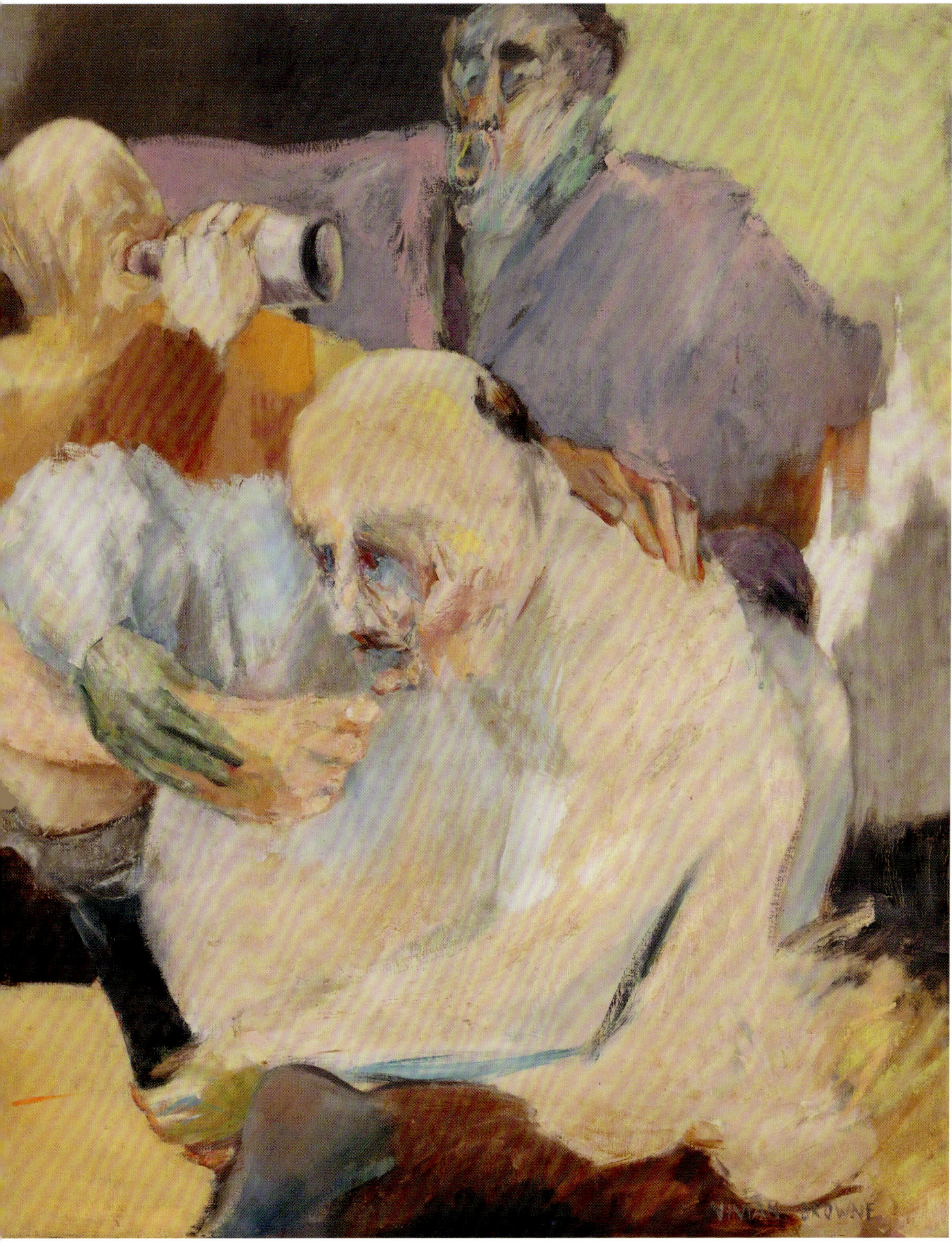

Plate 14
Seven Deadly Sins, c. 1968
Oil on canvas
59 × 112 inches
Adobe Krow Archives, CA
and RYAN LEE Gallery, NY

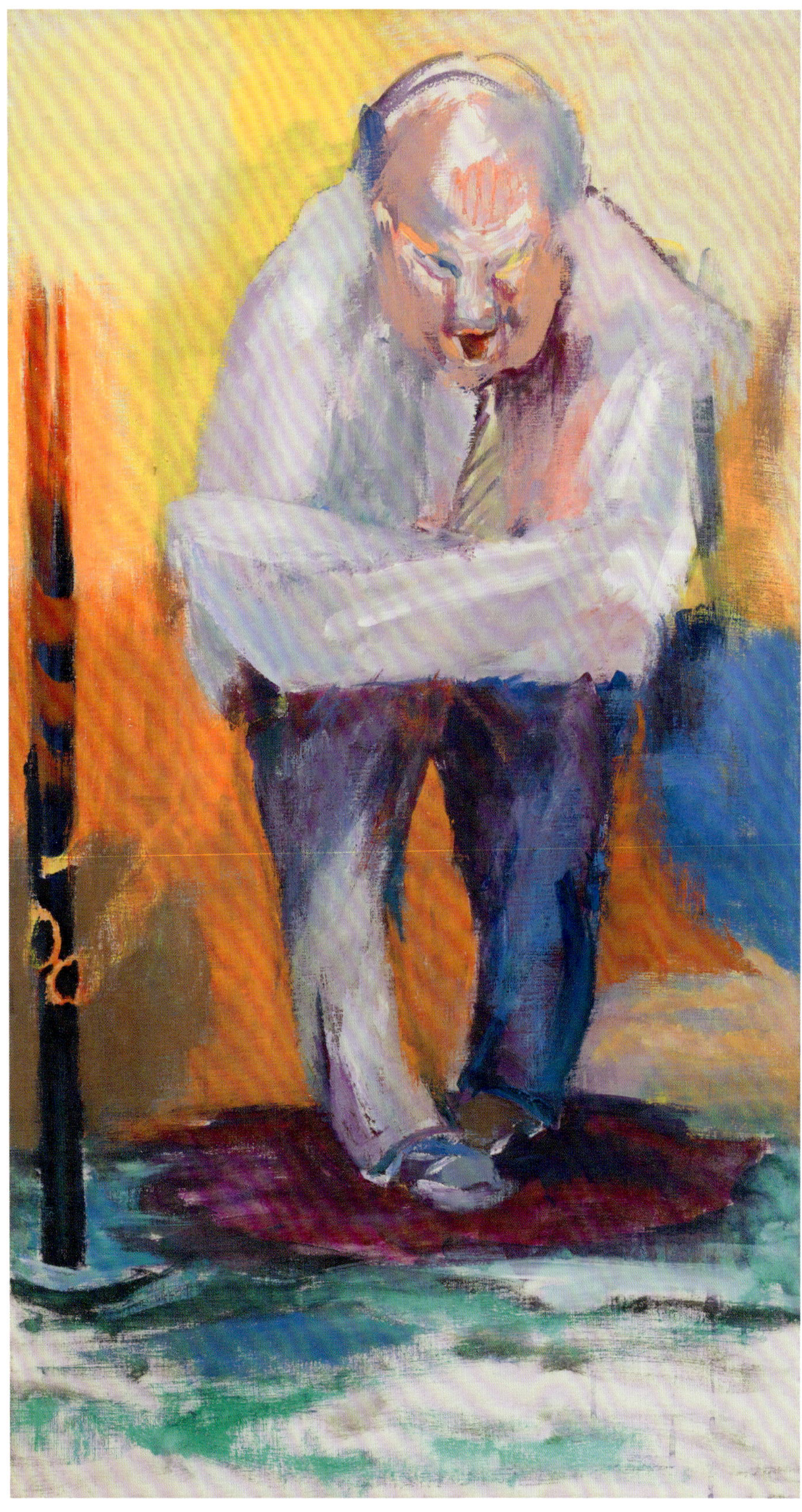

Plate 15
Untitled (Little Man with Arms Crossed), c. 1967
Oil on canvas
36 × 20 inches
Baz Family Collection, Colorado,
courtesy RYAN LEE Gallery

Plate 16
Wall Street Dancer, 1968
Oil on canvas
54 × 48 inches
Collection of Beth Rudin DeWoody

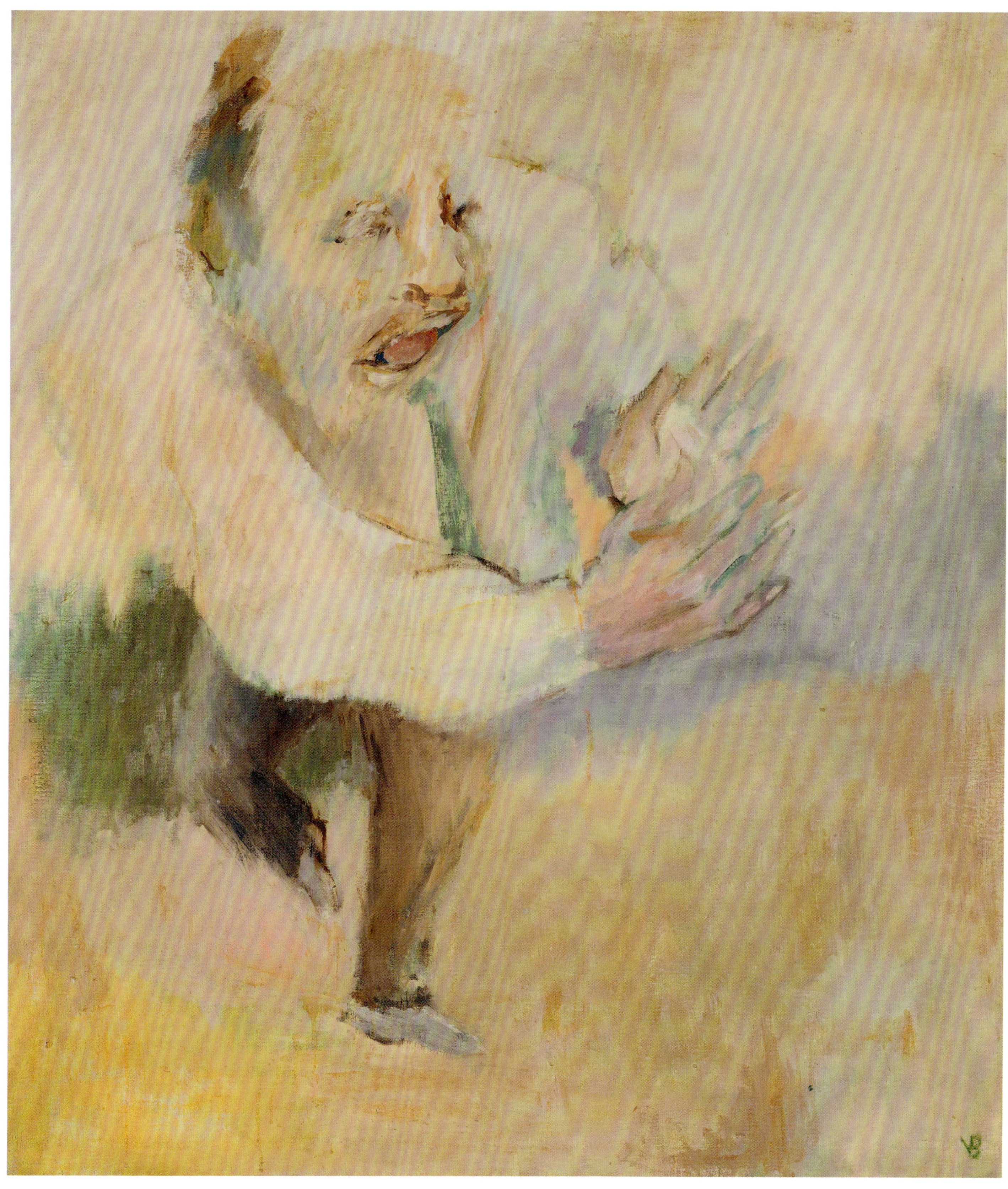

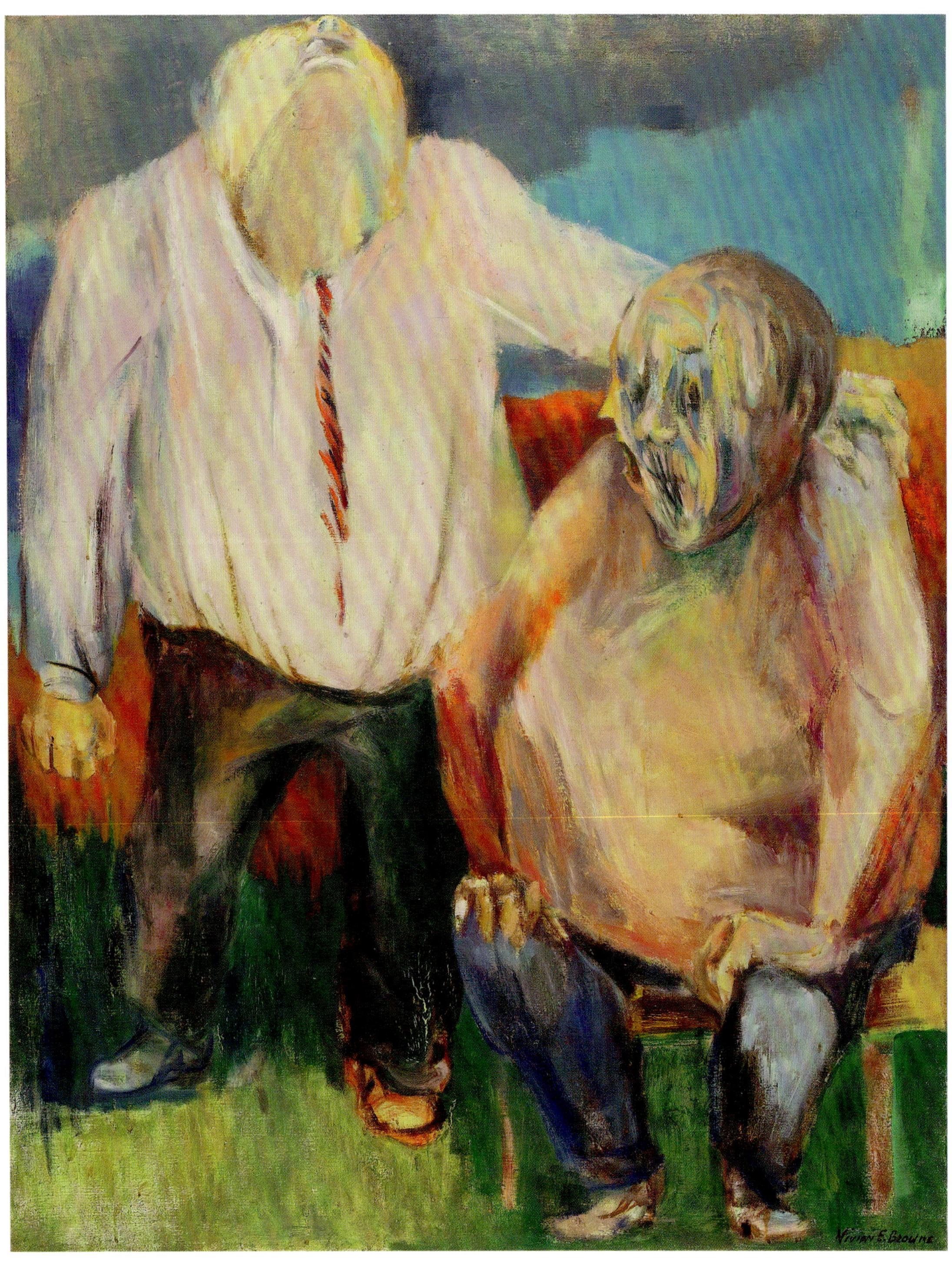

Plate 17
Two Men, 1969
Oil on canvas
61 × 48 inches
Baz Family Collection, Colorado,
courtesy RYAN LEE Gallery

Plate 18
Wall Street Jump, 1969
Oil on canvas
59 ¾ × 46 inches
Adobe Krow Archives, CA
and RYAN LEE Gallery, NY

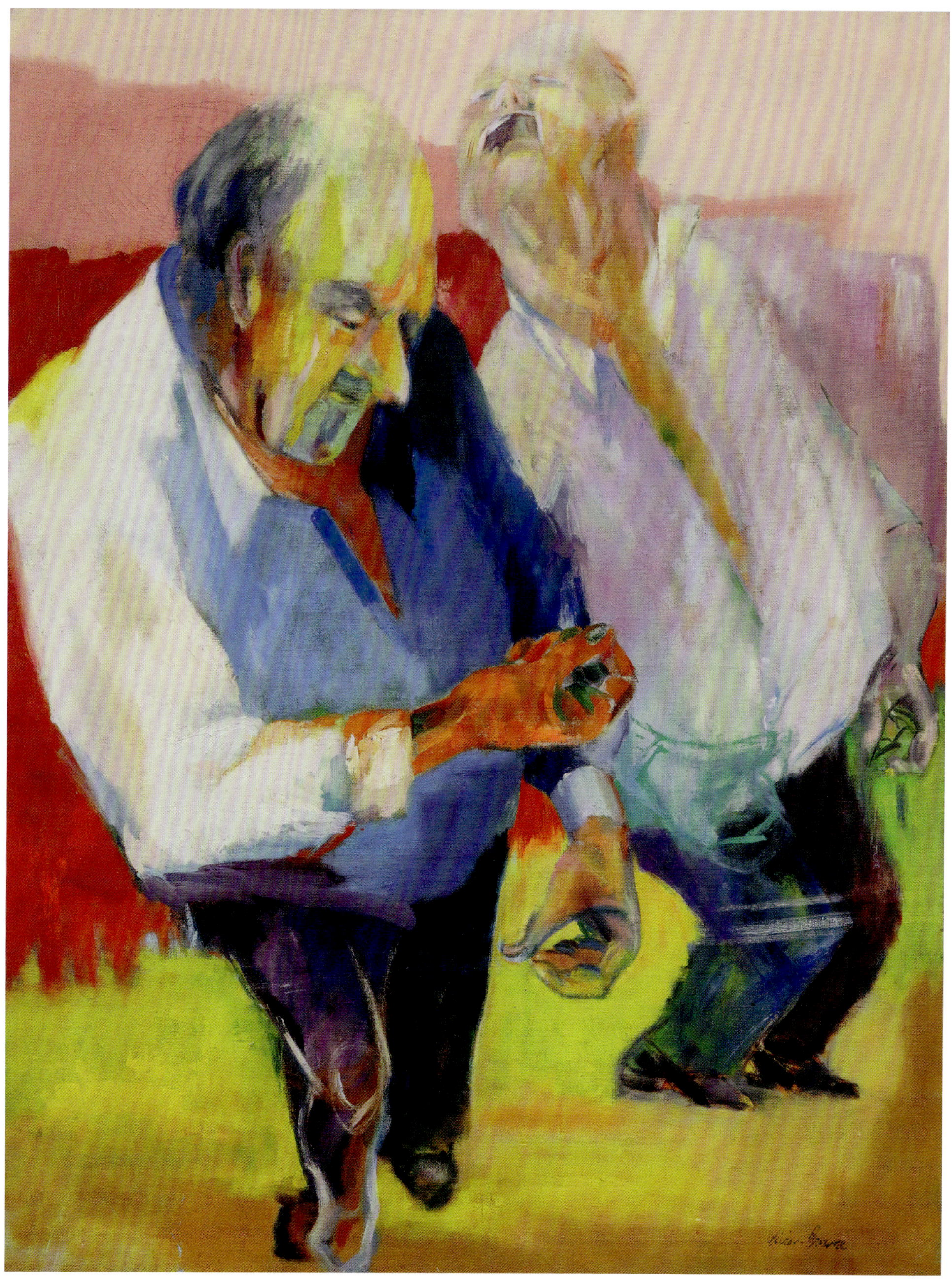

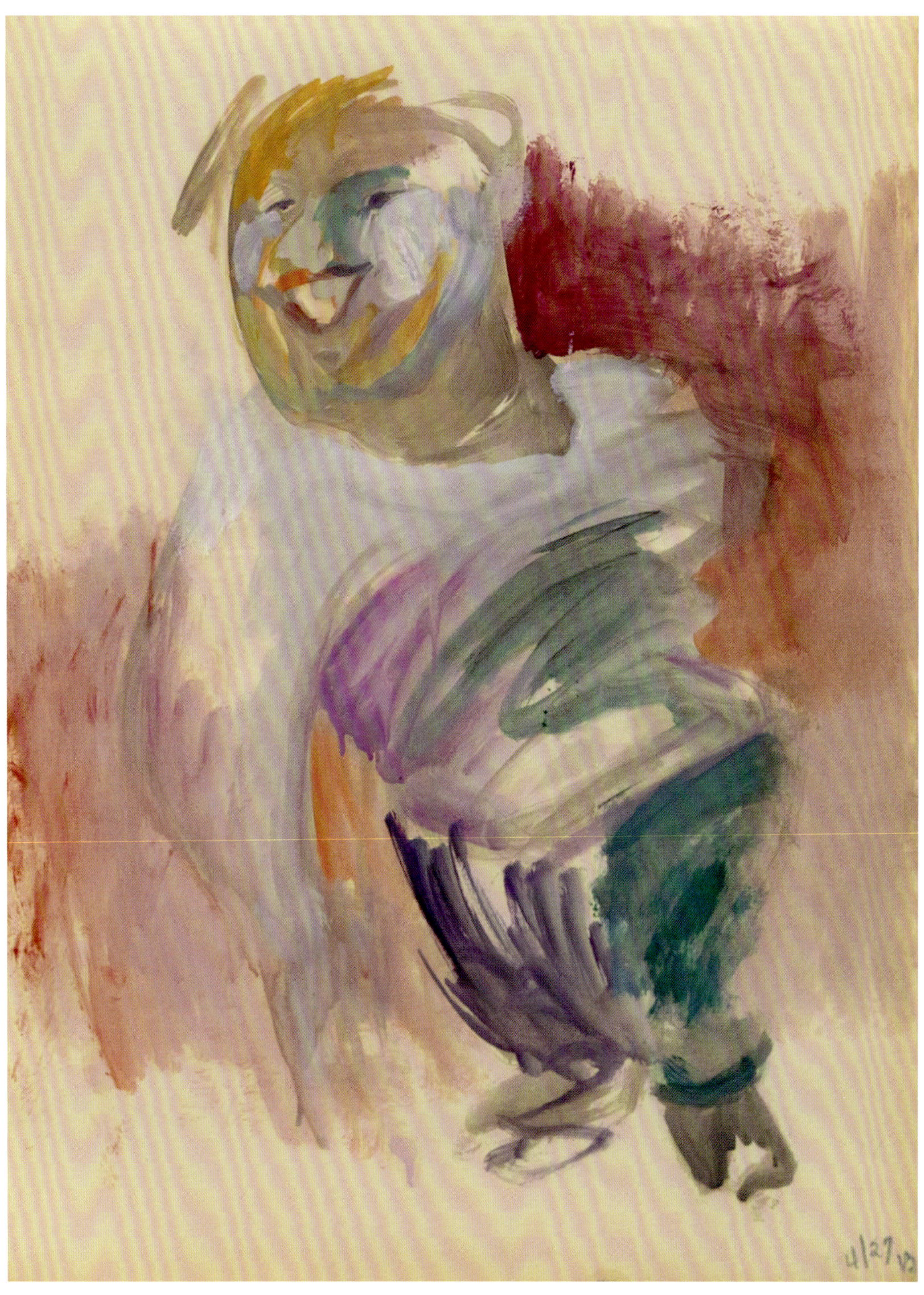

Plate 19
Little Men #12, c. 1967
Oil on paper
23 ¾ × 17 ¾ inches
Adobe Krow Archives, CA
and RYAN LEE Gallery, NY

Plate 20
Little Men #3, c. 1967
Oil on paper
23 ¾ × 17 ¾ inches
Adobe Krow Archives, CA
and RYAN LEE Gallery, NY

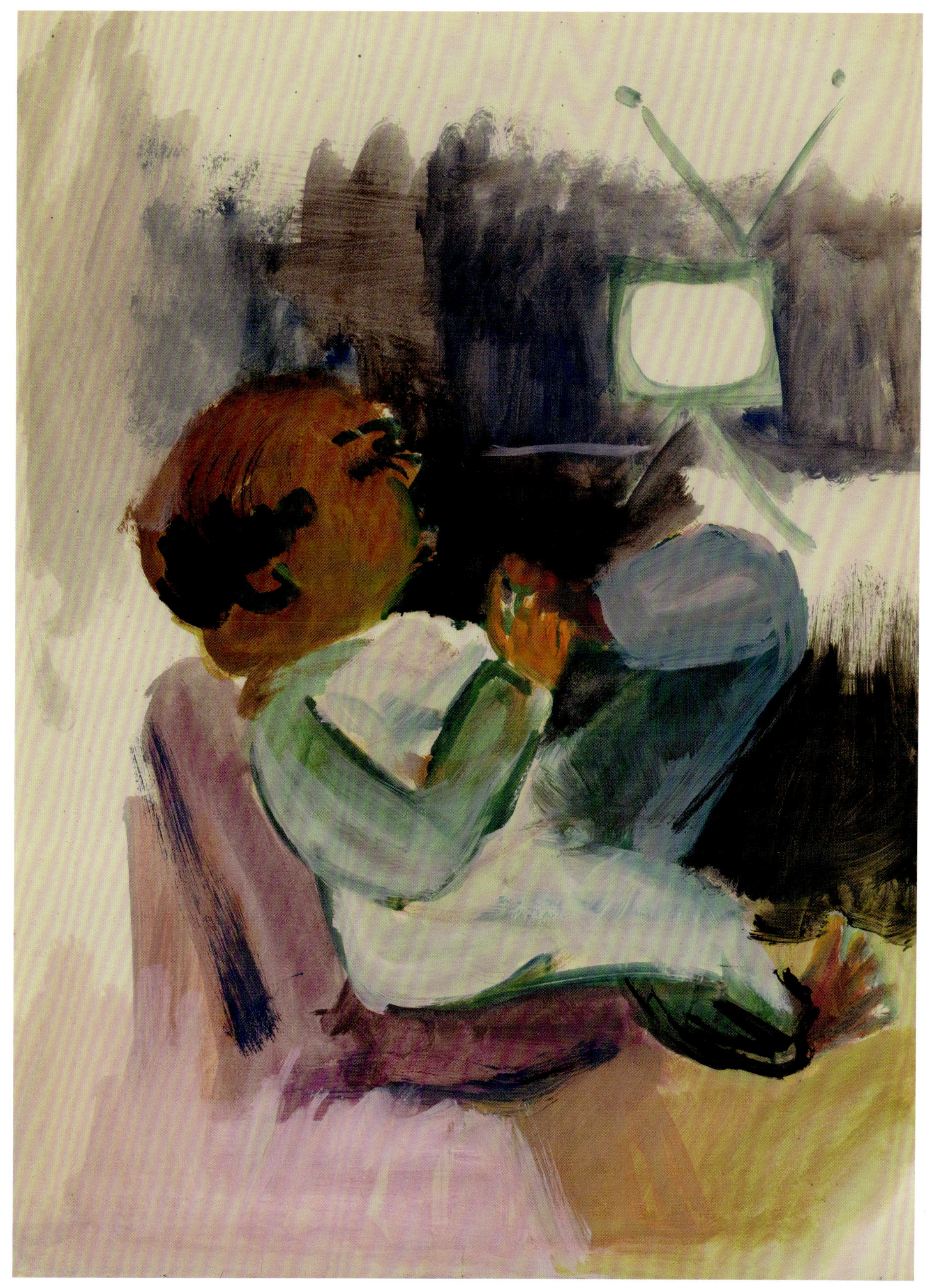

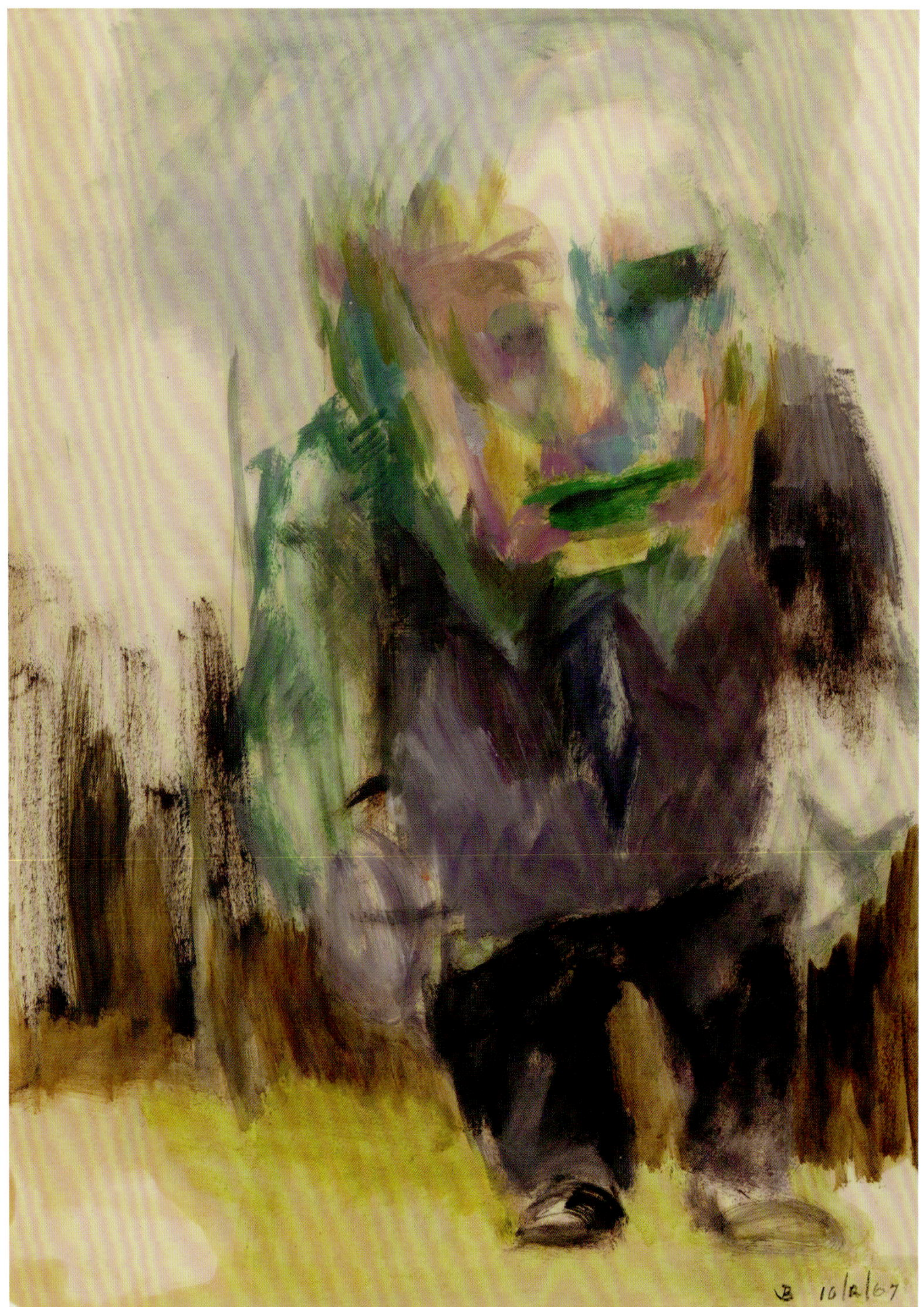

Plate 21
Little Men #77, 1967
Oil on paper
23 ¾ × 17 1/8 inches
Adobe Krow Archives, CA
and RYAN LEE Gallery, NY

Plate 22
Little Men #4, c. 1967
Oil on paper
23 ¾ × 17 ¾ inches
Collection of James Keith Brown and
Eric G. Diefenbach, courtesy RYAN LEE Gallery

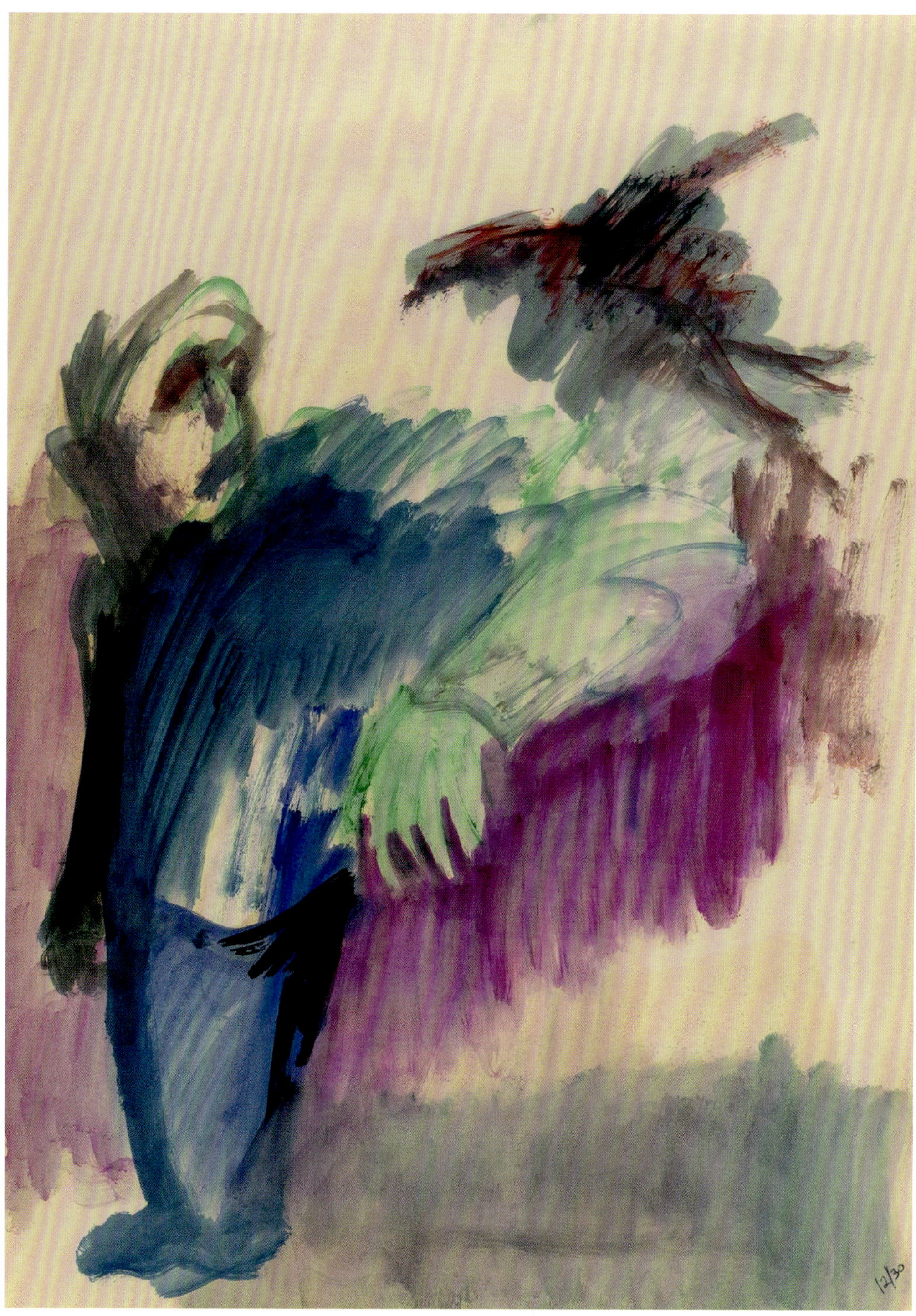

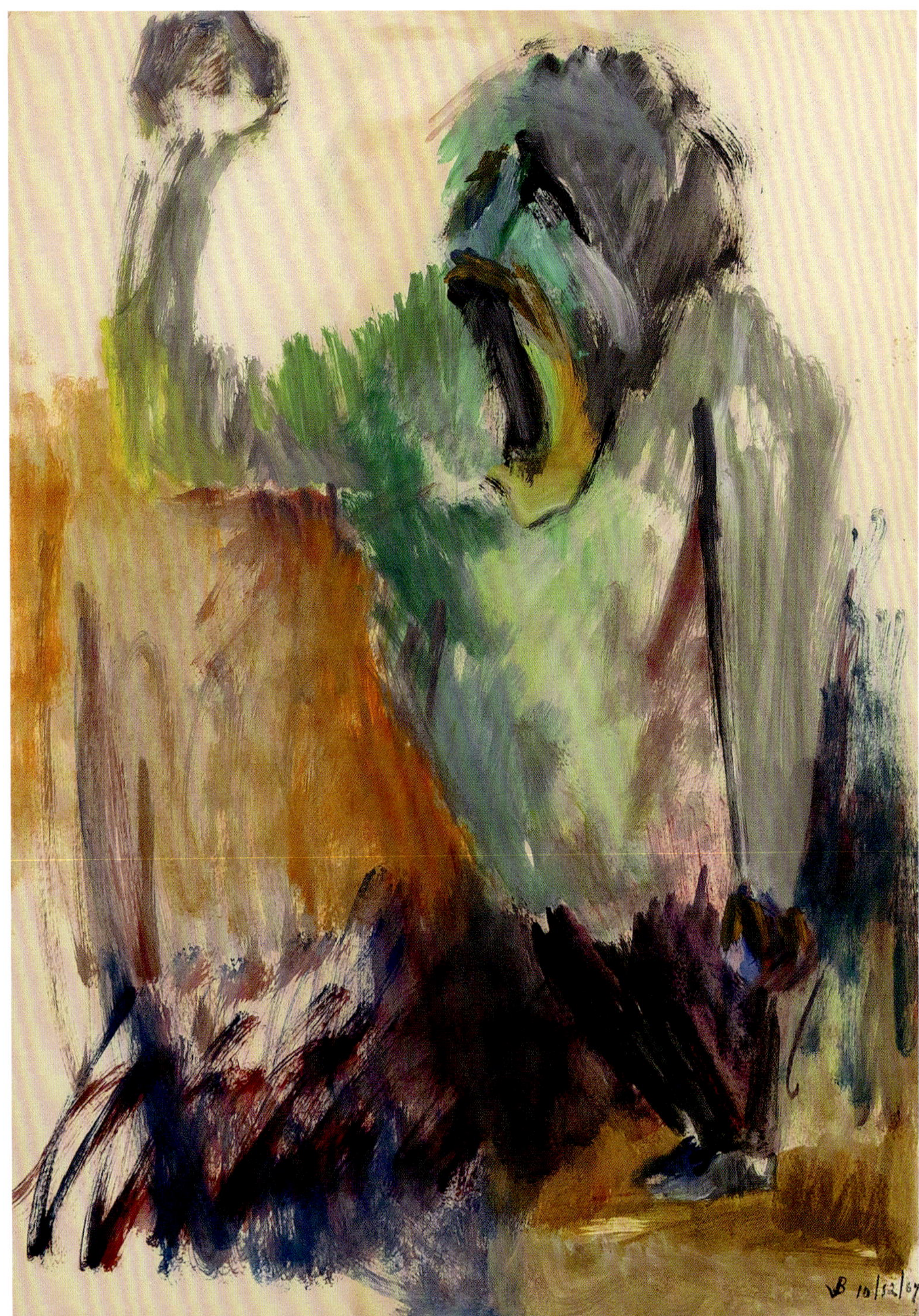

Plate 23
***Little Men #7*, 1967**
Oil on paper
23 ¾ × 17 1/8 inches
The Museum of Modern Art, New York.
Acquired through the generosity of
Marie-Josée and Henry R. Kravis, 2020

Plate 24
Little Men #86, 1967
Oil on paper
23 ¾ × 17 1/8 inches
The Museum of Modern Art, New York.
Acquired through the generosity of
Marie-Josée and Henry R. Kravis, 2020

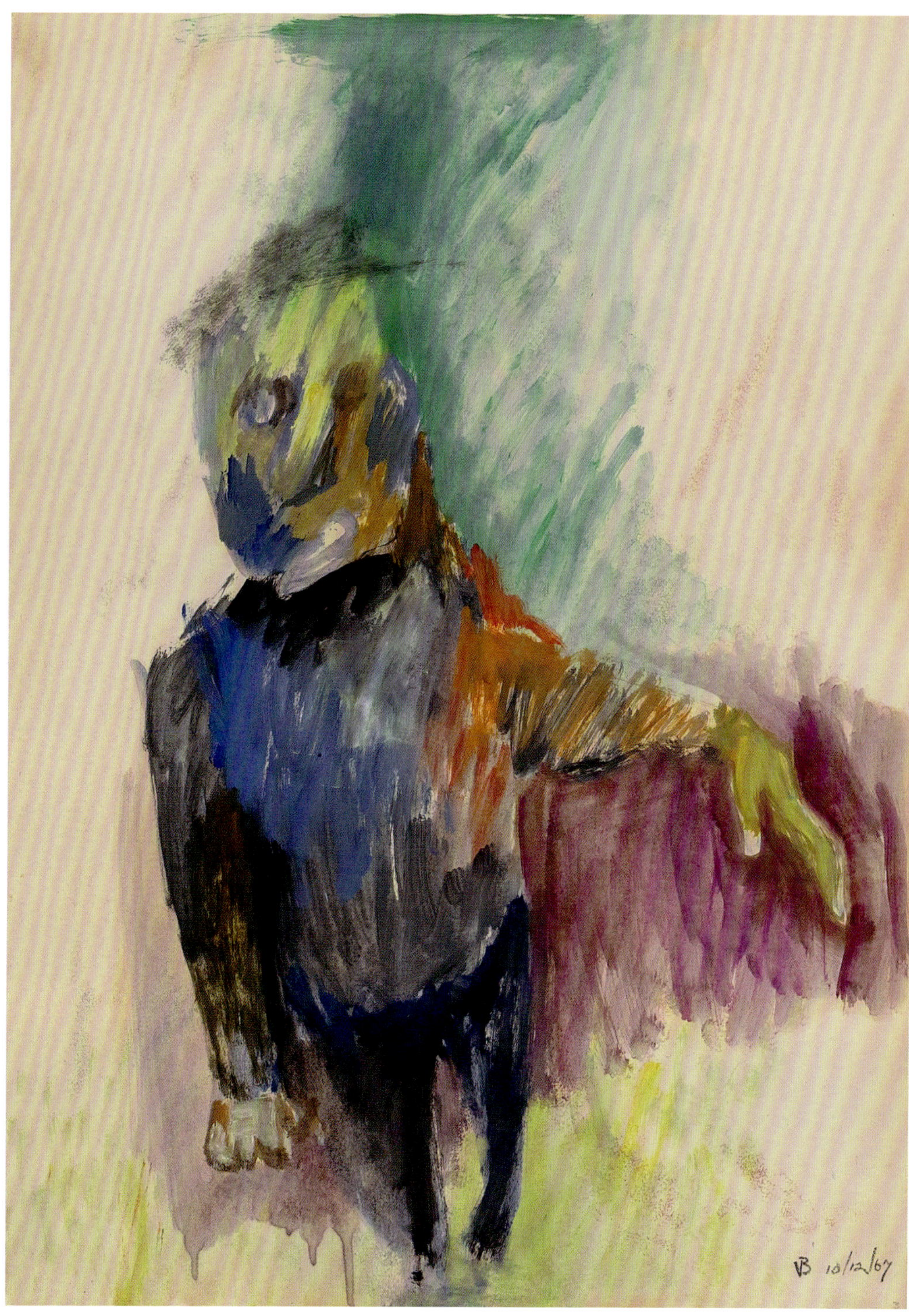

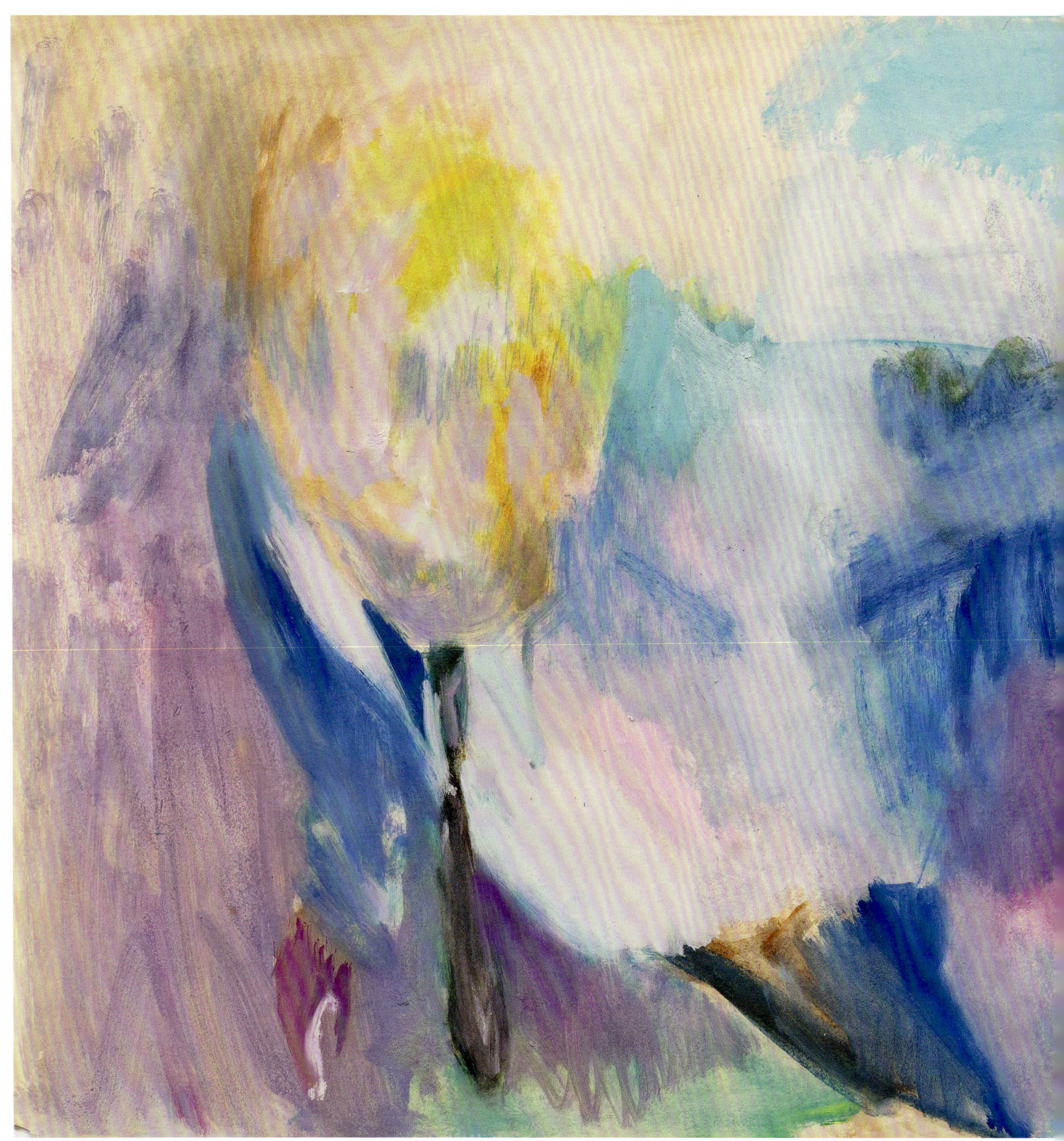

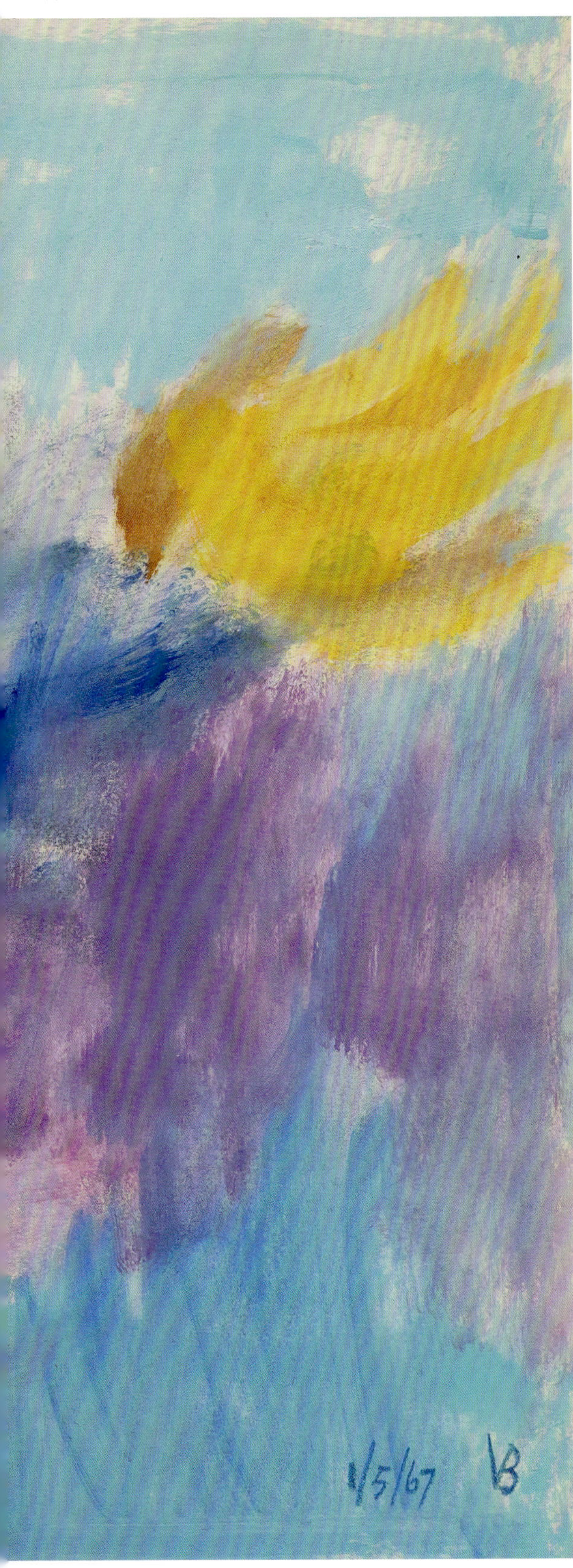

Plate 25
Little Men #30 / I Had a Dream,
1967
Oil on paper
17 1/8 × 24 inches
Adobe Krow Archives, CA
and RYAN LEE Gallery, NY

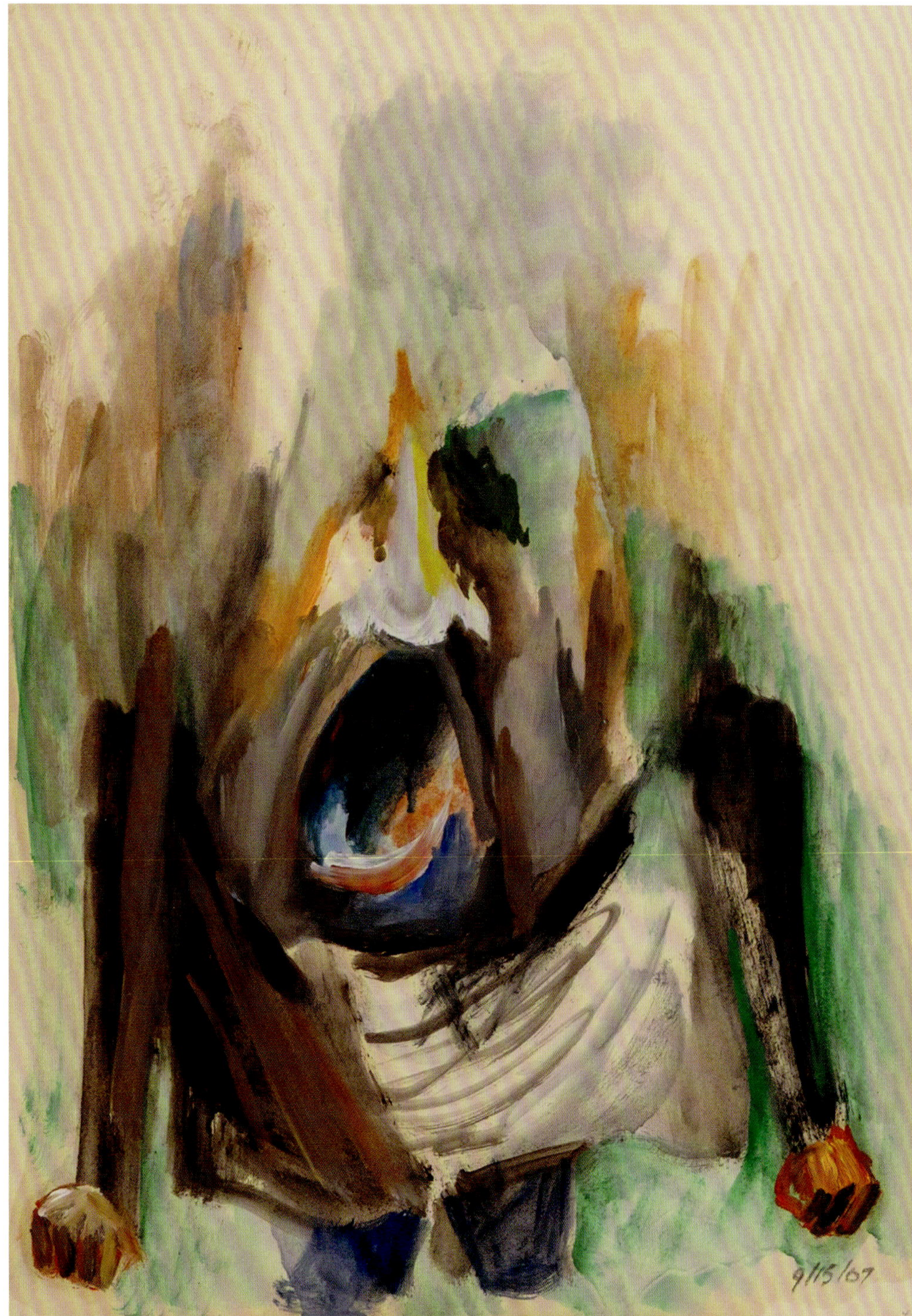

Plate 26
Little Men #102, c. 1967
Oil on paper
23 ¾ × 17 1/8 inches
Private Collection; Promised gift on long-term
loan to the Minneapolis Institute of Art.

Plate 27
Little Men #78, c. 1967
Oil on paper
23 ¾ × 17 ¾ inches
Adobe Krow Archives, CA
and RYAN LEE Gallery, NY

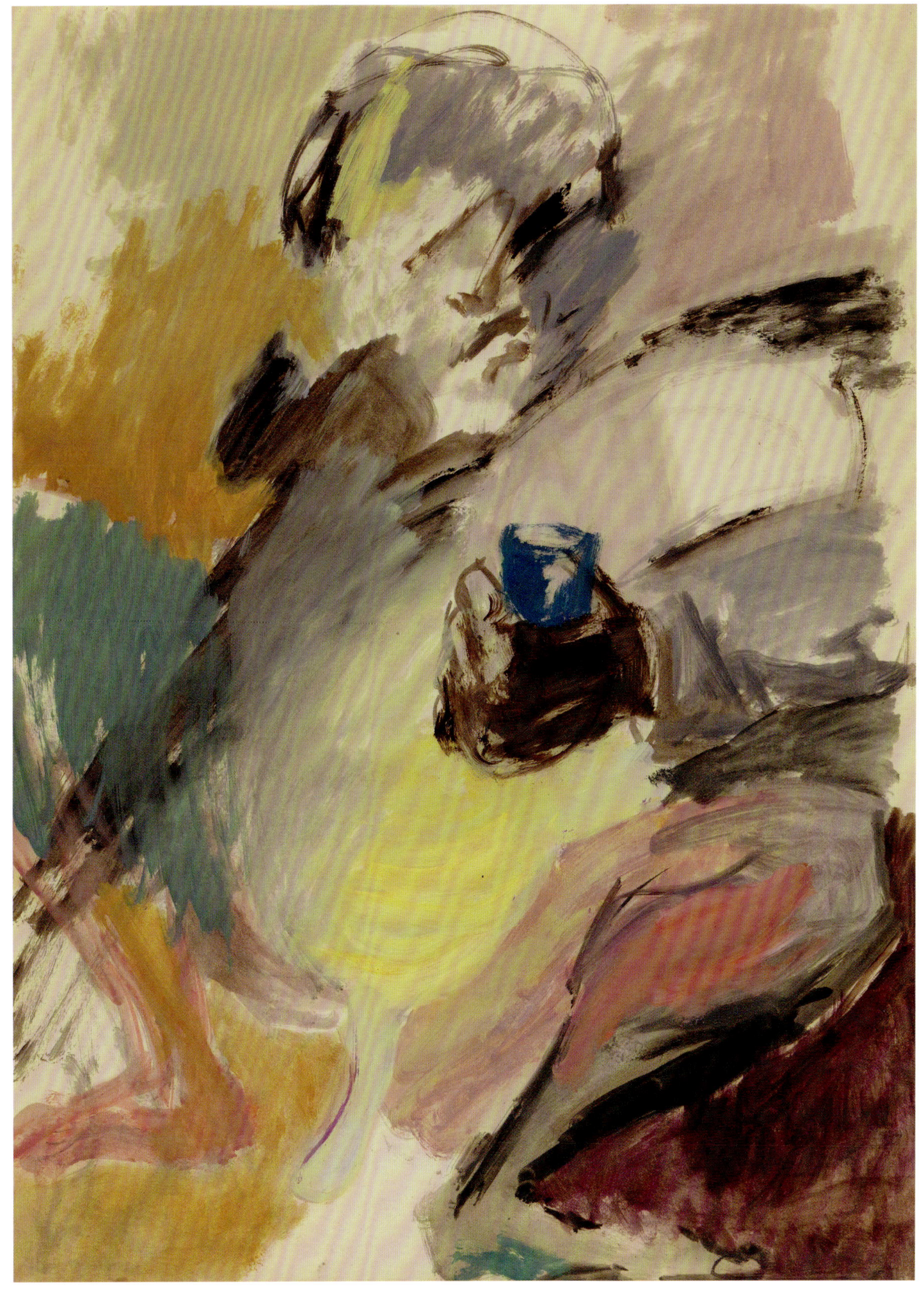

Plate 28
Warning, c. 1970
Etching
20 ¾ × 27 ½ inches
Adobe Krow Archives, CA
and RYAN LEE Gallery, NY

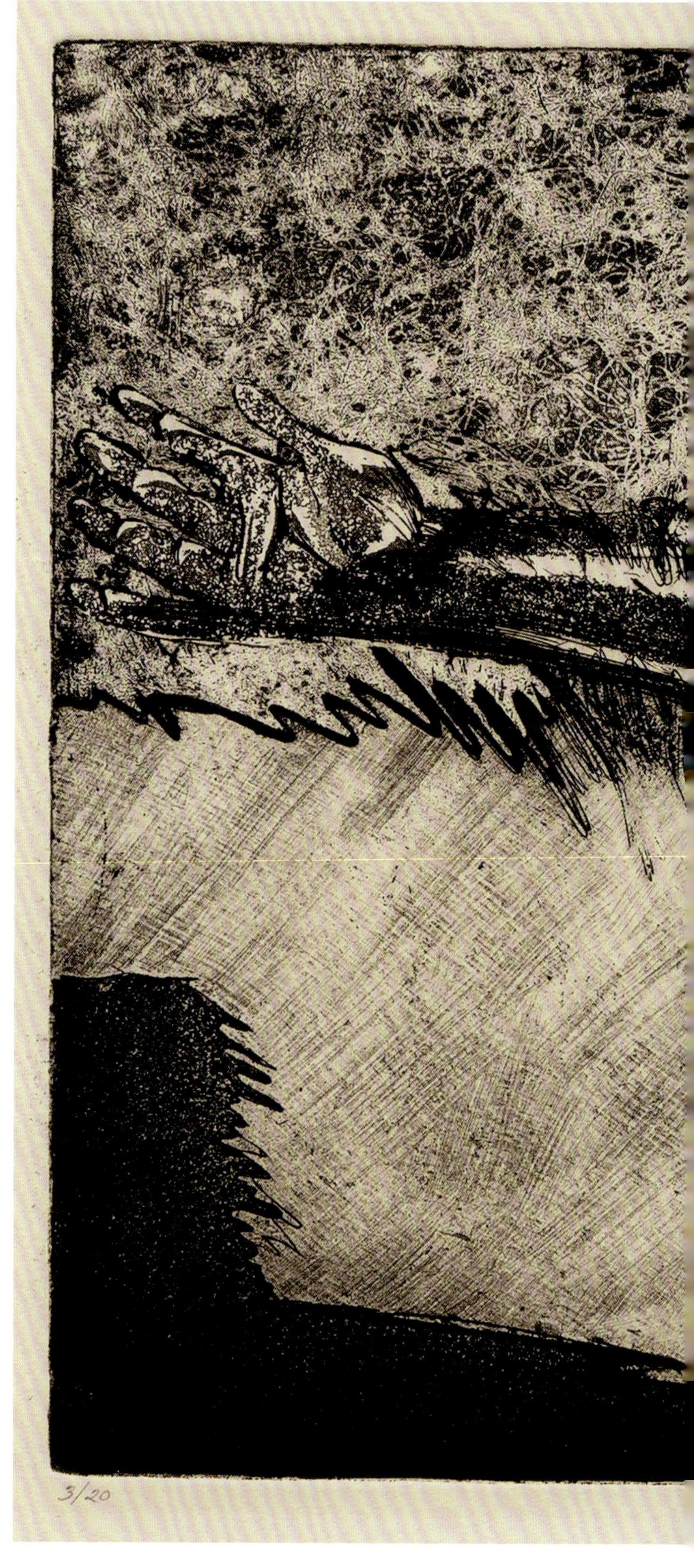

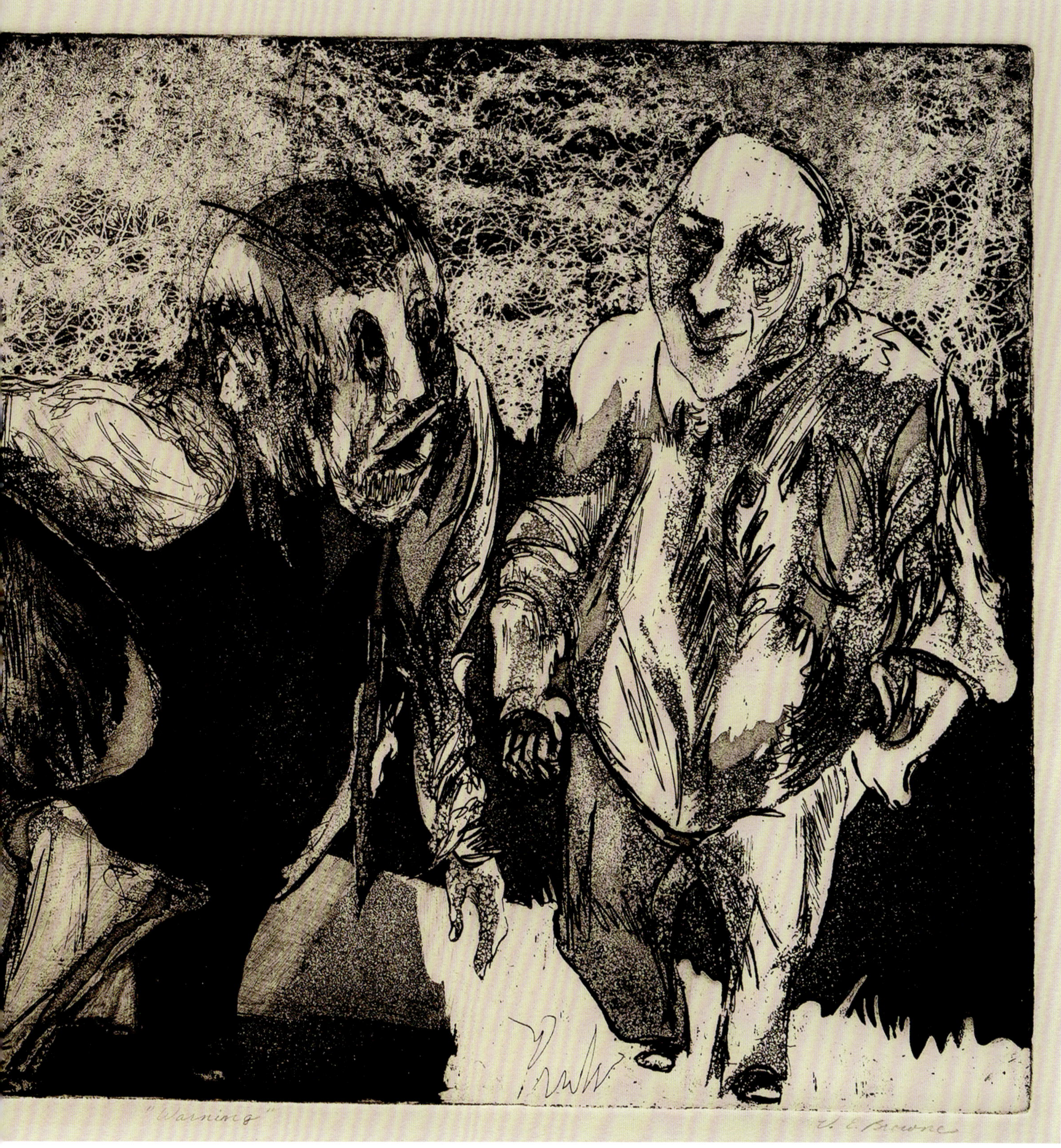

"Warning"

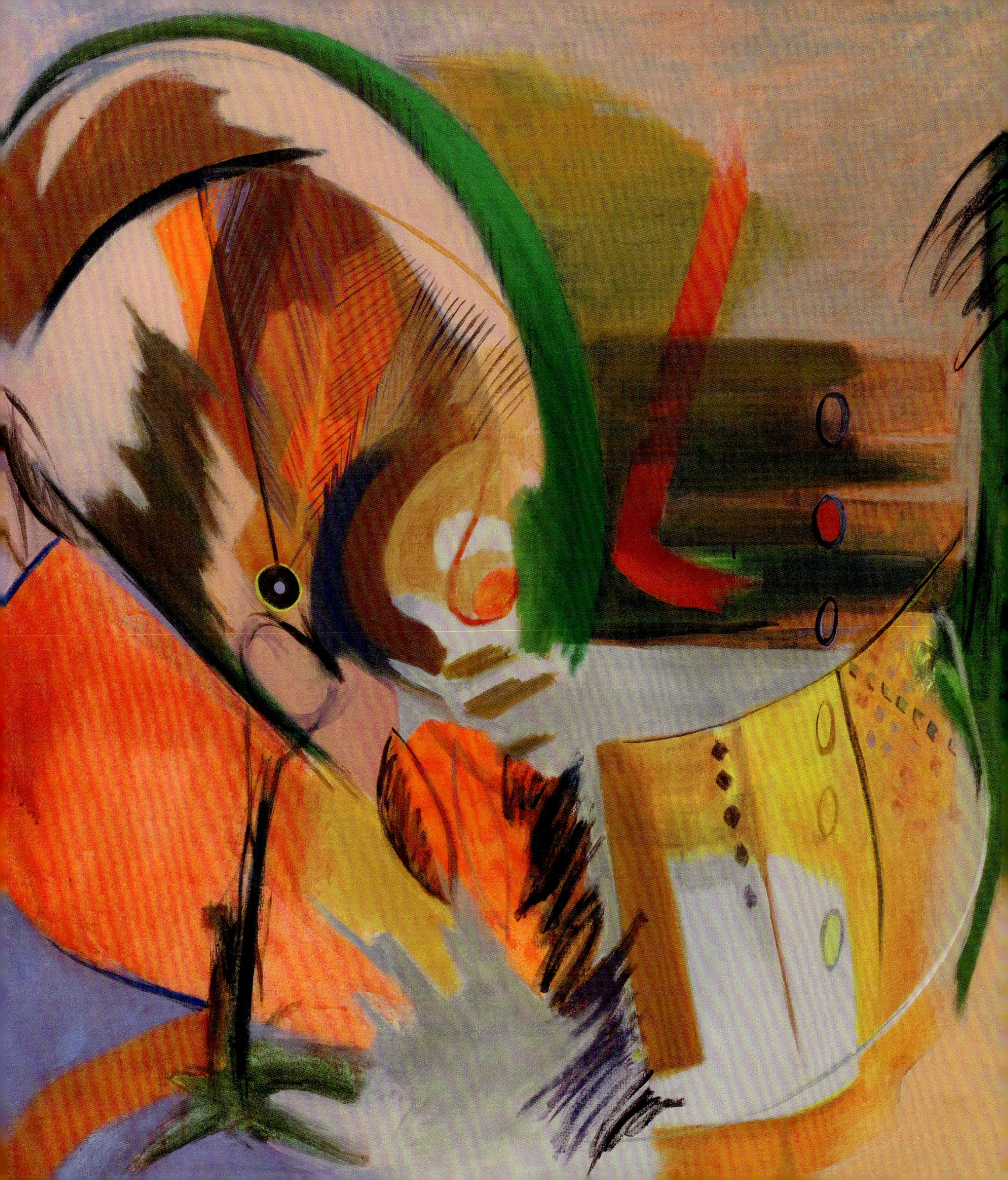

Intangible: Vivian Browne and the African Experience

Adrienne L. Childs

"My work changed from figurative to abstract. It changed without my deliberation. It changed because what I wanted to say changed. I had to paint differently in order to say it. My work began to be abstract after I came from Africa. The experience in Africa was such an emotional uplift that abstraction seemed to be the only way, manner, in which to work."[40]

A 1971 snapshot of Vivian Browne during her study trip to West Africa captures the artist in a moment of leisure, reclining on Victoria Beach in Lagos, Nigeria (fig. 1). With legs, arm, and head pointing distinctly to her left, she strikes a pose, showcasing her crown-like braided coiffure. While Browne's Nigerian hairstyle is an of-the-moment fashion statement, its decorative flourish reflects a Nigerian tradition of sculptural hair fashions dating back centuries. Browne's stylized hairstyle echoes those documented by renowned Nigerian photographer J.D. 'Okhai Ojeikere in works such as *Untitled (Ife Bronze)* (fig. 2). In this series of photographs, Ojeikere chronicles a post-colonial moment in Nigeria in which women's hairstyles reflected the interweaving of tradition, national identity, and cosmopolitan lifestyles. In fact, Ojeikere was involved in this documentary project during Browne's visit to Nigeria. In this era when many Black American artists touted their ties to Africa as an essential genealogy, Browne's hairstyle might signal a personal embrace of that lineage. Browne's sojourn in West Africa was indeed a meaningful experience for her, one that was uplifting and would inspire a significant shift in her artmaking. Yet Browne's enthusiasm for Nigerian culture was more exploration than homecoming, more observation and reaction than embrace of an unbroken cultural heritage. In a 1972 interview with James V. Hatch, Browne reflected on her trip to West Africa: "Now, after having been, I am even more aware of the fact that Americans—Black Americans—they're just not Africans. We are not Africans, and we have some link and it's intangible."[41] Although cognizant of intangible connections to Africa, Browne remained cautious about claiming her African-ness. This ambivalence, this flirtation with the intangibility of Africa, would come to characterize her *Africa Series*, a body of work as compelling, complex, and individual as the artist herself.

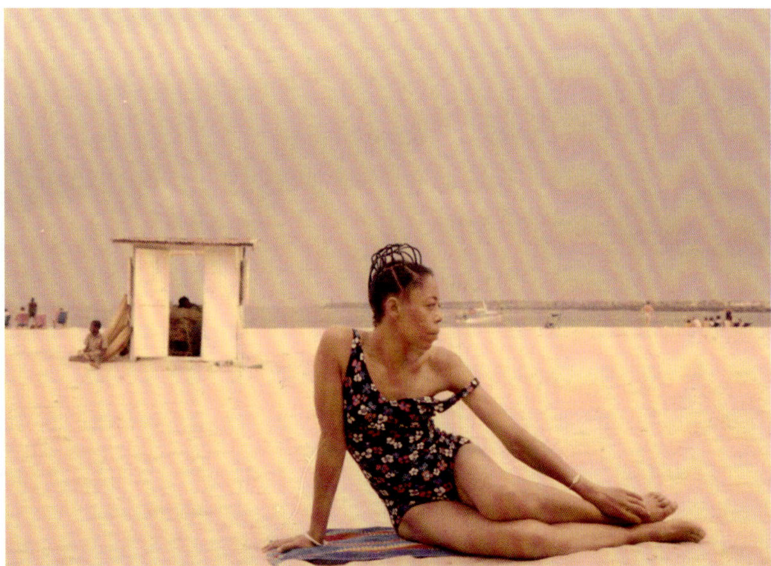

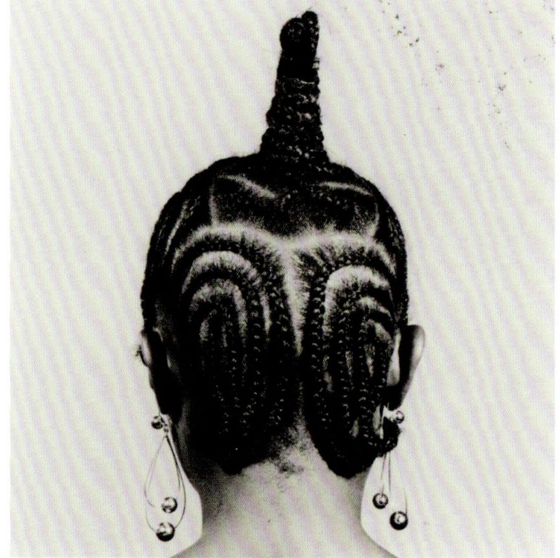

Fig.1
Vivian Browne on Victoria
Beach in Lagos, Nigeria, 1971

Fig.2
J.D. 'Okhai Ojeikere
Untitled (Ife Bronze), 1972
Gelatin silver print
The Phillips Collection, Gift of Julia J. Norrell, 2018

Artist, teacher, and activist, Browne was a consummate traveler who cultivated global experiences that took her throughout the United States and beyond to Mexico, Jamaica, Europe, the Middle East, North Africa, West Africa, and China.[42] Like many artists, travel deeply impacted her artistry, and her 1971 trip to Nigeria precipitated a critical turning point in her career as a painter. Accompanied by the artist and scholar Floyd Coleman (see plate 42), Browne spent six weeks at the University of Ibadan, a historic site for the development of modern African art, and two weeks in Lagos and Ghana. Browne often stated that as a result of her experiences in West Africa her work shifted from figuration toward a more abstract visual language, one that she would nurture and refine for the remainder of her career.

The mid-twentieth century saw a global movement throughout the Black diaspora to support and celebrate Black creativity and the synergies between Black artistic expressions in Africa, Europe, and the Americas. For many Black American creatives of the 1960s and '70s—the years in which Browne came of age as an artist and activist—the idea of Africa wielded powerful, multivalent implications.

In the U.S. a wave of Black artistic energy and agency known as the Black Arts Movement (BAM), occurring roughly through the 1960s into the early 1970s, animated the Black art world through which Browne navigated. BAM was assertively separatist, radical, and intent on defining a Black aesthetic. The movement called for a reordering of the Western cultural ethos.[43] AfriCOBRA—or the African Commune of Bad Relevant Artists, founded in 1968— was a collective of Black artists who embody the fullest expression of the movement. Their acronym centers the idea/ideal of Africa as a driving force in their practice. Their philosophical concepts included creating images "inspired by African people and their experience; Images performing some function that African people can relate to directly and experience."[44]

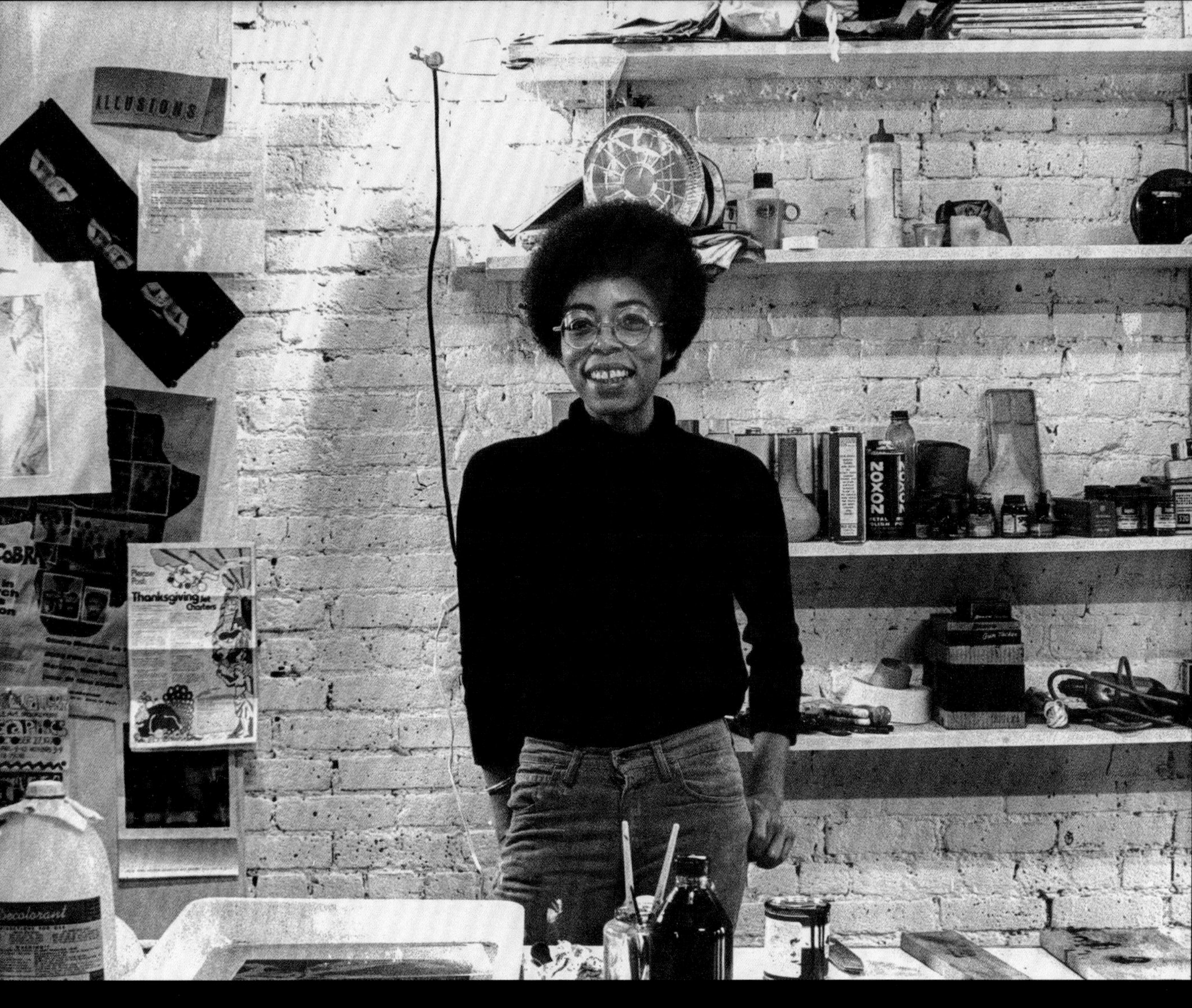

Fig.3
Vivian Browne in her studio, 1970

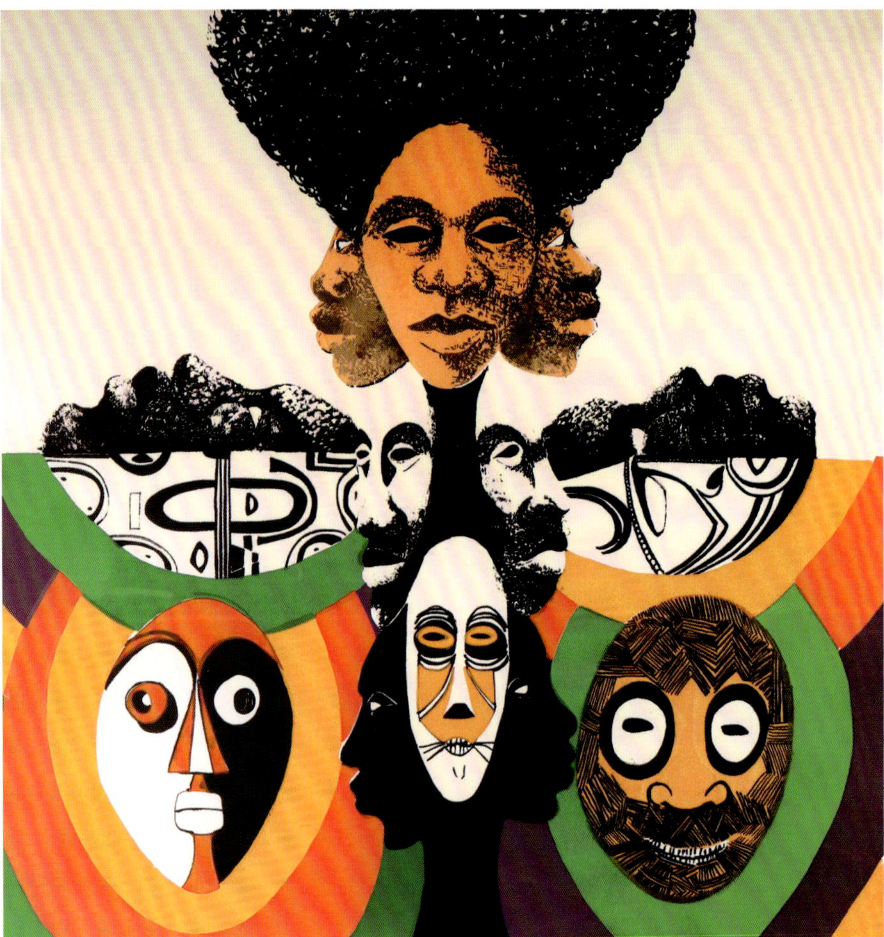

Browne was keenly aware of the afro-centric philosophies and aesthetics of AfriCOBRA, whose exhibition *Ten in Search of a Nation* was mounted at the Studio Museum in Harlem in 1970, a year before her trip to Nigeria. In fact, a poster for the exhibition is visible on Browne's studio wall in a photo dated 1970 (fig. 3). In *Ten in Search of a Nation*, Browne would have encountered brightly colored, dynamic figurative works by artists such as Jeff Donaldson, Wadsworth Jarrell, and Barbara Jones-Hogu, aimed at realizing the spirit of Black nationhood and representing a kaleidoscopic African family tree. Jones-Hogu's print *Heritage* was featured in the exhibition and reproduced on the poster in Browne's studio (fig. 4). The print makes explicit cultural connections between contemporary Black American identity, symbolized by naturalistic Black visages and the Afro hairstyle, and Africa as the motherland symbolized by schematized masks and patterns. Jones-Hogu and her cohort mounted a collective Black identity-making project that similarly occupied many of the artists in Browne's circle—albeit toward different aesthetic ends. Yet Browne forged her own path. In spite of her interest in the culture work of fellow artists, she resisted the Black nationalist bent driving BAM makers. Browne's would be a wholly individualistic approach to the idea and experience of Africa.

Black American artists of the period were consistently faced with navigating the notion of a conscious or unconscious engagement with African heritage and the supposition that it was *their* responsibility to express and amplify these heritable aesthetic traditions in their artistry. In this climate, it is not surprising that Hatch asked Browne if her trip to Nigeria was a "going home or looking for roots...."[45] Browne's response was characteristically ambivalent and demonstrated a resistance to the pull of these cultural forces:

> I think I was partially looking for roots, but not overly. A lot of people seem to go in a sense of going home and looking for roots. But I have somehow been always aware that my Western experience has been really the only one I have.... I have become interested in African art and I wanted to know about that firsthand.[46]

Browne was cautious about claiming an essentialist African lineage, but instead acknowledged the centrality of her Western experience as a Black woman. On one level, Africa's appeal to Browne was linked to her interest in traditional African sculpture; on another level, her engagement was tied to her visceral experience of West Africa, the sights and sounds. Eventually it would be these elements—traditional Nigerian sculpture coupled with her sensorial memories of her experiences—that would be the driving forces in her *Africa Series*.[47]

Finding the *Africa Series*: Memory and Abstraction
"And now I'm concerning myself more with form and color, but it's the form and color based on an African experience." [48]

Browne's six weeks at the University of Ibadan placed her and her companion Floyd Coleman in one of West Africa's most vibrant centers of artistic and literary production. It was a creative hub for some of the most important artists, musicians, and intellectuals of the era. Ibadan became a center for modernist African aesthetics when in 1961 the German writer and critic Ulli Beier, along with Wole Soyinka, Chinua Achebe and others, established the Mbari Artists and Writers Club—a collective that went on to become an influential space for artistic and literary production in 1960s Nigeria.[49] Interestingly, the artists and writers who were forging a postcolonial modernist ethos in Nigeria engaged in similar debates to the ones that Browne and her American colleagues were having regarding the politics of representation, tradition, identity, and the responsibilities of the modern African artist.[50] Even though Browne's visit to Ibadan followed the height of the Mbari activities, there remained an active artistic community.[51]

While in Nigeria and Ghana, Browne did not sketch or create work. Instead, she absorbed the multi-sensory experience in order to translate it into paintings, prints, and drawings. Upon her return she immediately began exploring her encounter with pattern. The 1971 painting *Umbrella Plant* (plate 30) references one of her beloved house plants and reveals the repartee between Browne's intimate environment and her memories of Nigeria. Browne stated that the patterns she observed while in Africa were overwhelming and all-encompassing. She designed her own patterns as a way to process what she encountered. Browne had a clear sense that, since she was not African, she could not "go where they go with pattern in their painting." But, rather, she could synthesize her own lived experiences, environments, and sensibilities.[52]

Although Browne often forefronted Africa's role in the abstract turn in her practice, she regularly incorporated figurative and narrative references such as classical Benin (present-day Nigeria) sculpture and Yoruba cosmology into the *Africa Series*. These often-elusive figural elements added a representational connective tissue that was a bridge to complete abstraction. In an untitled sketch we see Browne developing a figurative language for what would be a series of images of mounted Benin warriors (fig. 5). In the painting *Benin Equestrian*, the partially abstracted horseman emerges from a field of color, patterns, and expressive markings (fig. 6). In pale oranges and purples and other muted tones, Browne makes a clear reference to traditional Benin bronze sculptural forms—often considered some of the finest examples of early modern Nigerian artistic production. The facial features and sword in the sketch, as well as in *Benin Equestrian*, recall sixteenth-century works such as *Mounted ruler (so-called Horseman)* now in the collection of the Boston Museum of Fine Arts. Similarly, Browne's 1973 painting *The Gathering* features three figurative elements drawn from Benin equestrian bronzes (plate 34). The title points us to a gathering of horsemen. However, the composition is opaque, fashioned with fragments of bodies, equine-esque shapes, a disembodied face/mask, and a hybrid figure. This dream-like scene is executed in bright yellows, blues, and oranges, with interspersed abstract patterns and markings. Here, Browne hints at a narrative but pivots toward an almost surreal interplay of figures, objects, colors, and patterns.

Browne often incorporated references to Yoruba Ibeji into her paintings. Sacred Ibeji twins are divine Orishas (or deities in Yoruba cosmology) and the subject of one of the most enduring forms in Yoruba sculpture. In *Ibeji II* (plate 31) Browne conjures this cultural referent in the title, as she moves toward pure abstraction. The single eye and the suggestion of a head, neck, and arm in *Ibeji II* tease the figure. However, Browne reverses course and through abstraction disrupts the lure of narrative, diverting us from the seduction of tradition's familiarity. *Ibeji II* is largely a series of abstract passages, part gestural marking and part color field. *The Chief's Attendant* (plate 32) is a fully abstract painting with no reference to the representational source of the title. What Browne does offer in these works is a riot of color and expressive form that draw upon memories and experiences in a non-memetic mimetic language. Browne stated unequivocally that she is concerning herself more with form and color, "but it's the form and color based on an African experience."[53]

As she absorbed her dynamic multisensory surroundings, she was particularly impacted by the sonic environment:

> When I began thinking about music, the sound in Africa was such that it turned me around. I did not ever have an experience before of hearing that kind of call and response that [the writer] Amiri Baraka speaks of. I never had that experience; the dissonance became something that was just an extraordinary musical experience. I had to have all those things in the work.[54]

Here again Browne eschews the cultural politics embedded in Baraka's notion of call and response, in which he traces a direct line from African musical traditions (the call) to Black American musical artistry (the response).[55] Yet the experience of hearing African music 'turned her around' and she did respond to its call. In abstractions such as *Bini Apron* (plate 35) and *Guard of the Palace* (fig. 7), Browne creates images characterized by chromatic tensions between disharmonious colors, decentralized compositions, and arrhythmic movement. Like some forms of jazz music, these works feel immediate and improvisational. In a statement in the 1983 exhibition catalogue for *Jus' Jass* mounted at Kenkeleba House in New York, Browne describes happening upon a concert of choirs while in Ghana: "The rhythms, the dissonance, the off-up beat, the cacophony of sound were awe-inspiring. I was transfixed. I recognized the music. I knew that this was where Jass originated…. In these paintings the

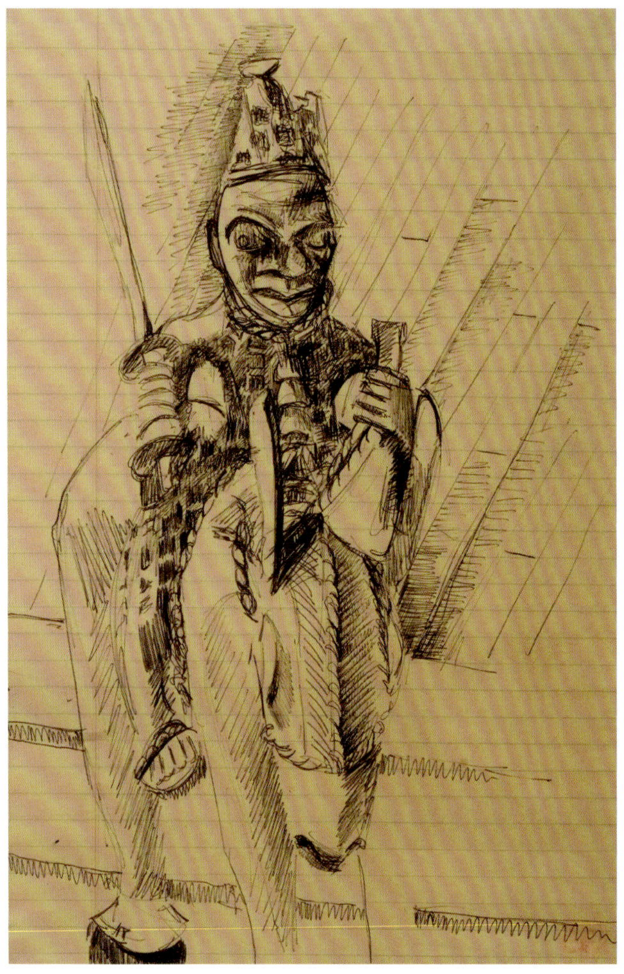

sounds, colors, lines, reflect the related order and rhythms between Jass forms and the African sounds to which we respond so completely and directly."[56]

Browne also produced works on paper that recall female adornment. *Tribes Woman* abstracts what seems to be a female form featuring "tribal" ornamentation (plate 37). In simplified shapes Browne suggests a multi-strand necklace and braceleted arm on a schematized body, all amid a decorative background of modular brushstrokes and hair-like serpentine patterns. Again, we observe Browne's flirtation with figuration. In the related work *Untitled #100* (plate 38), Browne revisits the form of a necklace and braceleted arm but abandons the conceit of a narrative title in this mostly abstract ink on paper. Here we see the way Browne's idiosyncratic, often opaque interpretations of African motifs radically

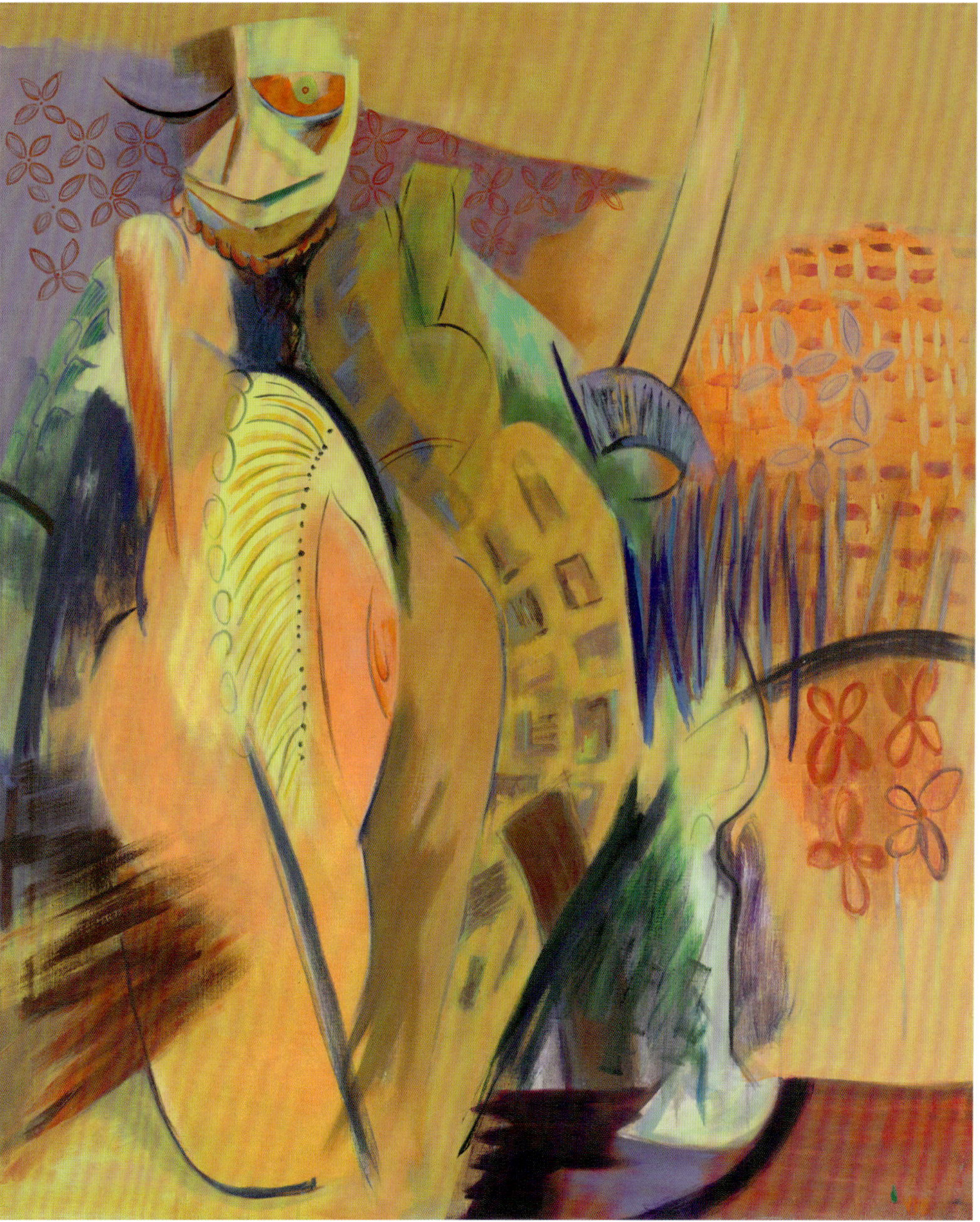

depart from images such as Jones-Hogu's *Heritage*—a work in which stylized but recognizable African masks are aimed at educating, celebrating, and uniting Black people through a shared and clearly articulated heritage.[57] Conversely, Browne's works are not didactic and their meanings are elusive. Hers is a highly personal reflection that fuses abstraction and figuration to materialize the intangible spirit of her encounters.

Between 1971 and approximately 1974 Browne's artistry responded to her experiences in West Africa in colorful and expressive oils, acrylics, watercolors, inks, and etchings. In 1973, her first solo exhibition, *African Memories*, mounted at the Adams Library Gallery at Rhode Island College, was dedicated solely to the *Africa Series* (fig. 8). The Africa works were exhibited widely in Browne's lifetime, in venues

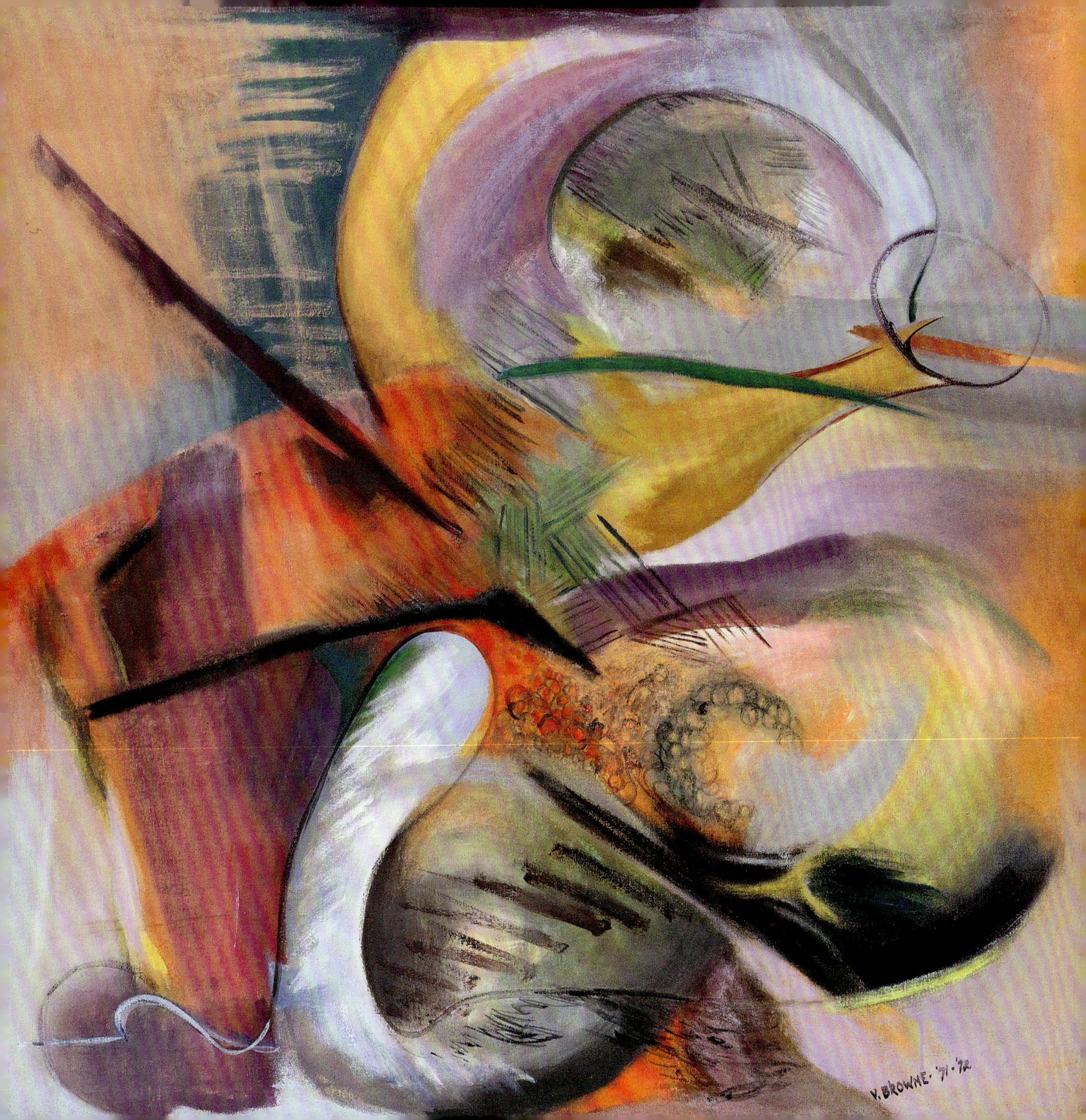

V. BROWNE· '71·'72

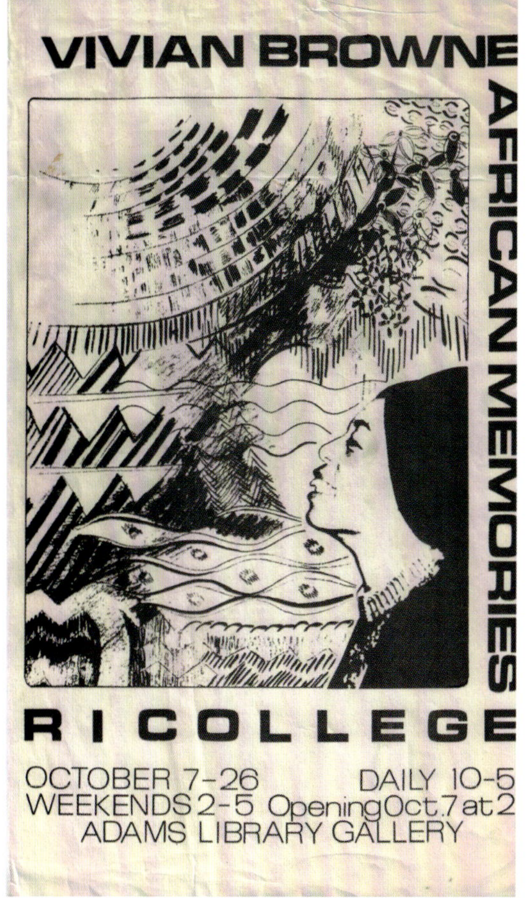

including the Just Above Midtown gallery, Ornette Coleman's Artist House in SoHo, Rutgers University Art Gallery, Robert Blackburn's Printmaking Workshop, and Kenkeleba House in New York. *Bini Apron* was even exhibited in the Afro-American Pavilion at the 1974 World's Fair in Spokane, Washington, representing Black artists of the United States.

Despite its exposure and success, Browne's *Africa Series* remained relatively unknown after her death in 1993. Indeed, much of her work remained under the radar. As the interest in art by African Americans grew over the last quarter of the twentieth into the twenty-first century, curators, historians, gallerists, and critics failed to consider Browne's work in the way they attended to artists in her cohort such as Benny Andrews, Faith Ringgold, Emma Amos, and Howardena Pindell. Perhaps it was due to Browne's refusal to succumb to the identitarian pressures to produce 'Black art.' Browne

was difficult to place in narratives that privileged art as an expression of racial identity above all else. "During the Civil Rights Era one had to paint black themes, black people, black ideas," Browne stated in 1985. "I didn't. I was painting my kind of protest, but it didn't look like black art."[58]

Browne's chromatically and formally exuberant *Africa Series* is perhaps the closest she came to producing 'Black art'. With no preconceived notions of how to represent her African experience, Browne stated that she let the colors, rhythms, and patterns "come to her."[59] Although she was cautious about claiming African roots, Browne's works possess a certain energy that she drew from the place. Perhaps what came to Browne through the *Africa Series* was animated by the Yoruba spiritual phenomenon *ashé*, the intangible force that many believe has stimulated global Africana aesthetics for centuries.[60]

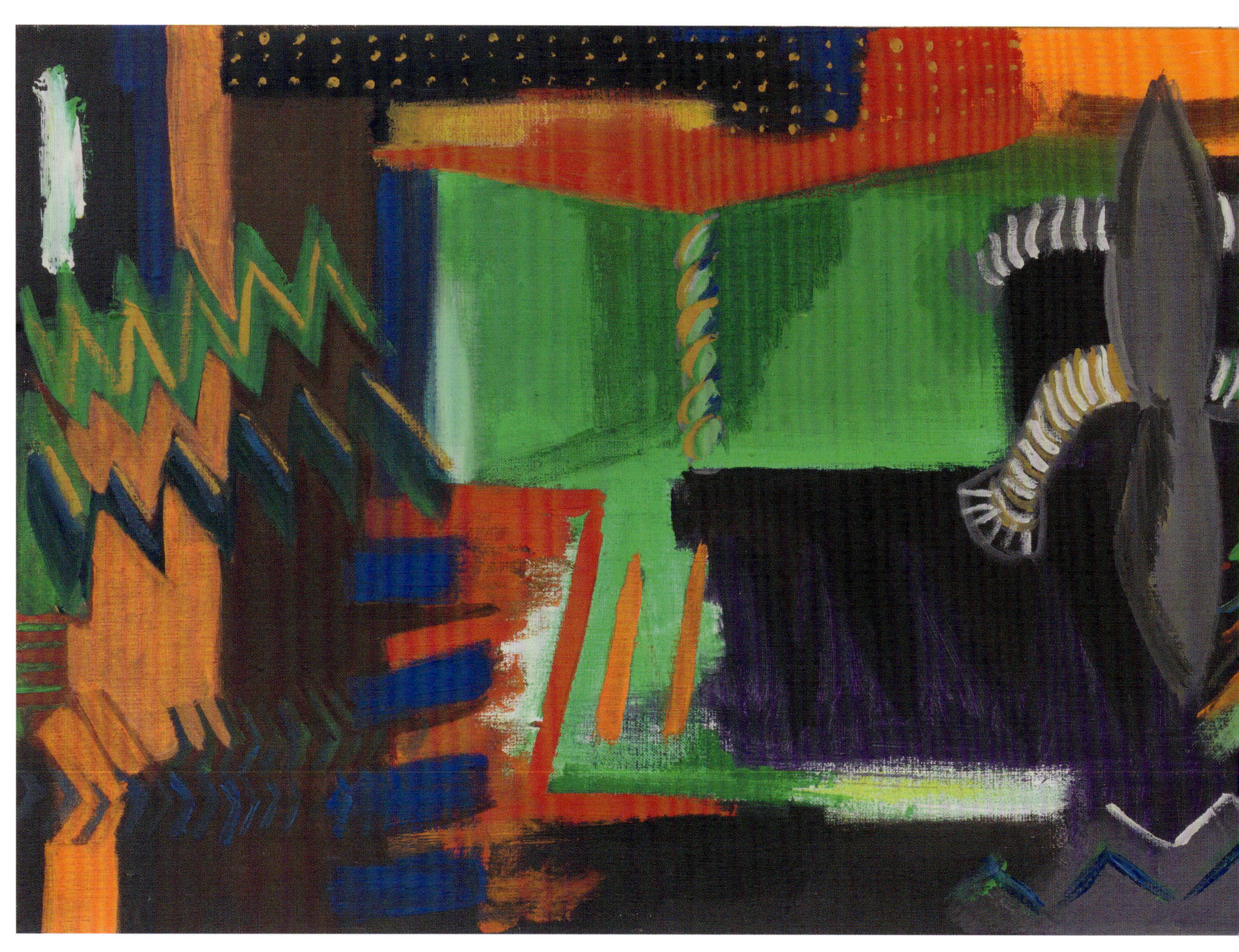

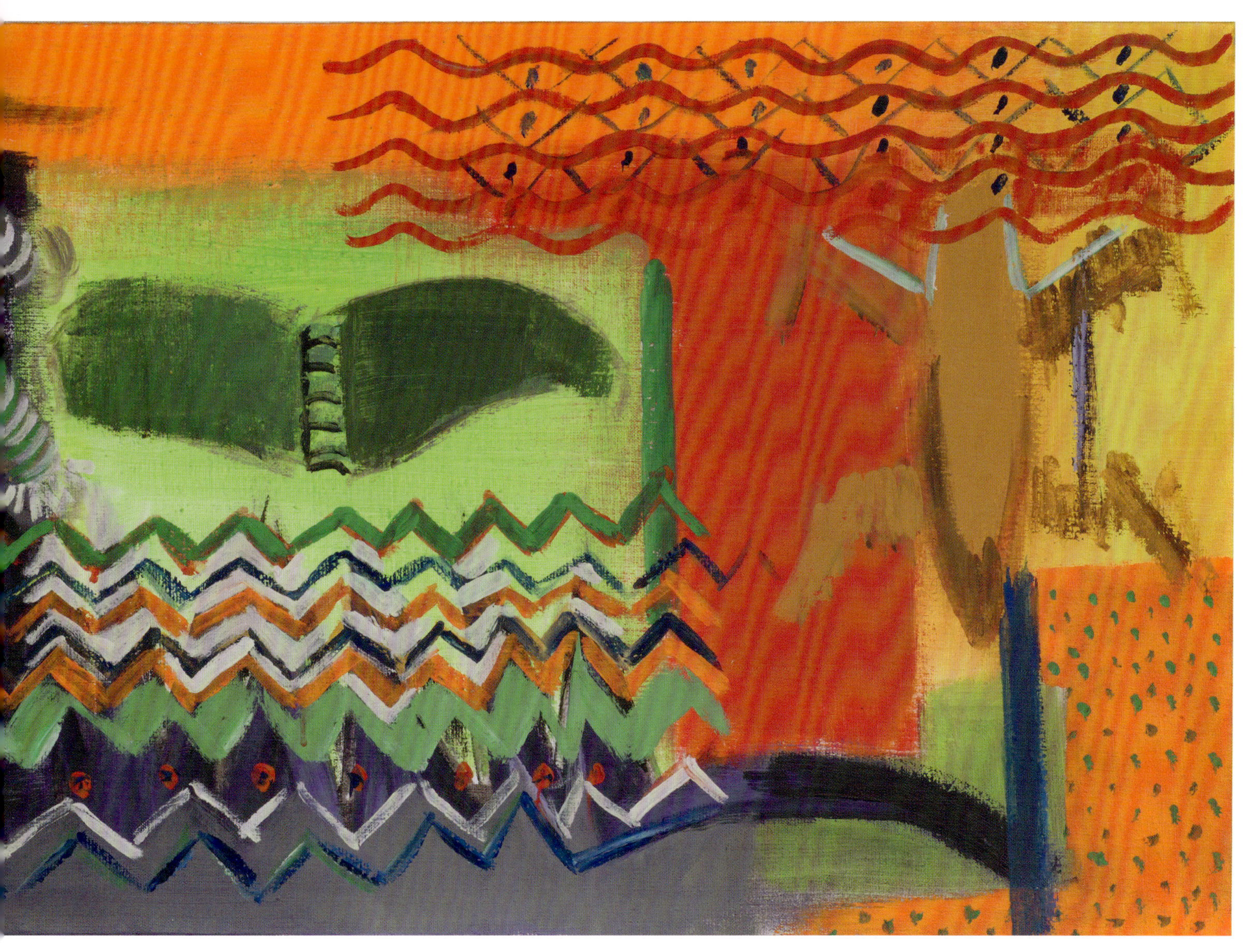

Plate 29
Shango Kingdom, 1972
Acrylic on canvas
17 ½ × 48 ¾ inches
Adobe Krow Archives, CA
and RYAN LEE Gallery, NY

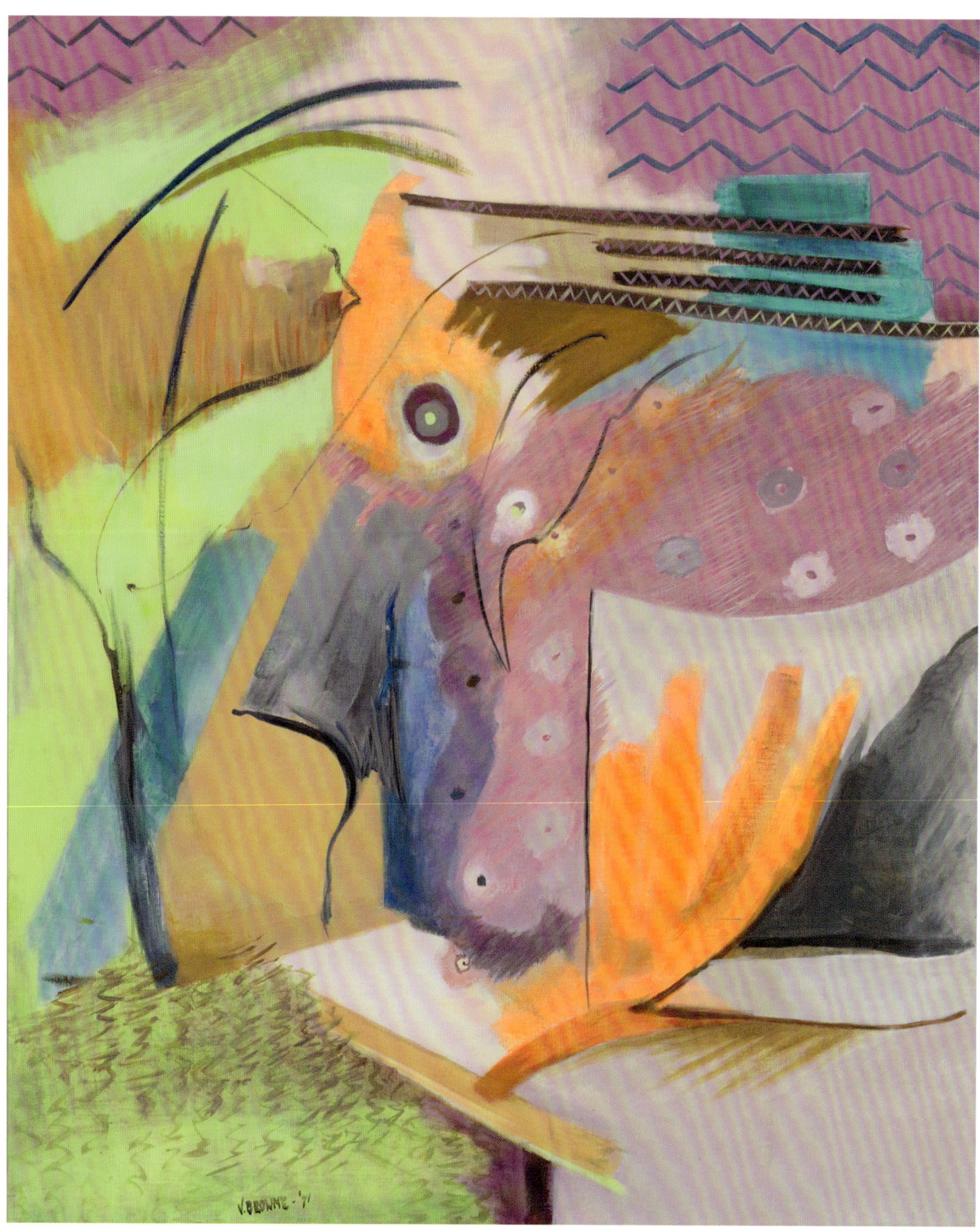

Plate 30
Umbrella Plant, 1971
Oil on canvas
48 ¾ × 40 ¾ inches
Adobe Krow Archives, CA
and RYAN LEE Gallery, NY

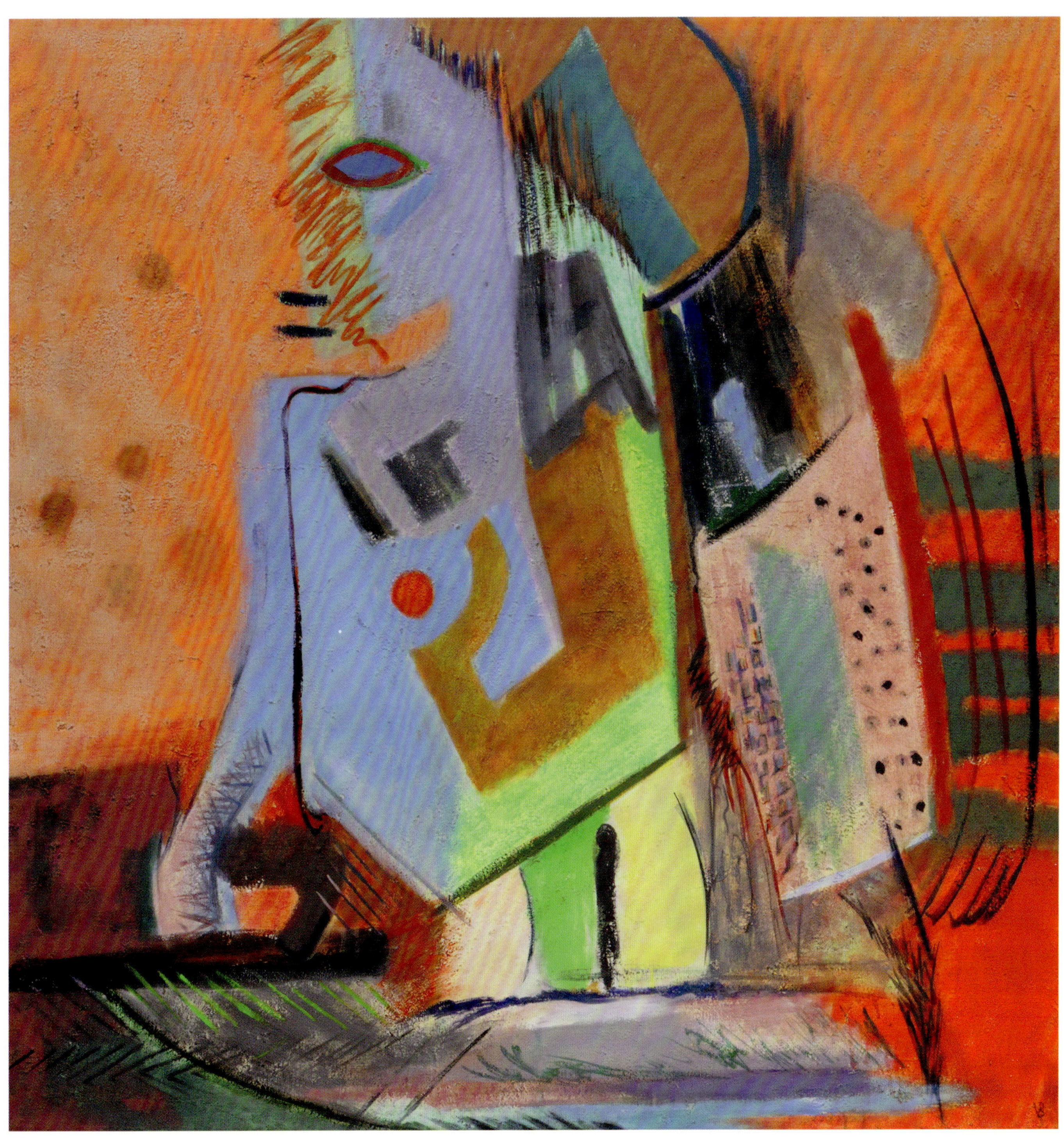

Plate 31
Ibeji II, 1972
Acrylic on canvas
48 ¾ × 48 ¾ inches
Detroit Institute of Arts, Museum Purchase,
Ernest and Rosemarie Kanzler Foundation Fund, 2024.7

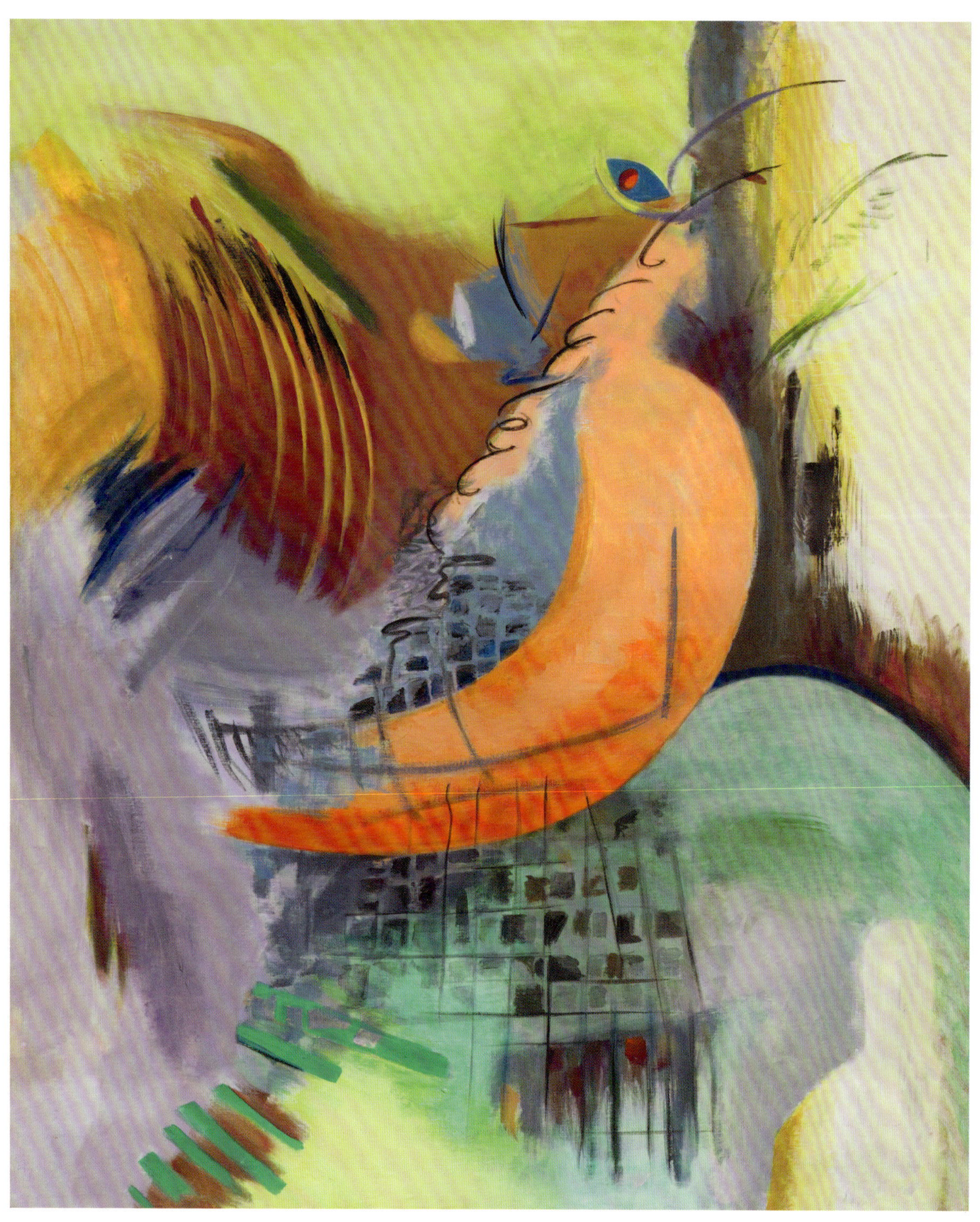

Plate 32
The Chief's Attendant, c. 1972
Acrylic on canvas
60 ¾ × 50 ¾ inches
Adobe Krow Archives, CA
and RYAN LEE Gallery, NY

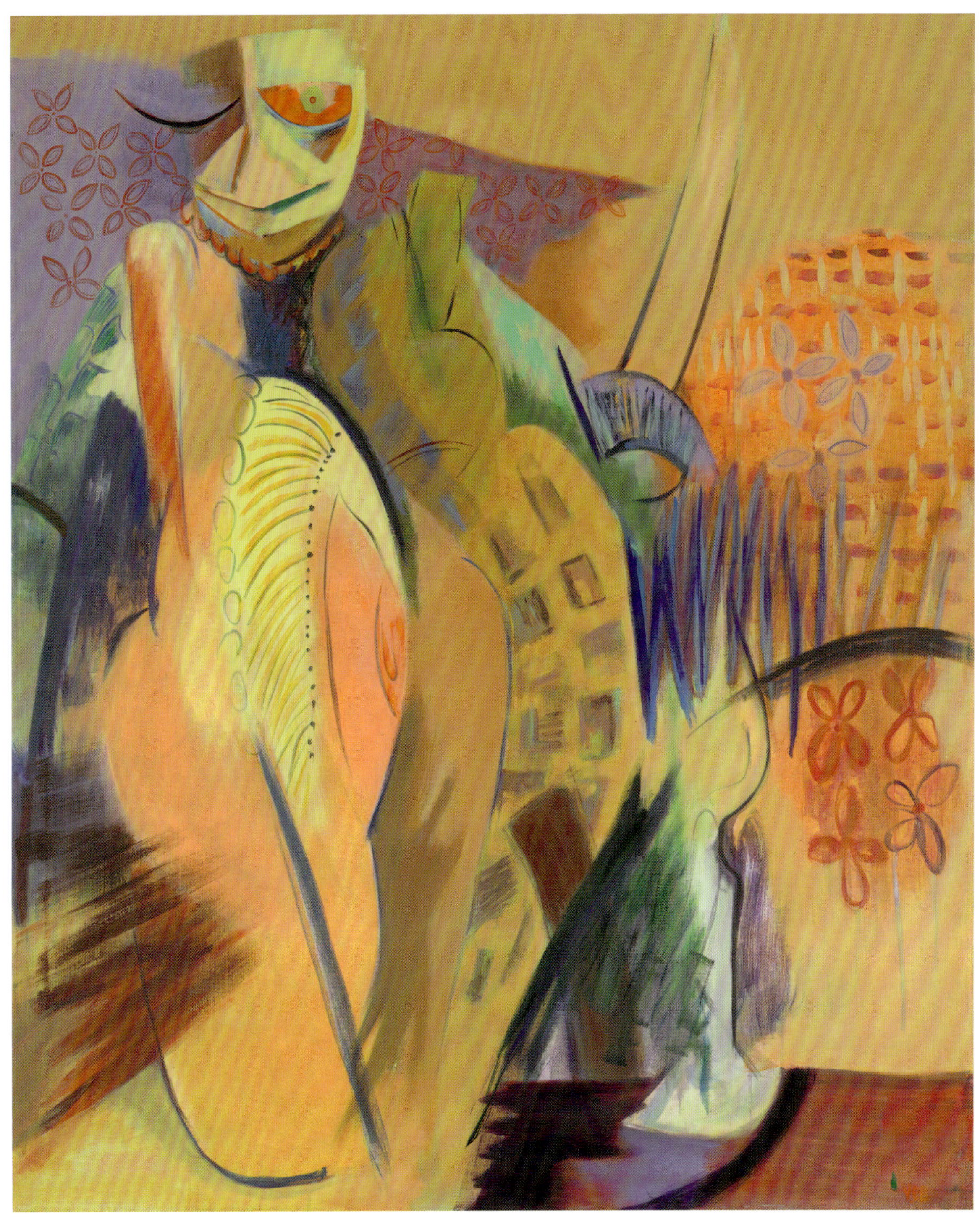

Plate 33
Benin Equestrian, 1973
Oil on canvas
61 × 51 inches
Art & Artifacts Division, Schomburg Center for
Research in Black Culture, The New York Public
Library, Astor, Lenox and Tilden Foundations

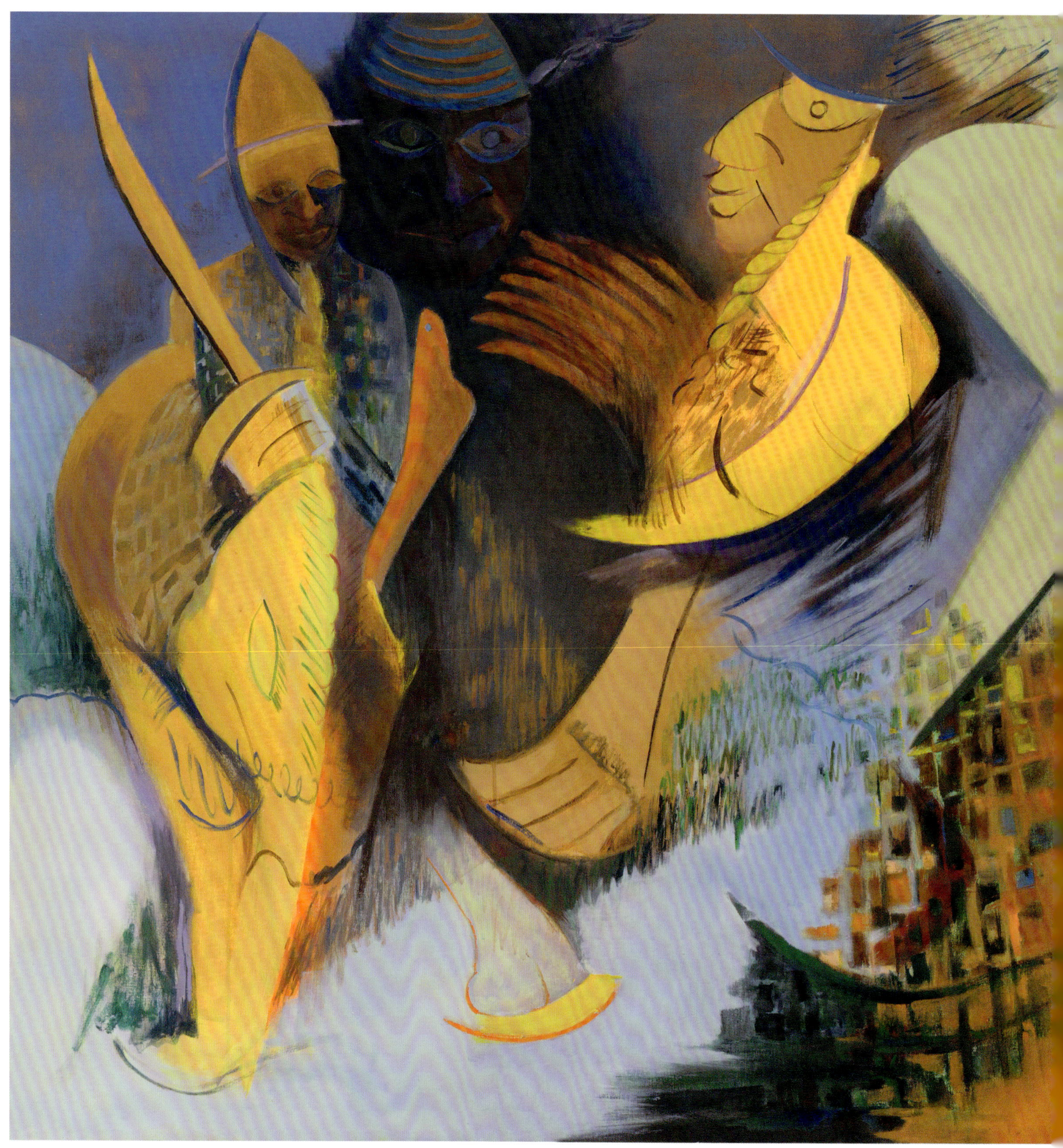

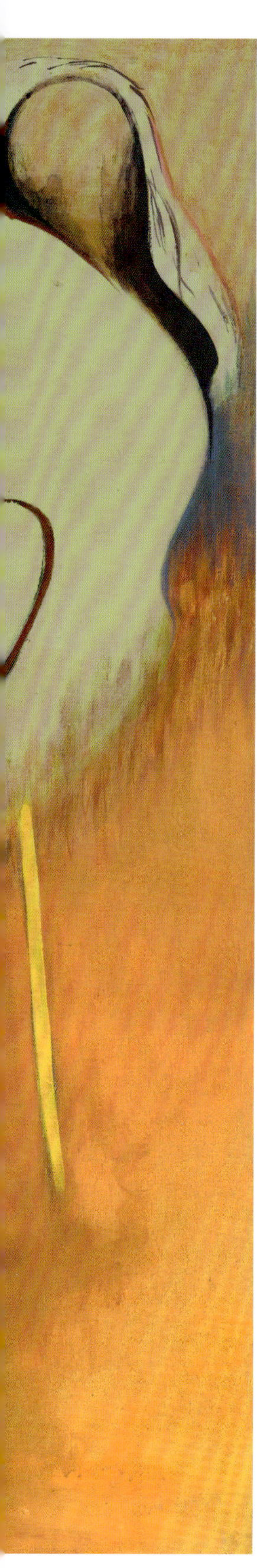

Plate 34
The Gathering, 1973
Acrylic on canvas
55 × 65 inches
Collection of William O. Perkins, III
and Lara Perkins, courtesy RYAN LEE Gallery

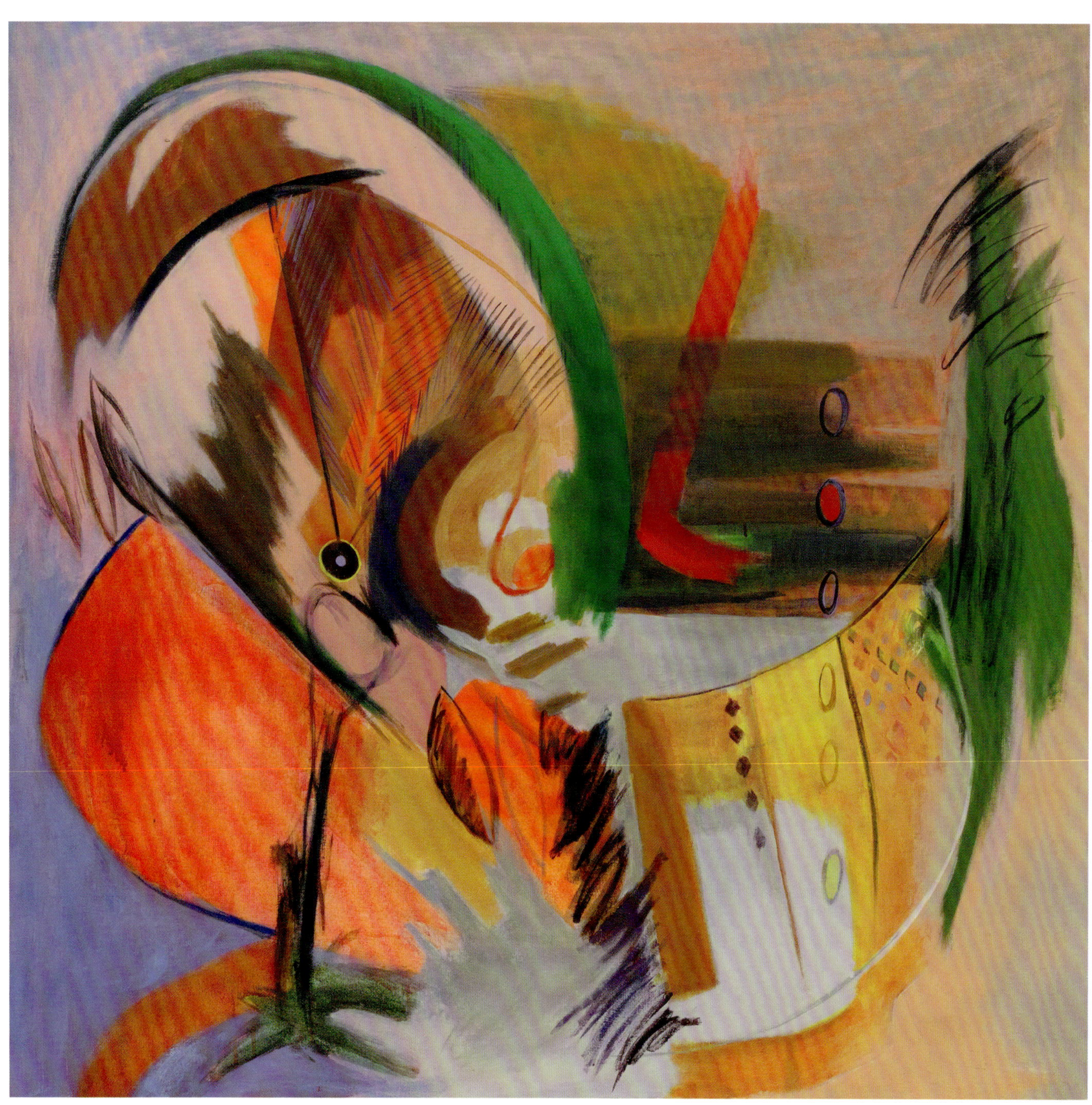

Plate 35
Bini Apron, 1973
Acrylic on canvas
48 ¾ × 50 ¾ inches
The Phillips Collection; Gift of Adobe Krow
Archives for Vivian Browne, Los Angeles, 2024

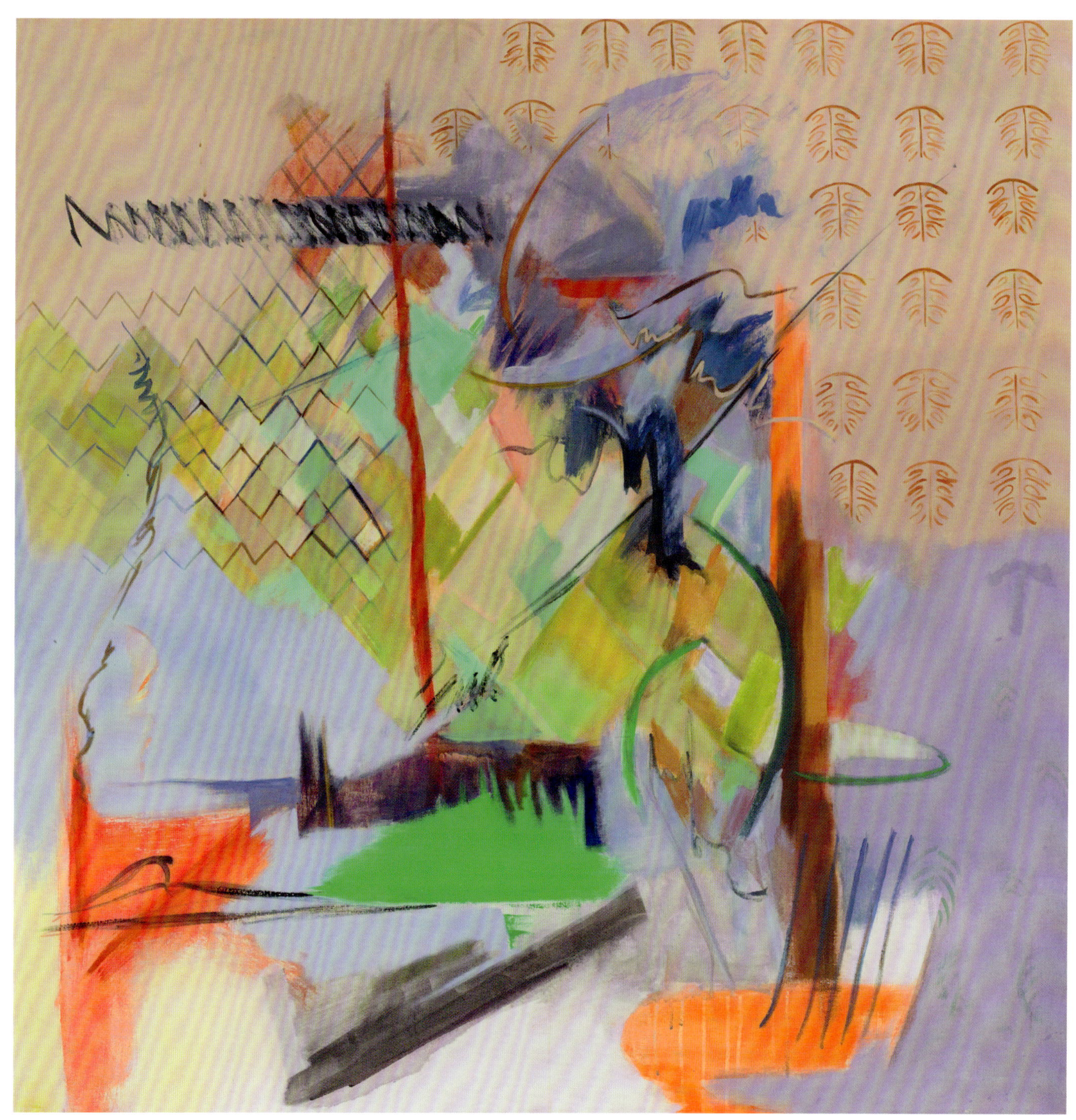

Plate 36
Diversities, 1973
Acrylic on canvas
54 ¾ × 54 ¾ inches
From the collection of Kenny and Elena Marks,
courtesy RYAN LEE Gallery

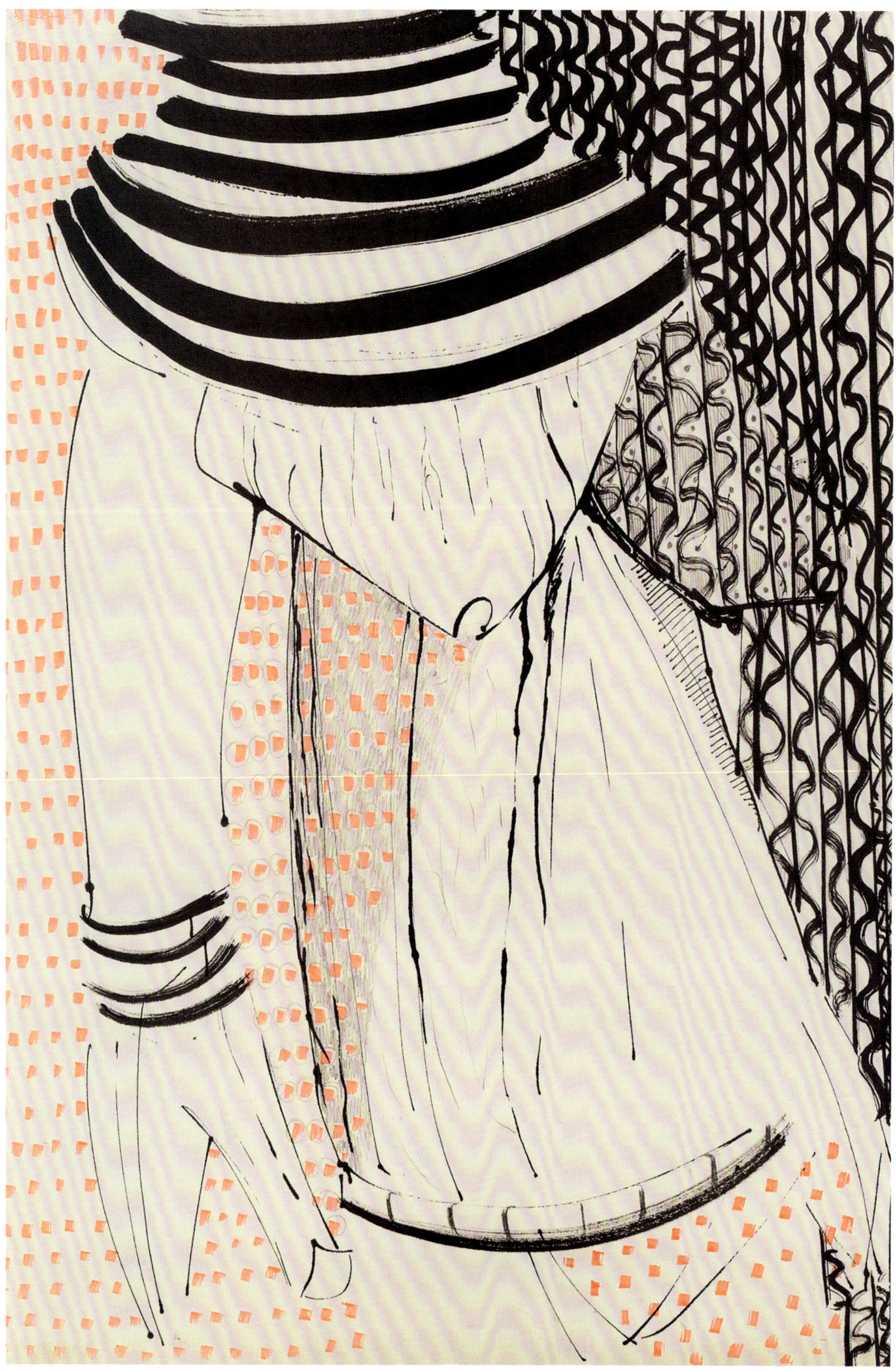

Plate 37
Tribes Woman, 1971
Watercolor and ink on paper
19 ¾ × 14 inches
Collection of Ruth E. Pachman and
Donald T. Fallati, courtesy RYAN LEE Gallery

Plate 38
Untitled #100, c. 1971
Ink and wash on paper
20 ½ × 13 ¾ inches
The Phillips Collection, Gift of Brenda A.
and Larry D. Thompson, 2024

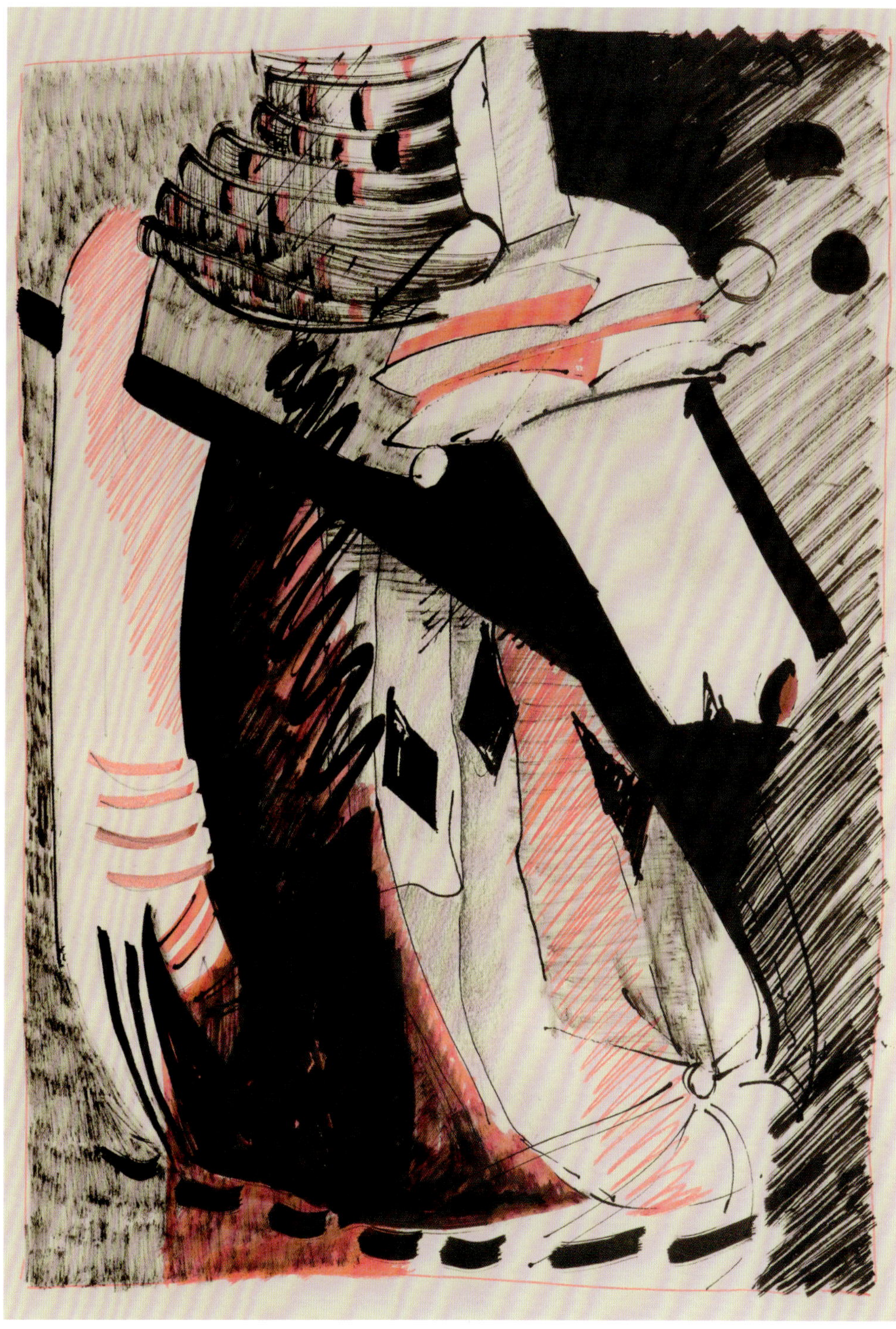

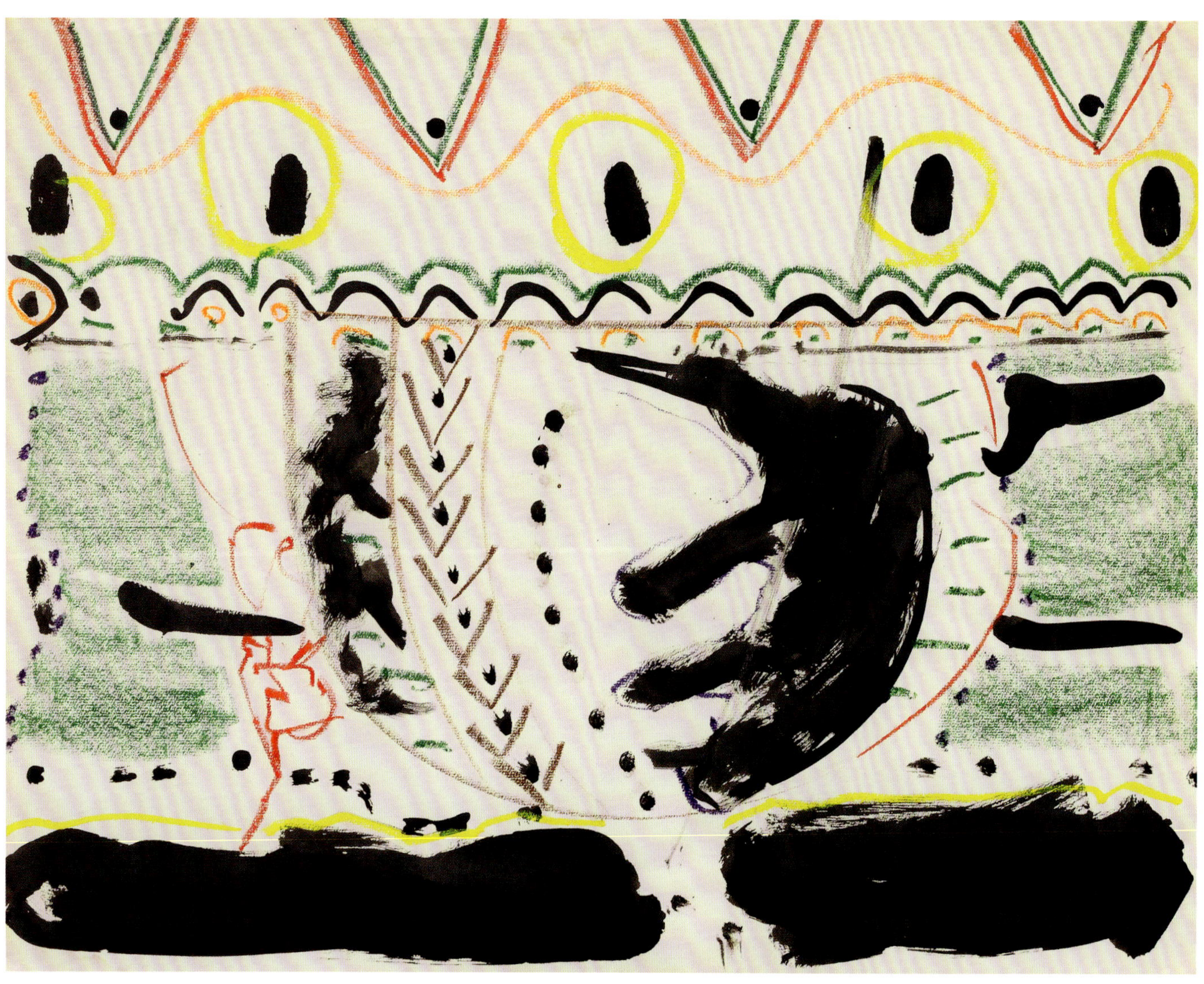

Plate 39
Africa Sketch #1, 1971
Watercolor and ink on paper
18 ¾ × 24 ¾ inches
Adobe Krow Archives, CA
and RYAN LEE Gallery, NY

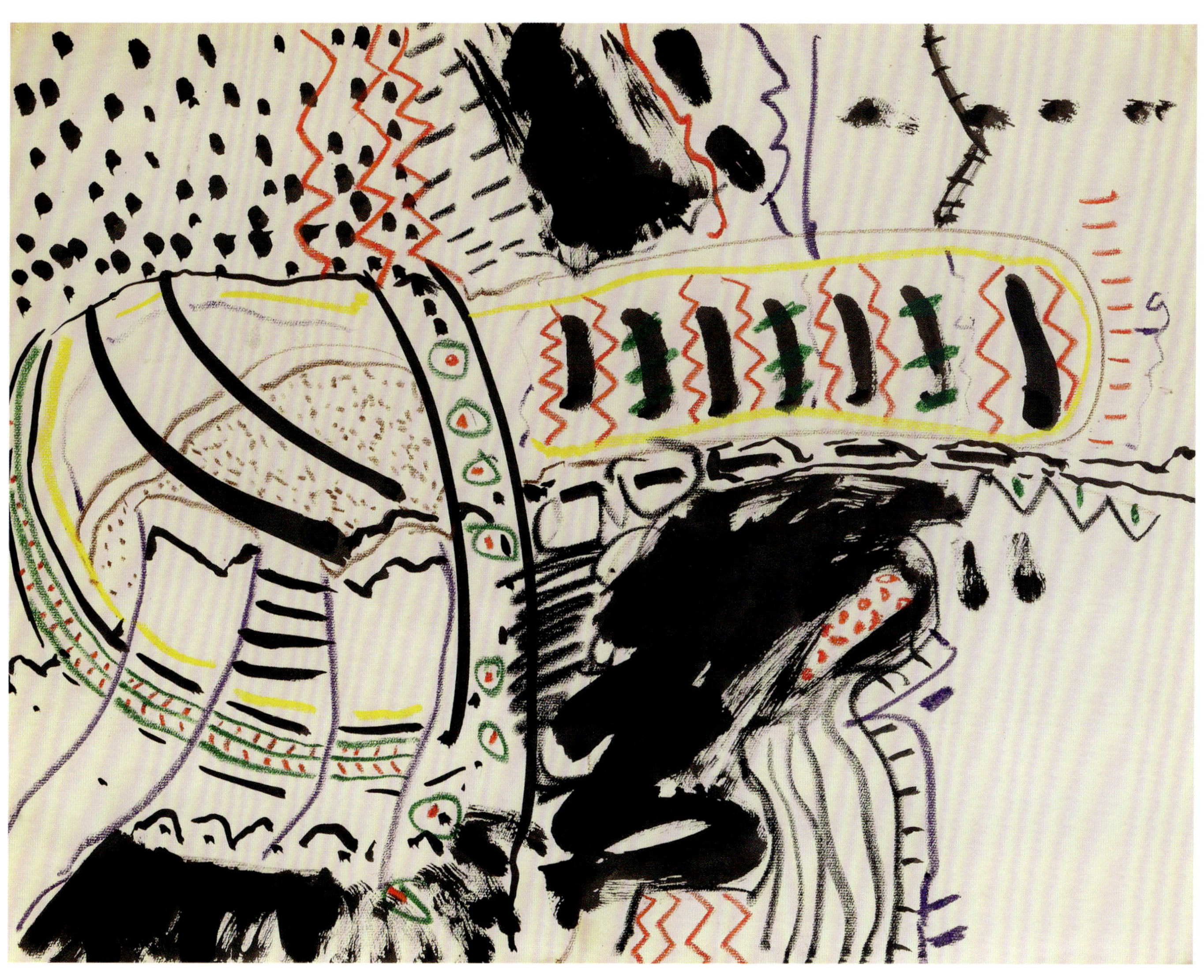

Plate 40
Africa Sketch #2, 1971
Watercolor and ink on paper
18 ¾ × 24 ¾ inches
Adobe Krow Archives, CA
and RYAN LEE Gallery, NY

Plate 41
The Bathers, 1971
Gouache, ink, and pastel on paper
19 ¾ × 28 inches
Whitney Museum of American Art, New
York; Purchase, with funds from the Drawing
and Print Committee 2024.49

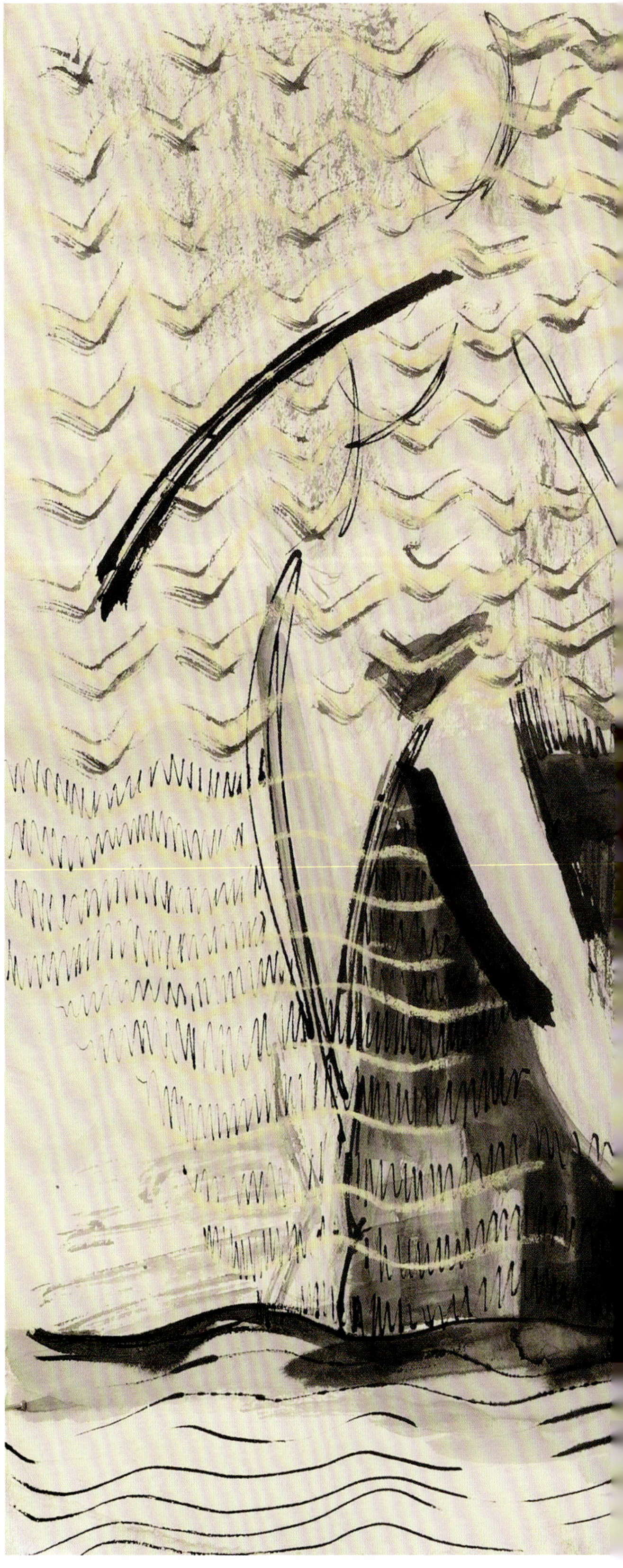

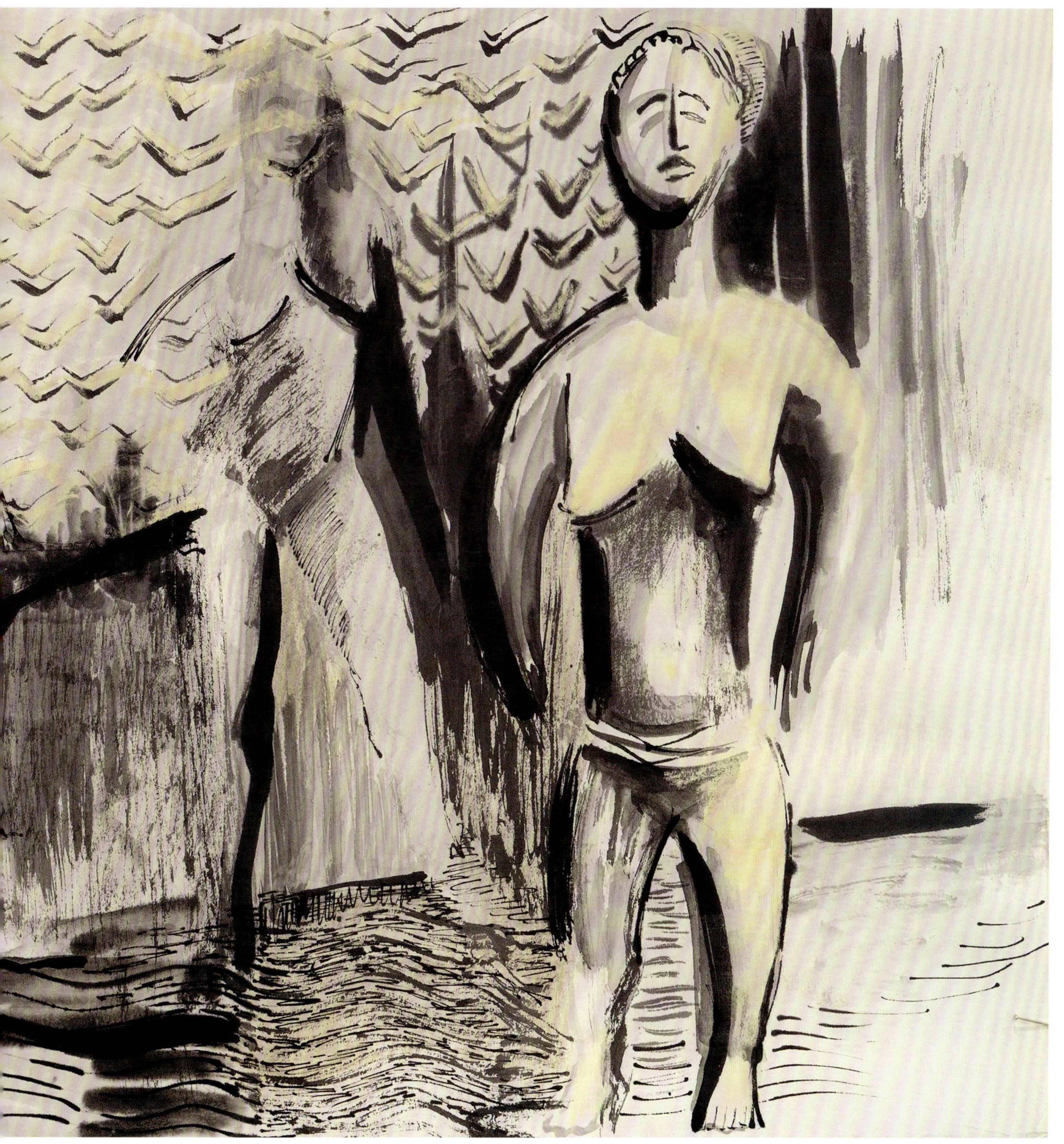

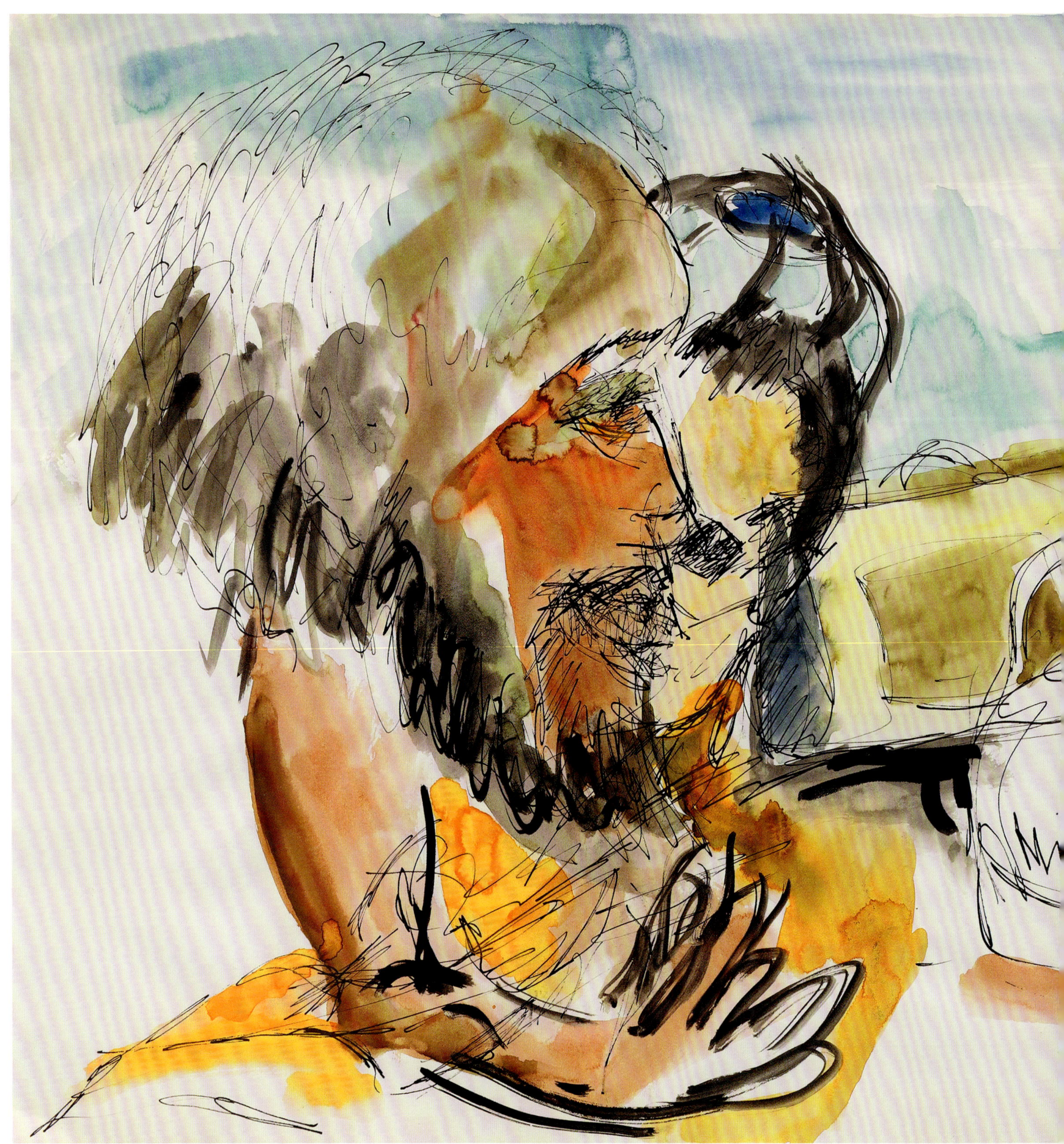

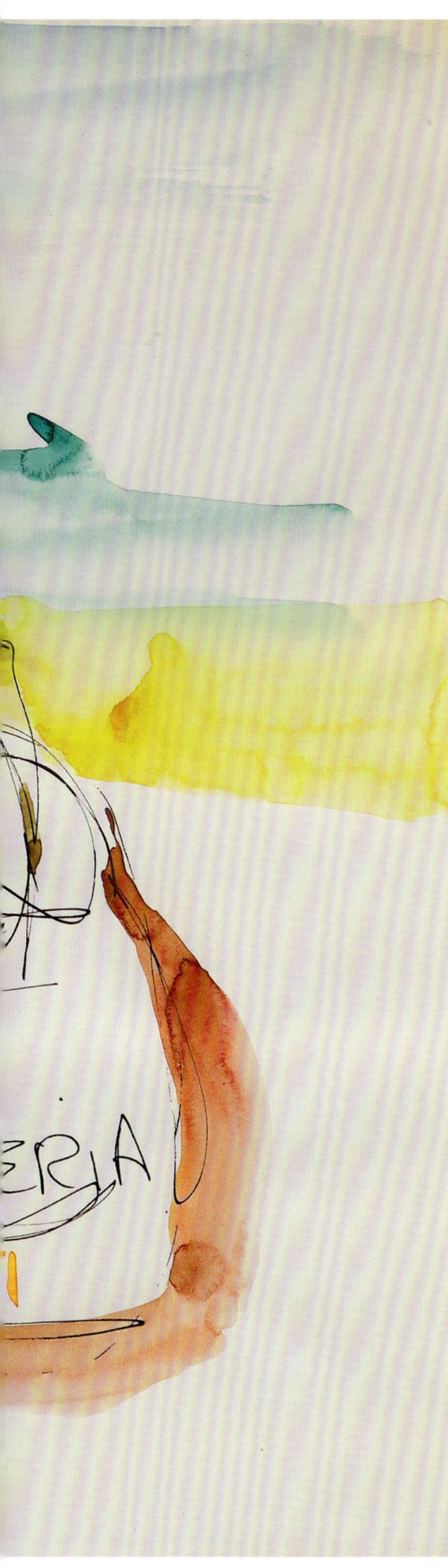

Plate 42
***Nigeria (Self-portrait with Floyd Coleman)*, 1971**
Watercolor and ink on paper
17 ¾ × 24 inches
Adobe Krow Archives, CA
and RYAN LEE Gallery, NY

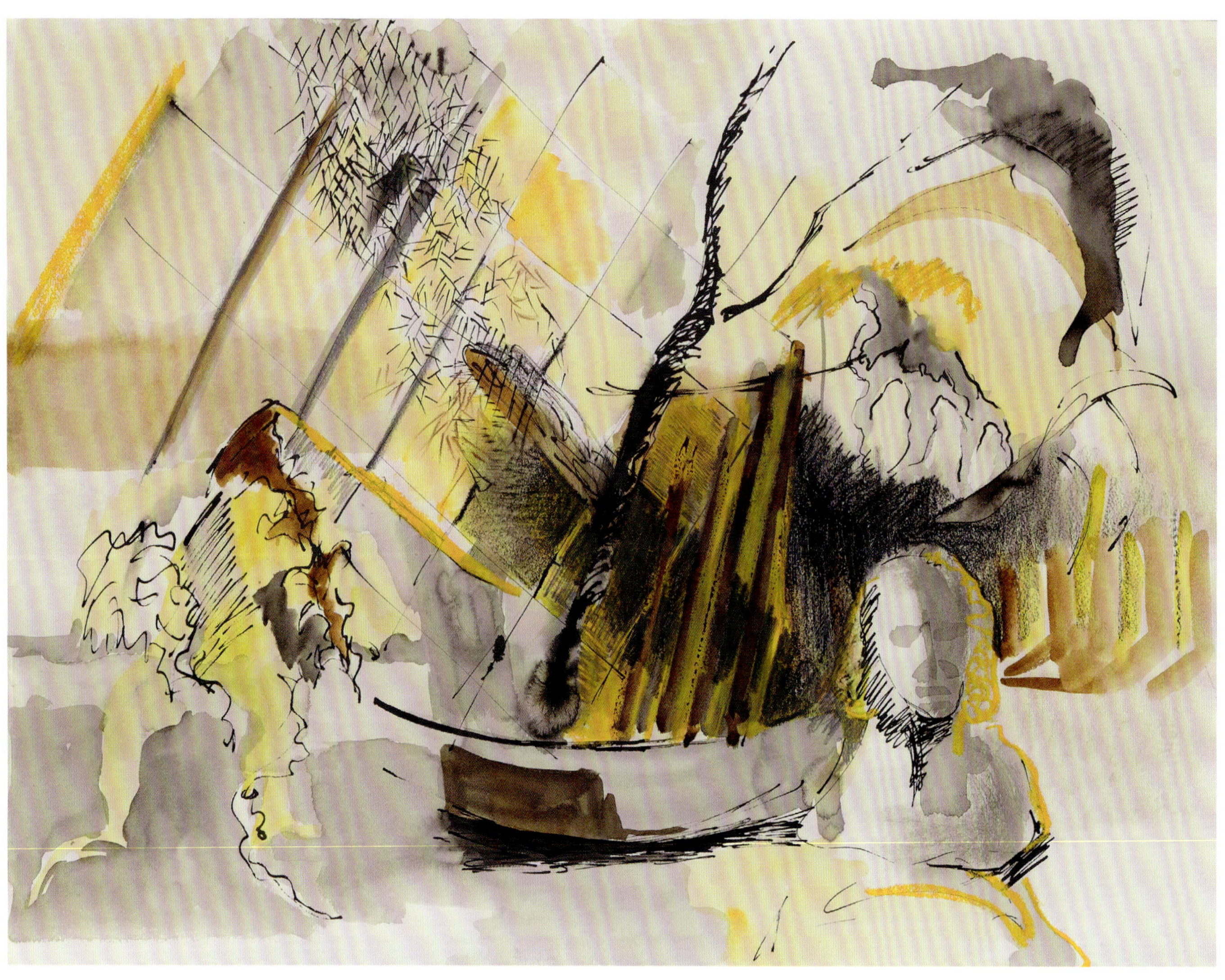

Plate 43
Egypt 71, 1971
Watercolor, pastel, and ink on paper
20 ½ × 27 ¼ inches
Adobe Krow Archives, CA
and RYAN LEE Gallery, NY

Plate 44
Equestrian, 1971
Etching and aquatint
22 3/8 × 14 15/16 inches
Whitney Museum of American Art, New York;
Purchase, with funds from the Drawing and
Print Committee 2024.46

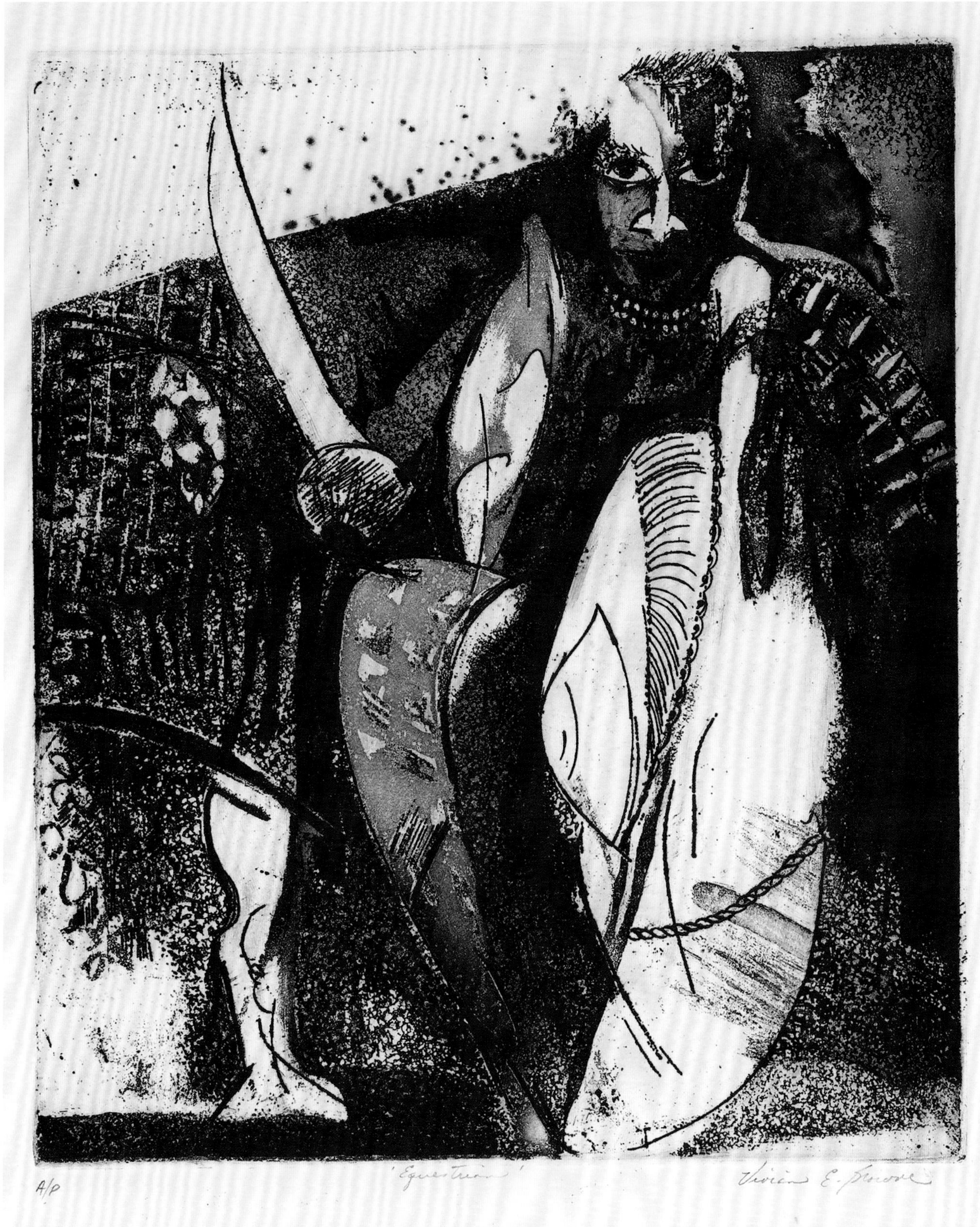

A/P
'Equestrian'
Vivian E. Moore

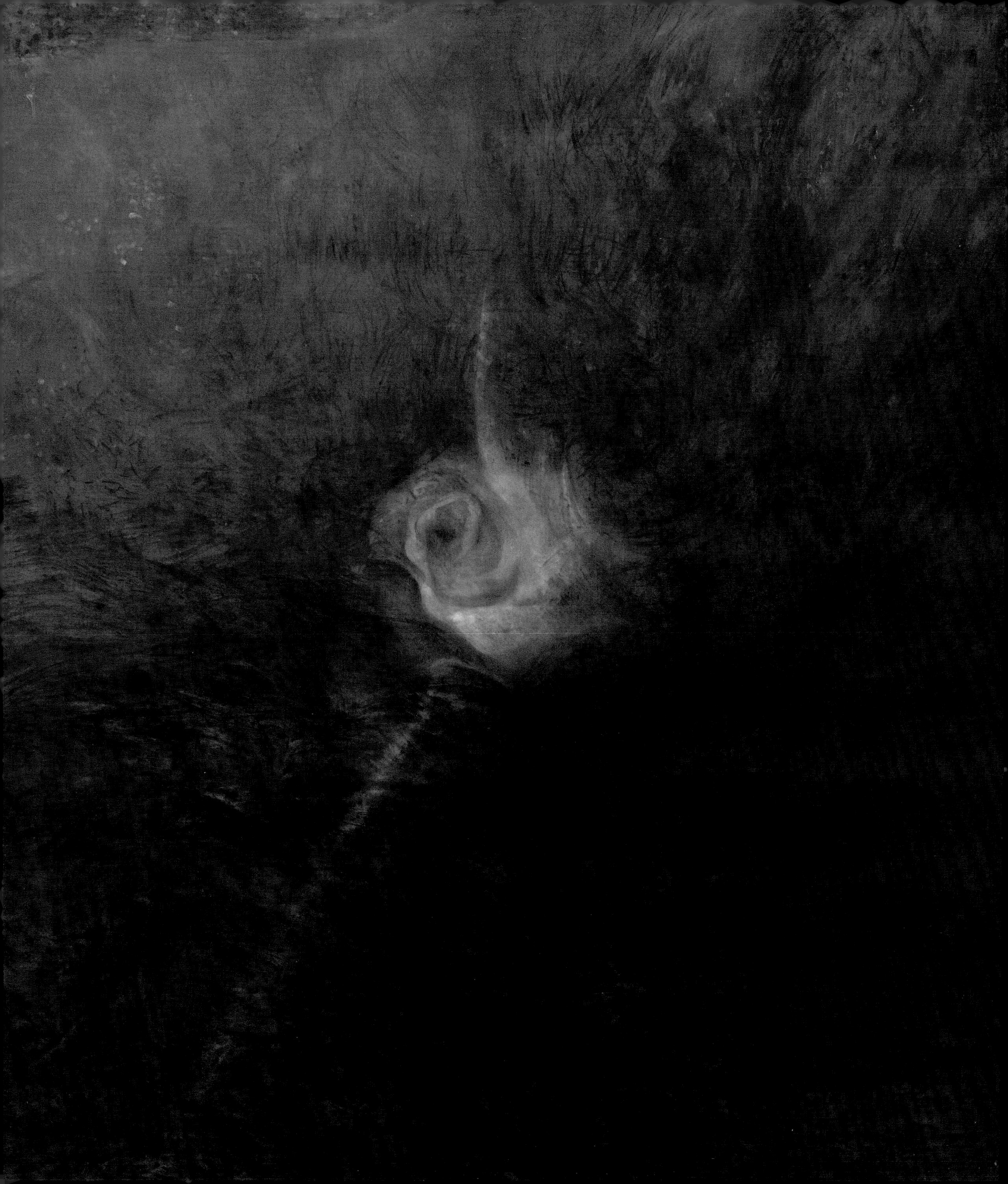

"The Other Things That Are"

Darby English

"I find that if I spend more time looking and feeling and accepting and relating, it becomes more a part of me and therefore more useful."[61]

1. The speaking visual artist usually is wasting their time: when it counts, they will be spoken for. This is a big problem and I want to avoid it here, because Vivian Browne has a message that we've failed to heed. It doesn't live in her pictures; Browne wasn't a messaging artist. She was Black, a woman, and a painter uninterested in messaging. More important, she was comfortable with uncertainty and painted towards an observer she credited with a similar tolerance.

2. What I call Browne's message lives in what she said, and how. Such as the comment above, about putting self aside in order to experience more—to have more to impart to her work and, thereby, to those interested in seeing it. In Browne's ideal, art operates the gap between experiencers. Browne's message concerns uptake; or, the act of using what is provided.

3. She said things like this, too, when invited to say what made her art go:

"I wanted to get the things that we see and the other things that are[,] together."[62]

Browne understood that only some of what we "see" comes from the brain processing waves of light; that much of one's worldly involvement doesn't involve seeing at all. The pull toward confluence, a hesitance to separate, tell of Browne's strenuous attempt to live creatively, to mine the outer limits of the given and provided. This attempt, to see now what one has not allowed oneself or been able to see before, belongs to art while also pointing beyond it. Only very deep respect for "the other things that are" places their being ahead of any identity that might be ascribed to them. How, then, could she also say and mean the following:

"In the final analysis, my paintings are about me, my dreams, my world, my way of transforming what I see and think and feel."[63]

Because if new perceptions—only some visual— ongoingly transform what one sees and thinks and feels, they also transform what one takes oneself-in-the-world to be. In other words, very heightened and considered external involvements expanded Browne's self-concept well beyond ordinary limits. In Browne's thought, as in dreams, "me" remains in question: strung along, left unfinished. Browne's "final analysis" eludes finality, and does so of necessity since it combines the known with that of which we must remain ignorant. Her painting often does, too: going over and over the work, I still have only fragments of ideas about what's going on. Sometimes I'd rather do anything but admit that.

4. Browne found that she had to be open in order to make art that she believed in. This may have been a development upon the existential openness she first experienced on exiting the stifling racism of American society at midcentury.

"You feel open. You feel like you can think and, if you like, you can be. Not necessarily be somebody, just be … yourself."[64]

There, in the Europe of the day, who and what she bounced off did not first inscribe her within an instituted identity and set of lifeways. Browne experienced herself anew, as open, able to think. This meant more than a little to her once she returned to the U.S., in whose political system she had withdrawn her faith. "I don't think that we really are living in this place. It's very hard to have any say in what happens to you."[65] Browne's story is not unique among Black Americans lucky enough to enjoy the privilege of comparison. I cite the story to draw out her use of the terms "be," "feel," and "open"—particularly the release from prescription that would shape and sustain her life's work.

5. The art world offered Browne little relief. When other Black artists answered to men handing down sources and imperatives, Browne could be found elsewhere: "I was painting my kind of protest, but it didn't look like black art."[66] Browne's inconstant, even equivocal "my" articulates dissent when it should speak assent: you don't personalize protest. In fact, personalization is the weak, perpetually available justification for minority groups disowning those they're sworn (though only implicitly) to recognize. In Browne's idiom, 'black art' connotes an environment that confers recognition in exchange for product with a predetermined artistic character—a nonstarter for her. Being an individual personality wondering how to become itself was Browne's protest.[67]

6. While speaking to Henri Ghent in 1968, Browne thought to tell a story to tell about being considered too avid a reader for a person of her kind. So Browne stifled her intellectual curiosity in reply to a mother and sisters who thought her too bookish to attract boys. Compliance with judging authorities and peers, Browne later realized, postponed her arrival in the very personality that was hers all along.

"I think what happened was, I, in hiding it, you know, I began to hide it from me so that I wouldn't go as far as I could go in intellectual curiosity." [68]

I hid it from me. Still more heartbreakingly, Browne's interlocutor, Henri Ghent (who's taking the oral history for the Archives of American Art), terminates Browne's reflection, seeking data about her technique. "Getting back to your early artistic leanings…," Ghent abruptly intones, hoping to build out his picture of Browne's inclination towards external objects, purposes, results—the literal definition of "leanings." A truer picture of Browne's occupations would emphasize the interplay between inside and outside things that informed her theory of art, and particularly her fervent interest in the self's always developing relations to its world—a form of curiosity well exceeding the intellectual sort. And it would heed Browne's insight, on another occasion, that serious watching and learning about the self have the inevitable consequence of improving one's ability to manage the density of others. Rather than dwell on Ghent's misstep, then, it's well to appreciate that by the time his questioning began, Browne had found a personal environment where there was self-respect in continuing curiosity and pursuing questions without answers.

7. Browne's discourse inclines towards the internal: "Each new painting is a whole new pulling and digging; it is very, very, very real and meaningful."[69] "It" does a lot of work for Browne here. It first describes each painting in connection to a fresh campaign of self-seeking, self-study, self-testing. Second, it figures a prerequisite for working at all, the sine qua non of work itself: "the fact is I couldn't paint, so I had to do that."[70] Third, it raises the stakes, for Browne and a caring observer alike, of the putting-oneself-out-there that follows work upon as such. "It" attempts to translate facts of feeling that one (artist or viewer) cannot perceive sensually and must, therefore, imagine. For Browne, it seems being with art meant being subject to the reach of the other.

8. Browne intensely regretted the general lack of sympathy for this elemental difficulty and opportunity of art, which she expected uptake to reflect. For art, Vivian Browne bore extremely high hopes:

"I think that as a painting that's what it should do. It should help you to do those things. But when people turn away from it, then obviously they're not able to do that in their smallest hours [e.g., the time a picture takes], to say nothing of any expansive qualities they may have. It's disappointing." [71]

9. Becoming a teacher refined Browne's already trenchant criticisms. Her disappointment gained scope to encompass much of the Black community. Speaking in 1969 to Cecilia Davis, Browne said:

"I'm interested in making artists. And I think that we have … certainly in the black community such a lack of knowledge about being an artist, about what art—not what art is, but what it can be for black people. Some of them will be artists and some won't. But more of them will if we encourage them." [72]

That would mean encouraging interest in and dedication to the kind of radical self-knowledge which meets self-ignorance with grace and dogma with doubt. Art represented the possibility of existing in the realm of fact as opposed to that of a political theory. Existing totally for community meant less space in an artist's life for spontaneous exercises of curiosity, to Browne the very stuff of that life. "What art can be for black people" carries no large, communitarian or therapeutic meaning for Browne. She might have said, 'For a black person,' since in her ideal the artist, in a social arrangement otherwise not offering this, always finds a divergent historical trajectory and follows it without apology.

10. An artist's problems do not exist prior to work, or are not handed to the artist, or are not externally regulated for the artist. An artist encounters their problems as they live them. They need only wonder who they are, then let their dealings with the world help them find out. As Browne thought it, you can't do art by knowing who you are in advance. When asked to address the relationship between Black Nationalism and her art, Browne had nothing to say about Black Nationalism and everything to say about art, which always belongs to a historico-social context:

"An artist has problems which are set for him as he works, or she, and the working out of the problems takes every single part of the artist and his life and his society and all that stuff. But that problem and that painting is where the artist should be. I have a big problem with this…." [73]

11. What's Browne's "big problem" with this? We'll never know for sure. I have my own idea: Browne's art would never represent protest to the deciders because *her* protest ranked too low in the table of shared grievances, and this obligated her to withdraw from a certain kind of involvement with the project of engaged art. (Her work as a feminist reformer was also somewhat adjunct to her art.) I suspect that Browne's "big problem" stemmed from an issue not with the politics of protest, but with groups—and particularly the prevalent notion that the answer always lies within the group. The sheer convenience of the idea constitutes its main flaw: to assume that the group always finds its answers with relative ease is to restrict the area of search in advance, to limit the group to answerable questions, to kill the curiosity that distinguishes Browne's searching way as a thinking artist. [74]

12. "Go and live and paint" was how a teacher dismissed Browne from his charge. She later recalled this rudeness as a goad, which seemed to say, *You can merely exist and paint or you can be very emotionally alive and paint.* Browne "entered upon the struggle of painting very soon after." [75] This oft-told commencement story encodes an attitude that is also a form in history, and already was by the time Browne embarked. While I feel a twinge to contextualize this historical form— the painting artist's struggle—I feel it more urgent to hold a focus on the idiosyncrasy of Browne's version. The truest history of this struggle will be a disinterested report of its versions: the irreducibly different ways irreducibly different people devised to face it down. Browne tried "very, very, very" hard—her words are digging, pulling, looking more, feeling more, relating more, accepting more—to give us more to look at than we can possibly see at one go. It's recognition of the profound character of such an attempt that demands when she urges "this country to heed what the artist gives to people, what the artist's purpose is." [76] Browne's artist doesn't give people *art*—Browne made art because she *didn't* know what art was. The artist organizes an experience (you can't say how and stay on a logical, rational level) that we experience. Art is an experience that

we experience; that's how it seeps from form and person and place, becomes something wondrous, terribly hard to handle, necessary to reexperience.

13. Like some others of her era, Browne complicated matters further when she suggested that the experience she organizes as a painting may arise from her experience of another's art, from a discrete inner-outer-inner negotiation. Conversing with fellow artist Emma Amos in 1985, she spoke of poetry as "soul food," not a *source* for her paintings so much as nutriment for what she brought, conceptually and experientially, to the making of them.

"I put … the words … more and more into the paintings. Not the words as much, but … the sense of continuing an experience. [T]o read poetry is to experience the work of an artist, and I meet that experience with my work." [77]

To meet Browne's work would be to enter a chain of experiences that resonate and sometimes compel without being harmonious, revealing, affirmative, or helpful. Browne saw deindividuation as the threat. She was serious in her belief that "it's only the artist who can save people from this, if only just letting them look and see." [78] Just? Really to look and see leads inevitably to the ongoing revision of one's views, given the actually-always-varying character of all "the other things that are."

14. "Yes, we have these artists like Charlie White, and Romy, and all that. The one thing that you must notice is that this society does not encourage them to change, that they don't get to change, that they get to do the same thing." [79] Not so Vivian Browne.

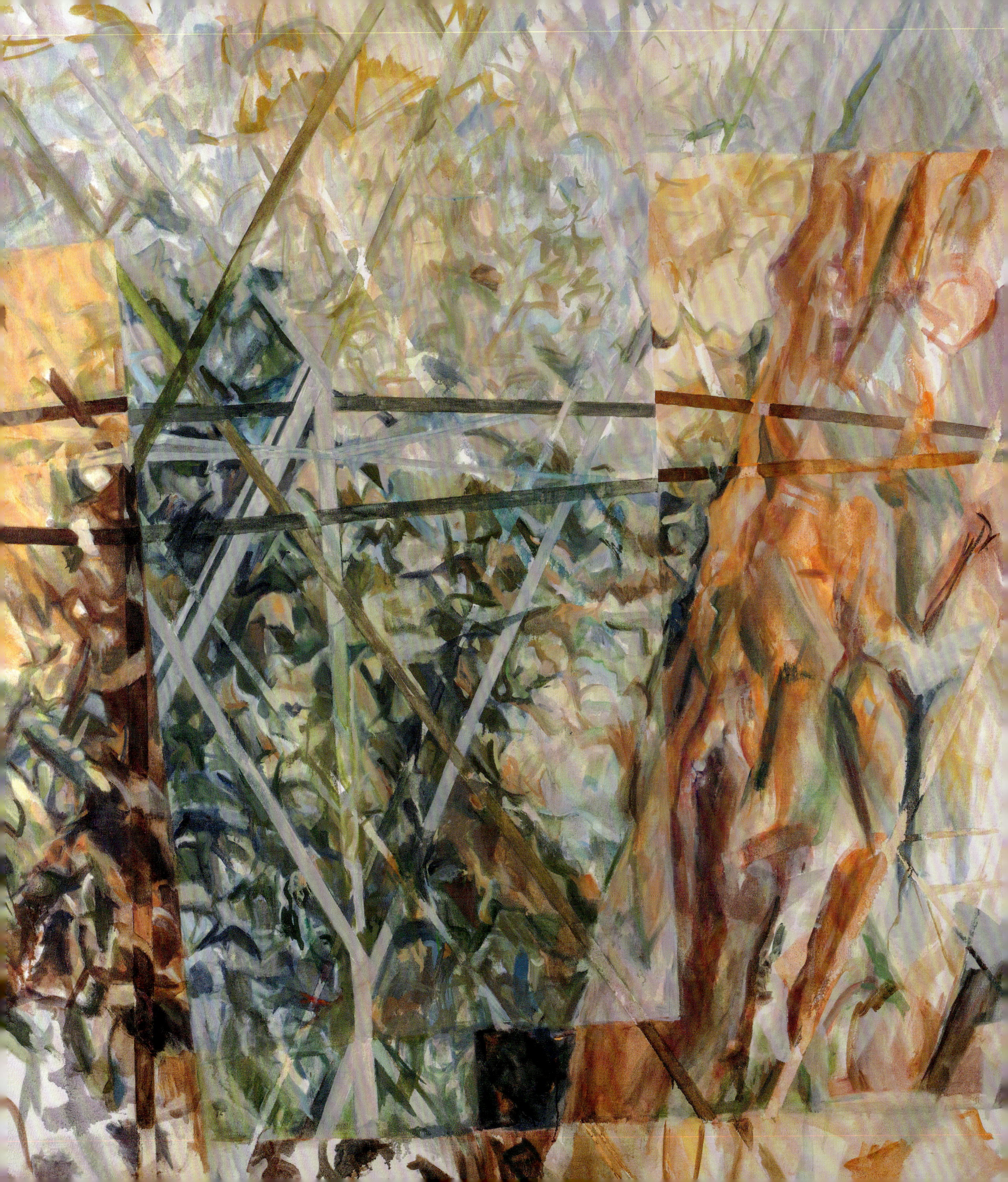

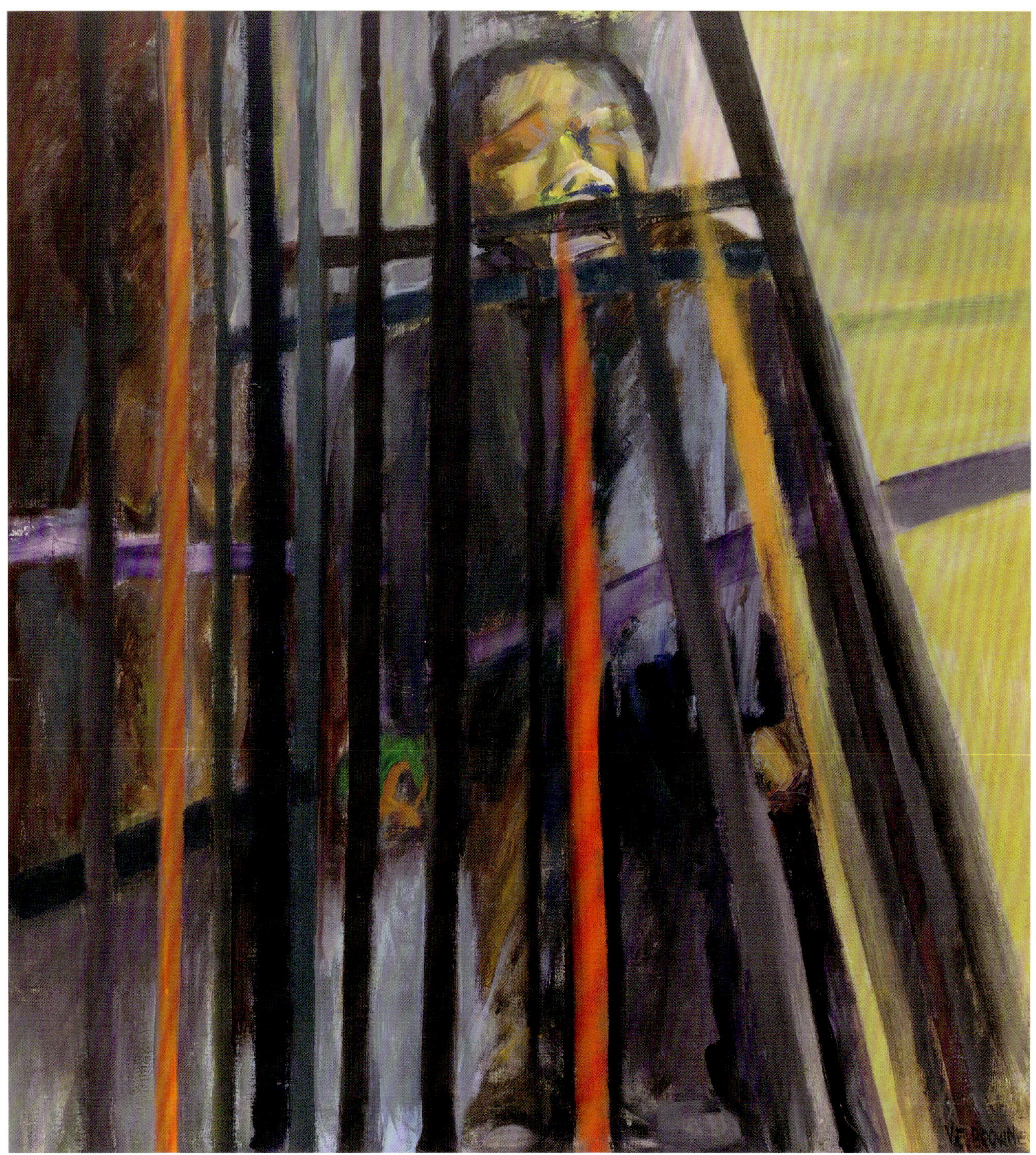

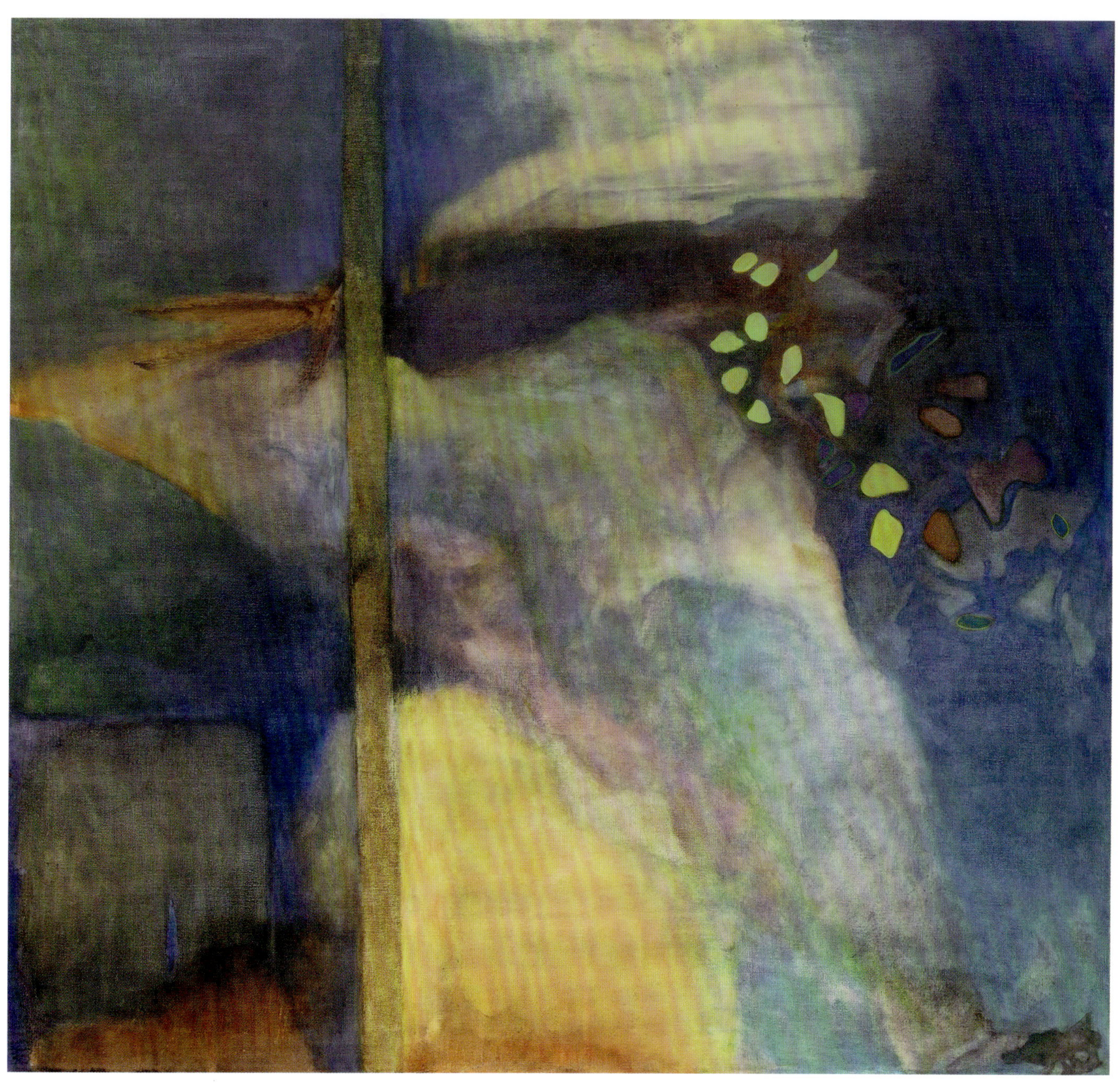

Plate 45
The Prisoner, 1972
Acrylic on canvas
45 ½ × 42 inches
Adobe Krow Archives, CA
and RYAN LEE Gallery, NY

Plate 46
For You, 1974
Oil on canvas
46 ¾ × 50 ¾ inches
Adobe Krow Archives, CA
and RYAN LEE Gallery, NY

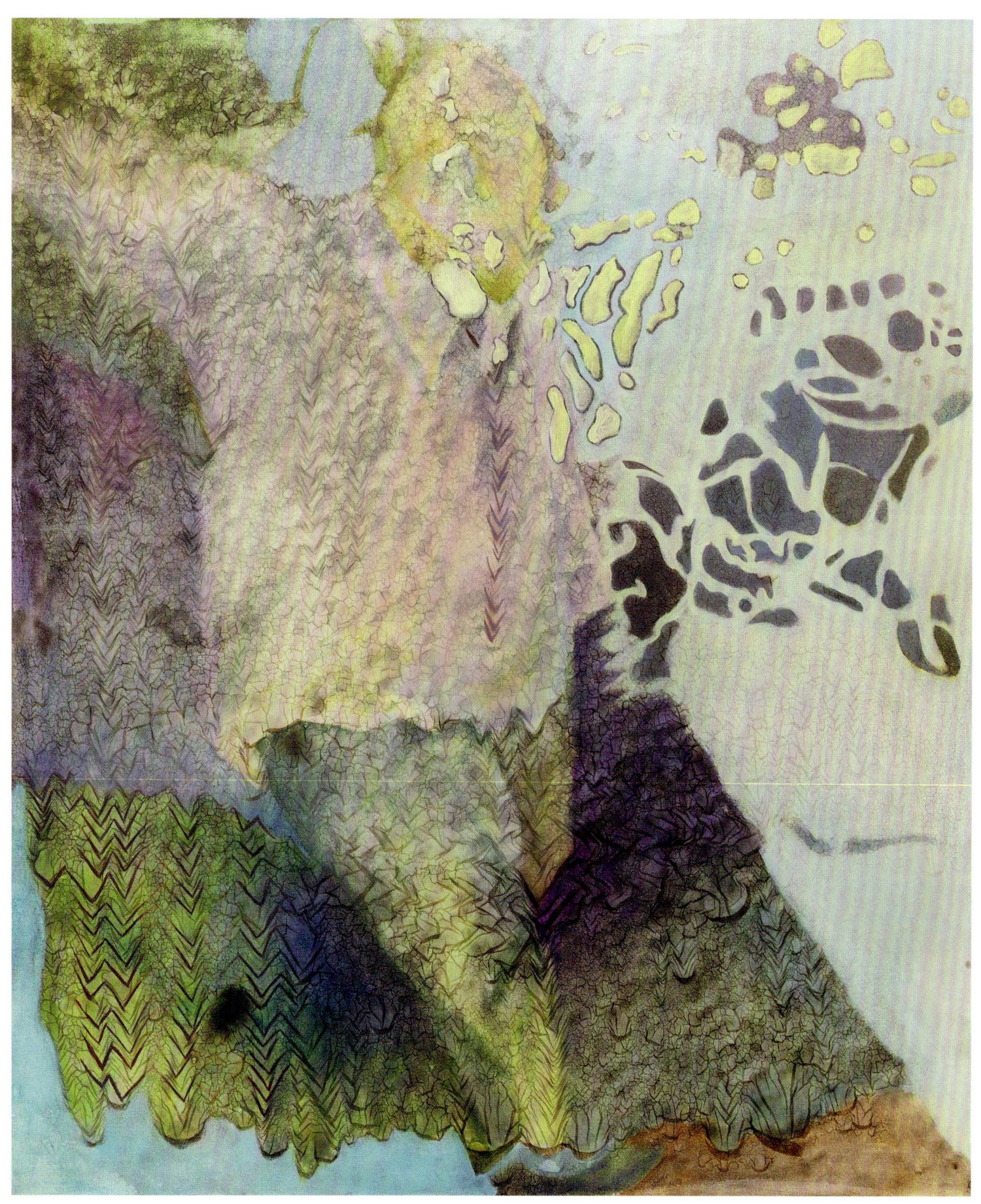

Plate 47
Untitled (Man in Mountain), c. 1974
Oil on canvas
40 ¾ × 34 ¾ inches
Adobe Krow Archives, CA
and RYAN LEE Gallery, NY

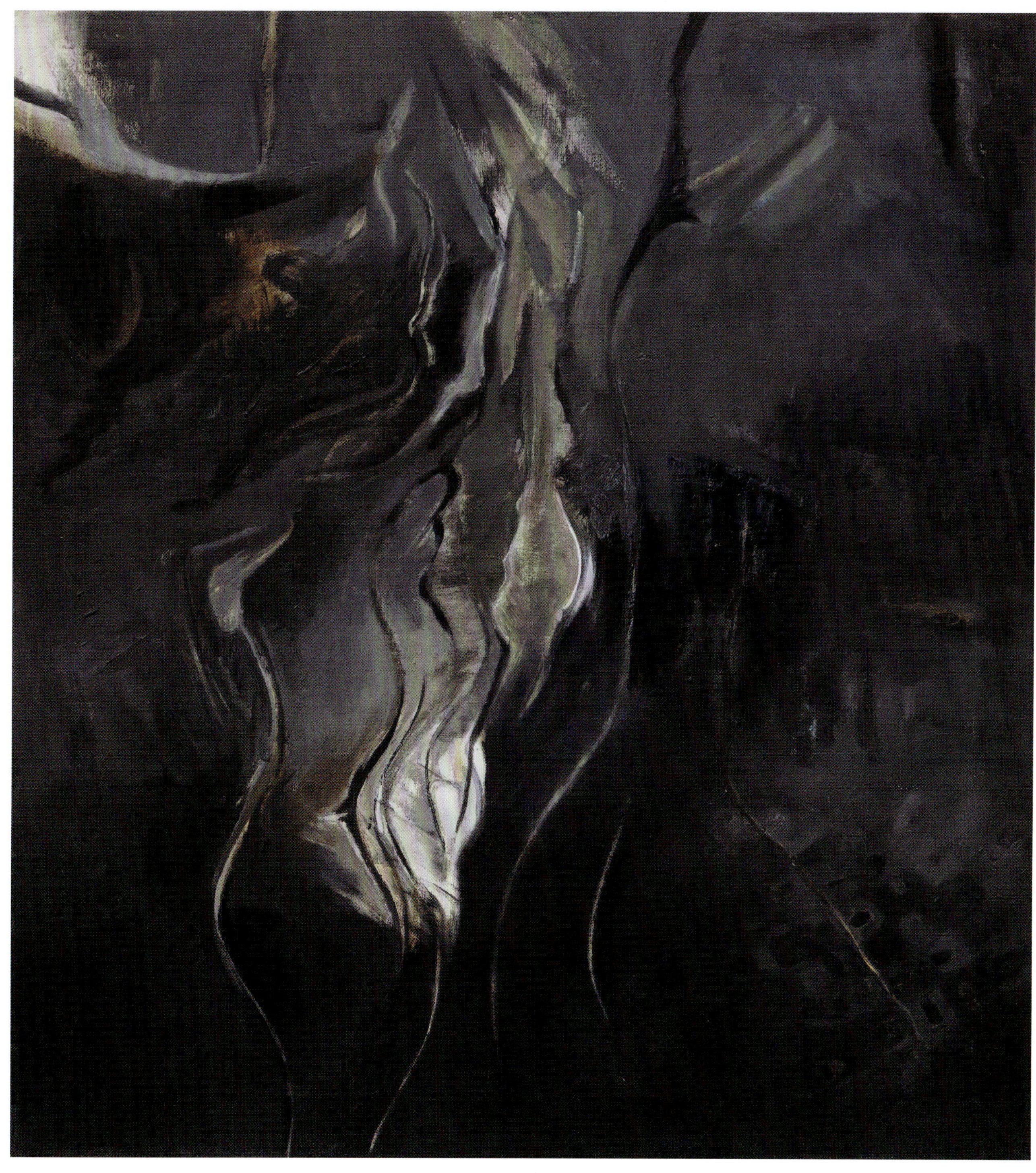

Plate 48
Sea Forms Abstract, c. 1978
Oil on canvas
25 × 27 inches
Adobe Krow Archives, CA
and RYAN LEE Gallery, NY

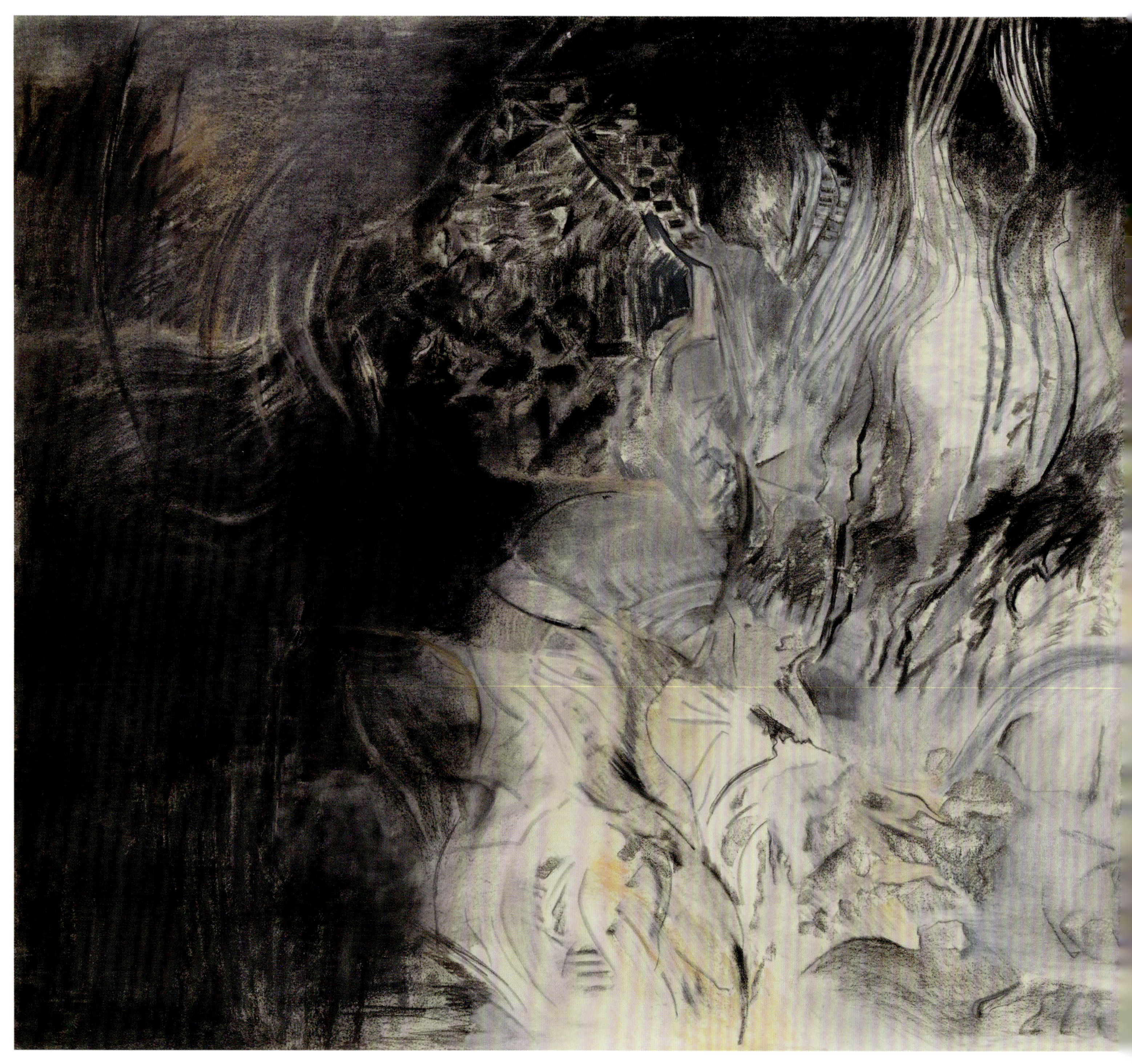

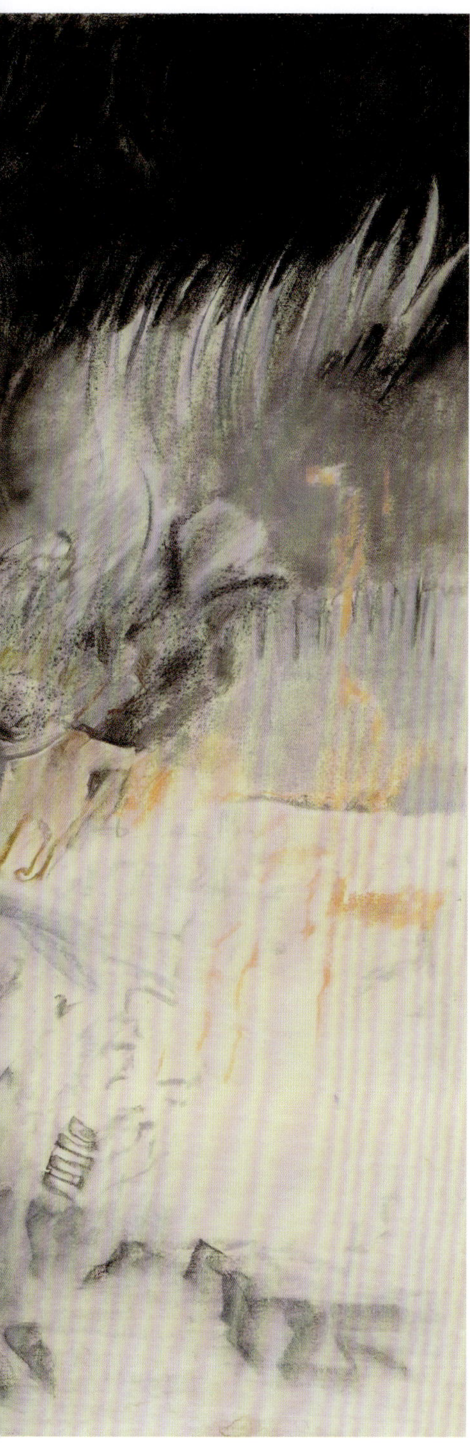

Plate 49
Ocean Forms I, 1978
Pastel on paper
40 7/8 × 58 5/8 inches
Adobe Krow Archives, CA
and RYAN LEE Gallery, NY

Plate 50 (opposite)
Shanghai Morning, 1980
Oil on silk and canvas
56 × 40 inches
Adobe Krow Archives, CA
and RYAN LEE Gallery, NY

Plate 51 (right)
Candy Memoriam, 1980
Oil on silk and canvas
56 ½ × 38 ¼ inches
Adobe Krow Archives, CA
and RYAN LEE Gallery, NY

Plate 52 (overleaf)
Clear Particles Floating Free, 1982
Acrylic on silk and pastel on paper
60 × 132 inches
Adobe Krow Archives, CA
and RYAN LEE Gallery, NY

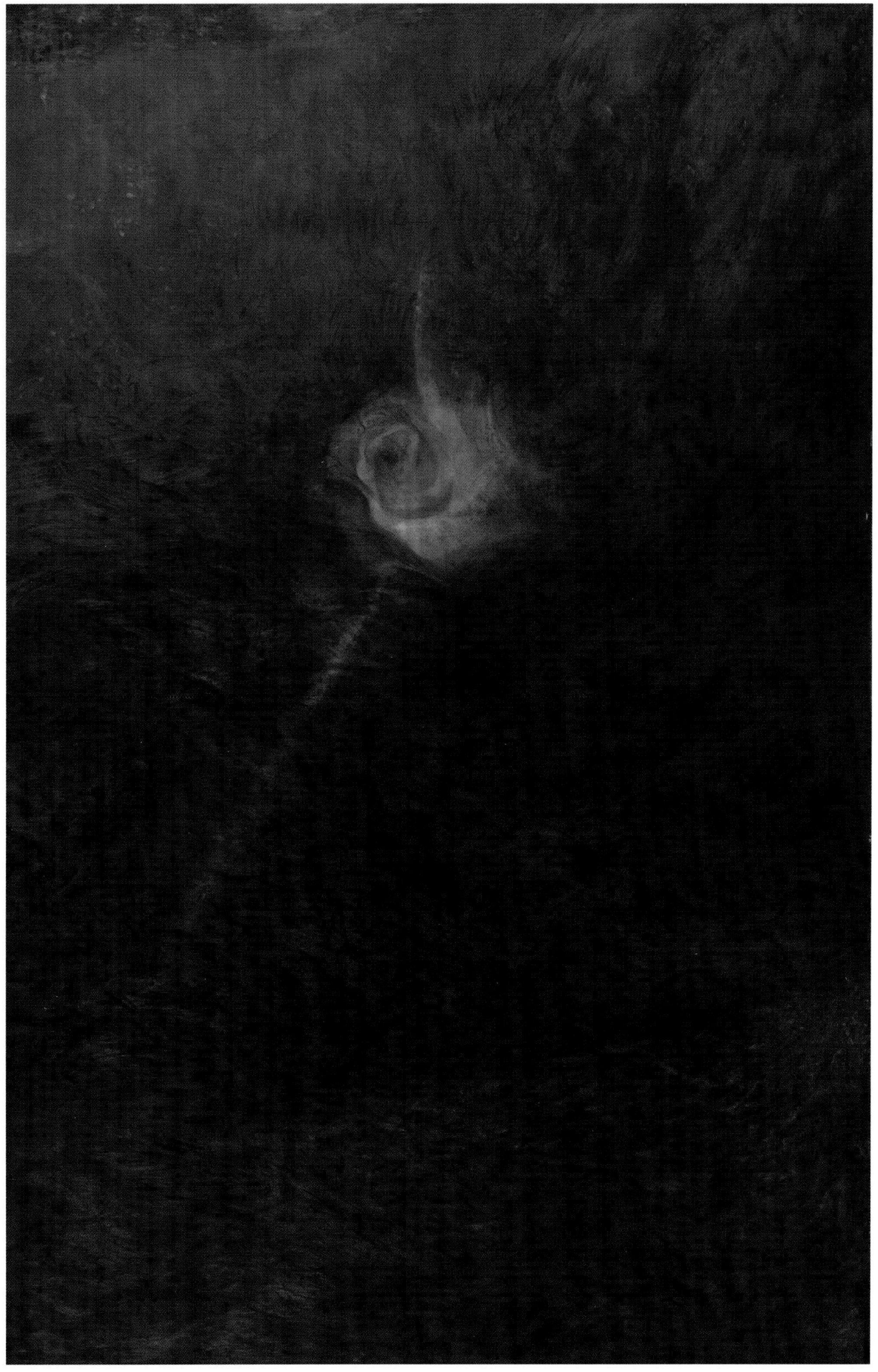

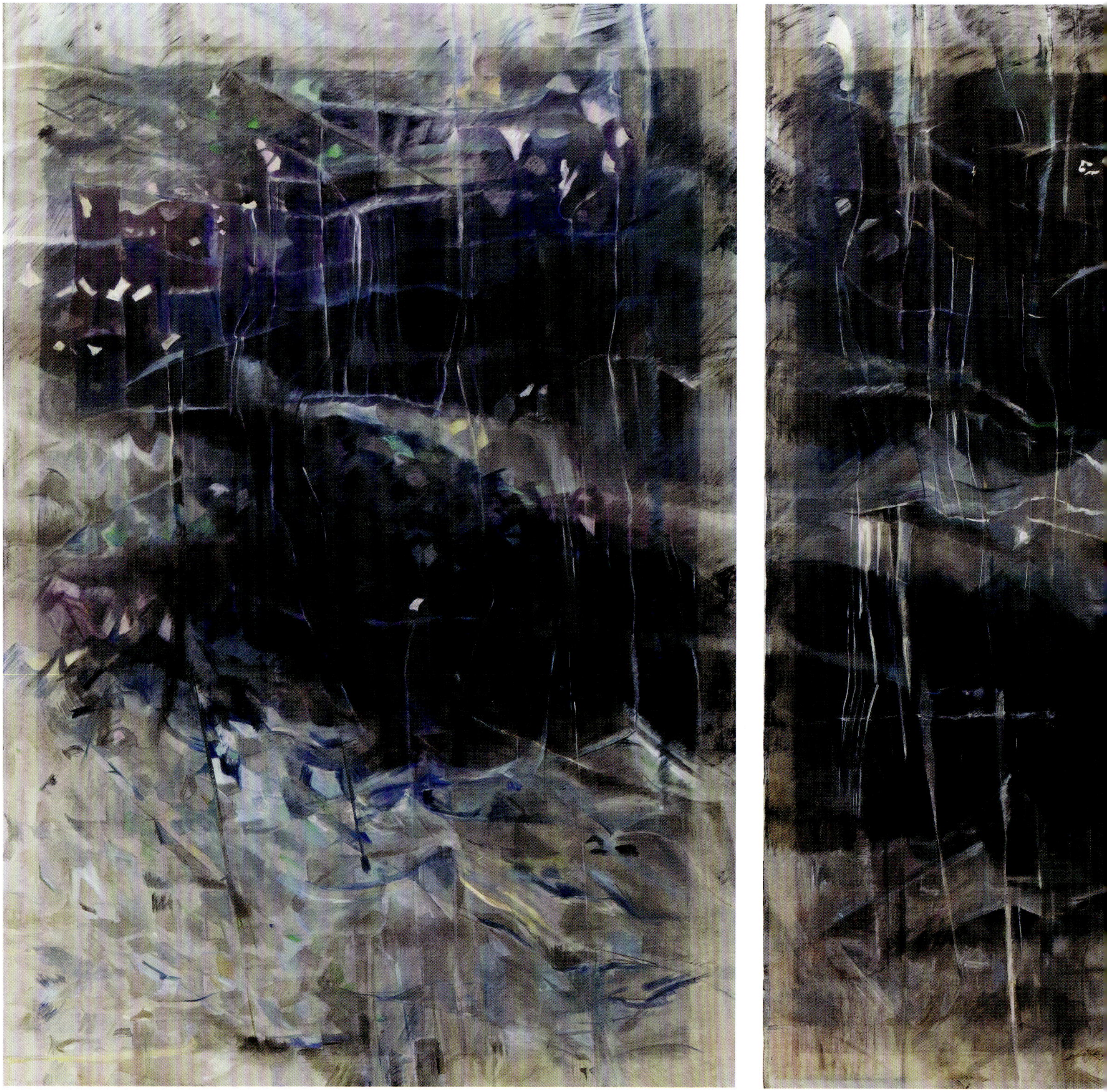

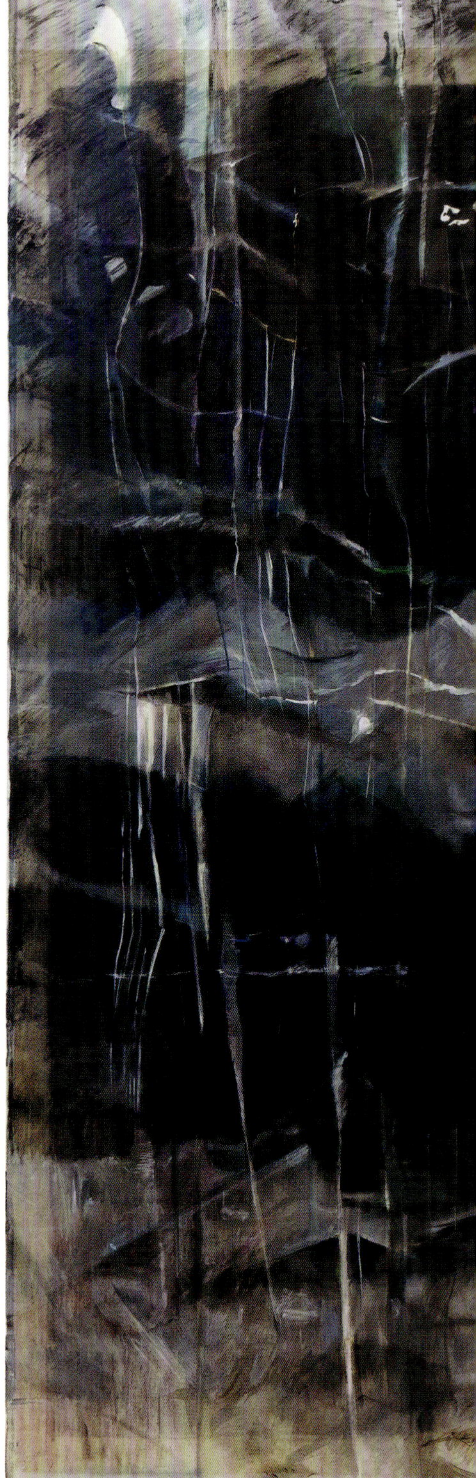

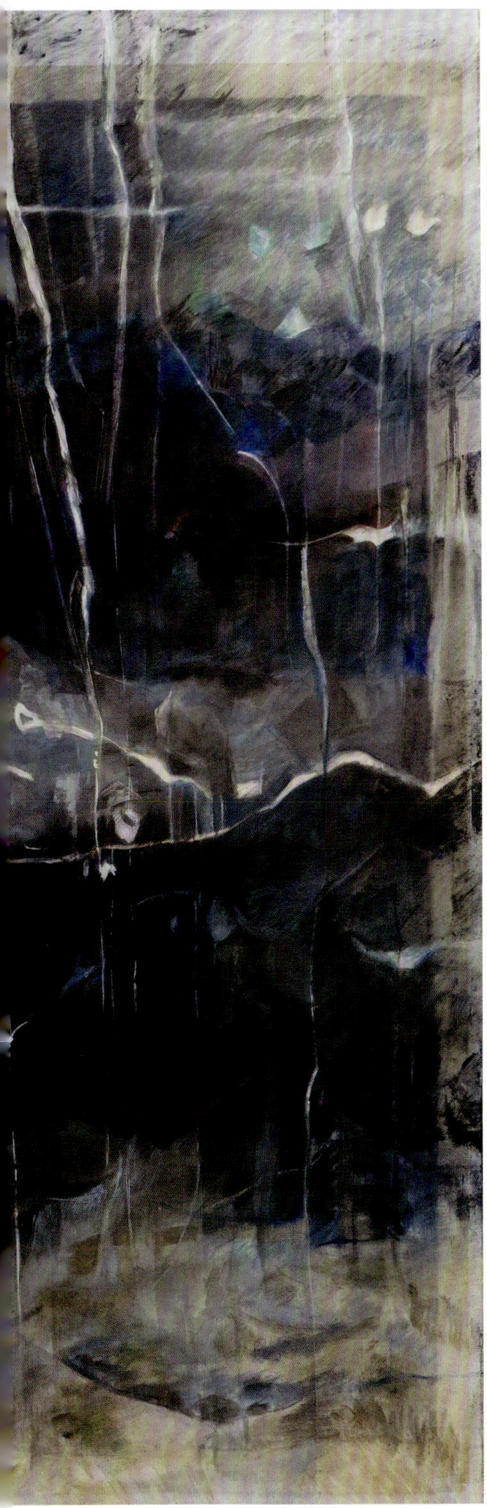

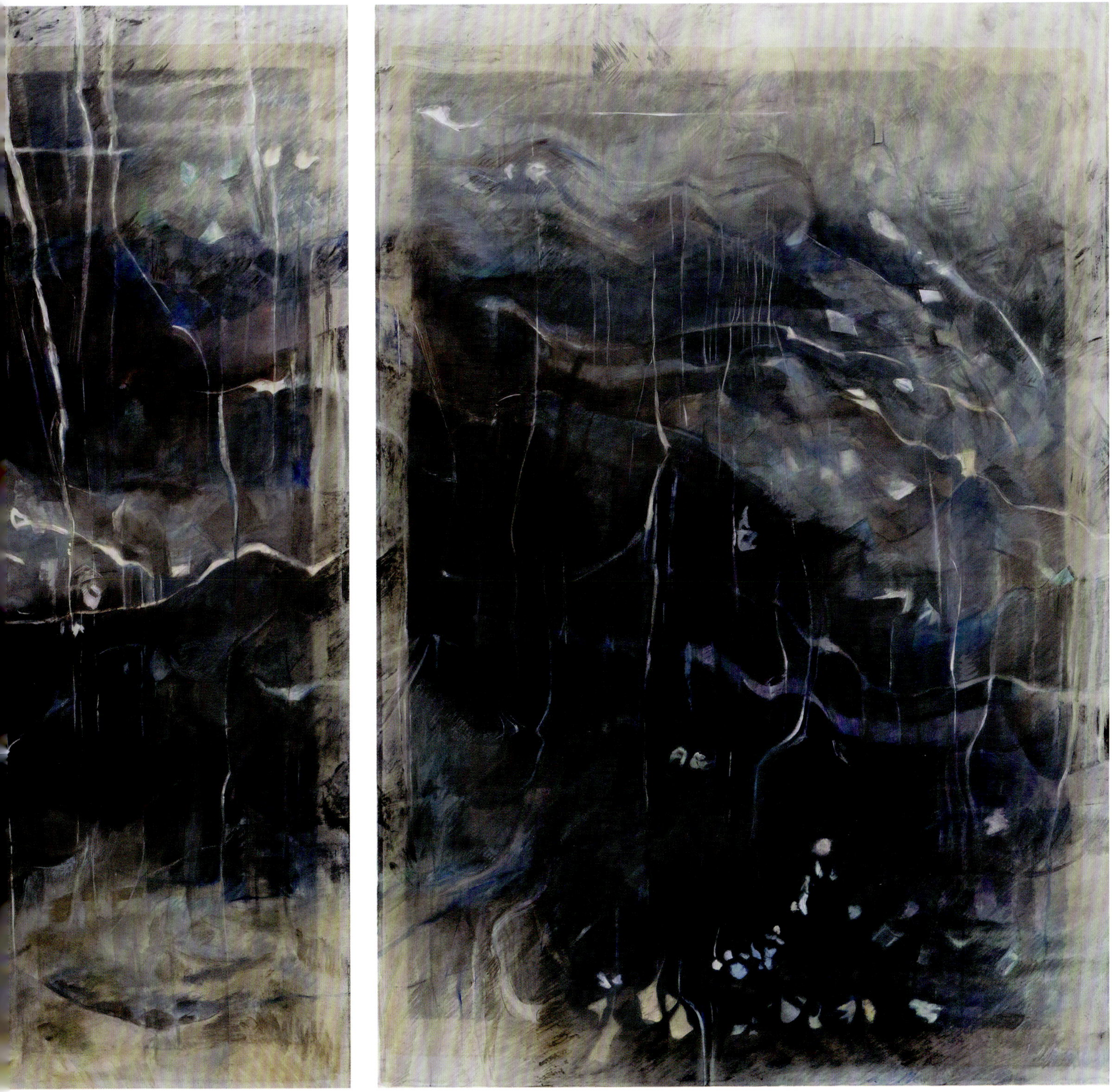

"Vivian Browne and William T. Williams"

Lowery S. Sims

I first met Vivian Browne in the early 1970s at the annual meetings of the National Conference of Artists, a black arts organization that has provided a forum for issues [germane] to black visual artists for over thirty years. Her work was figurative then, and often featured rather bloated figures of men—inevitably, white men—who were meant to be allegorical references to the excesses and unjustices [sic] in society. These works were contextualized within the contemporary civil rights and feminist movements. By the early 1970s these compositions, already characterized by their painterliness, became more abstracted and some motifs referring to African art forms could be discerned.

A few years ago Browne's work took a rather dramatic turn, and she began exhibiting wonderfully evocative abstractions that portrayed vaguely biomorphic forms engulfed by and emerging from a misty ambiance in which color was subsumed by black and white. Their delicate, sensuous quality was enhanced by Browne's use of silk as a support on which to create her images, whose titles often evoked elements in nature that approximated the qualities of a finely woven textile. Critics alluded to the associations with water, light and air, as well as to the artist's working method which contrasted with the more controlled aspects of her earlier work. "The surrealistic quality in the work is related to the 'automatic' process; working without a preconceived idea for the content of the painting. Browne works intuitively and '... [m]any memories and impressions from her extensive travel around the world find their way into the paintings'."[2] These aqueous ambiances took on a more concrete and expressionistic quality by the mid-1980s. Browne used a more vigorous and coloristic hand to create interwoven patterns whose "dissonance" and "jagged, gnarled and irregular"[3] quality contrasted with the more dreamy aspects of the work that immediately preceded it. References to natural plant life such as wild grasses and trees began to become more specific. A stylistic and technical affinity with Abstract Expressionism was more evident, and the pictorial agendas of the New York School were married with the artist's own interests in Native American nature mysticism and environmental issues.[4]

The work exhibited here shows that Browne's approach to imagery has come full circle. An emphatic realism has re-emerged, as the trees assume a foursquare position in her compositions. These landscapes and treescapes betray a variety of concerns. Her exercises in abstraction are evident in the skillful disposition of our point of view of the trees from directly below so that the branches emanating from the main trunk of the trees form a network that creates an all-over pattern connecting the side of the picture plane with the central areas. In a few of the paintings such as *Down to Earth* and *Scattered Conifers*, both executed in 1987, Browne has forthrightly stated the relationship between abstraction and figuration by pairing a naturalistic rendering of the tree with a more schematic, abstracted one that features a network of linear elements intersecting with each other and the limits of the picture plane. In her monumental triptych *Metasequoia*, Browne has interjected quotations from various Black American women writers in and among the multitude of brush strokes that comprise the images of the trees. One is reminded of any number of associations of female nature spirits, as well as the souls of human beings that are said to reside in the trees around us. Through this work, Browne has achieved a poignant tribute to her "womanist"[5] roots, as well as captured the wonderment of a child's first infatuation with trees, encapsulated in the dramatic upsweep of the perspective in many of these paintings.

Excerpt from Vivian Browne/William T. Williams,
The Jamaica Arts Center, New York, January 1988.

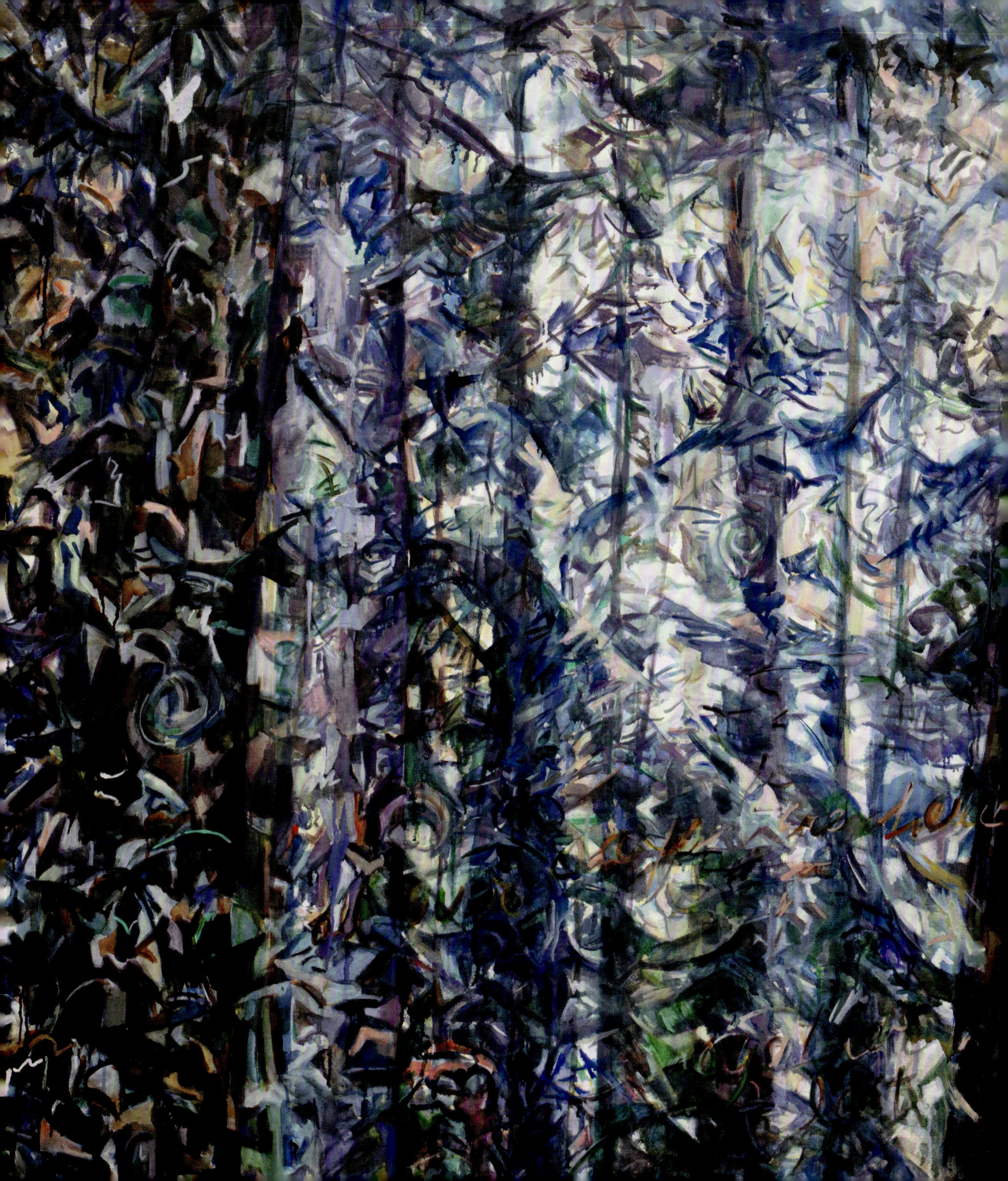

Artist Statement, 1988

Vivian Browne

In my recent paintings, I have tried to convey a sense
of movement and energy by utilizing a charcoal grid
(a preconceived arrangement of lines) emphasizing the mark.
This underlying grid has also been used to "find" the subject
matter and to maintain a linear counterpoint, i.e. a network
of linear elements intersecting with each other and the limits
of the picture plane.

In a series of acrylic paintings on paper based on Yosemite
conifers I have explored ideas of the written word, Native
American symbols, color and the Mark. Such issues as social
inequities, language and environment inform the paintings. To
[sic] most recent paintings, VERSATILE SOURCE and DOWN
TO EARTH, for example, involve juxtapositions [sic] of natural
symbols of power, strength and endurance (big trees), to those
of the technological world (power towers) in our environment.

As a child growing up in Queens, N.Y. when it was still
possible to walk through open fields and small orchards, I
became fascinated with trees. That compelling attraction
combined with a growing concern for environmental issues
has led to references to plant life in much of my work of the
past ten years.

Adobe Krow Archives

Plate 53
Adobe I, 1987
Woodcut on paper
40 × 27 inches
Adobe Krow Archives, CA
and RYAN LEE Gallery, NY

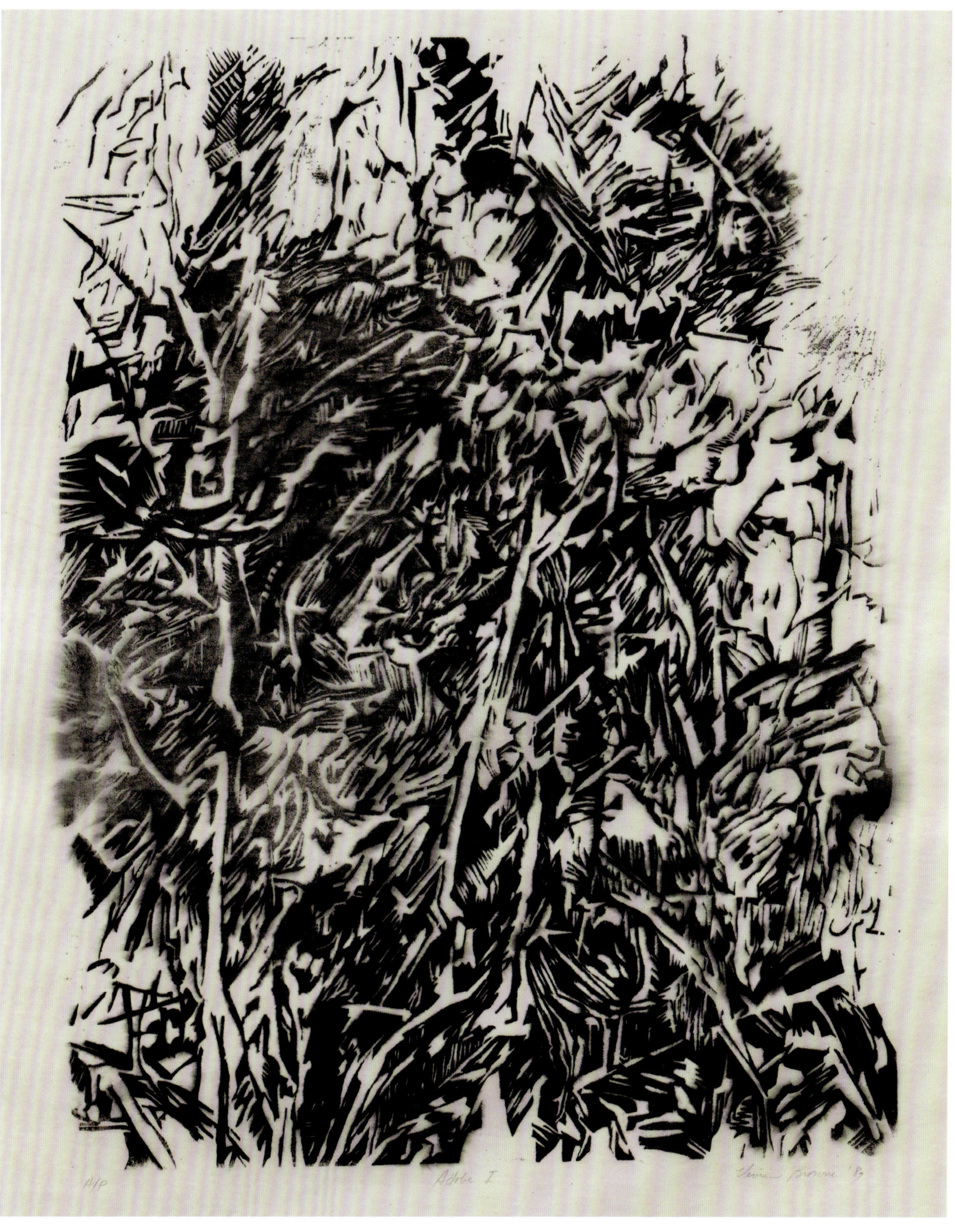
A/P
Adobe I

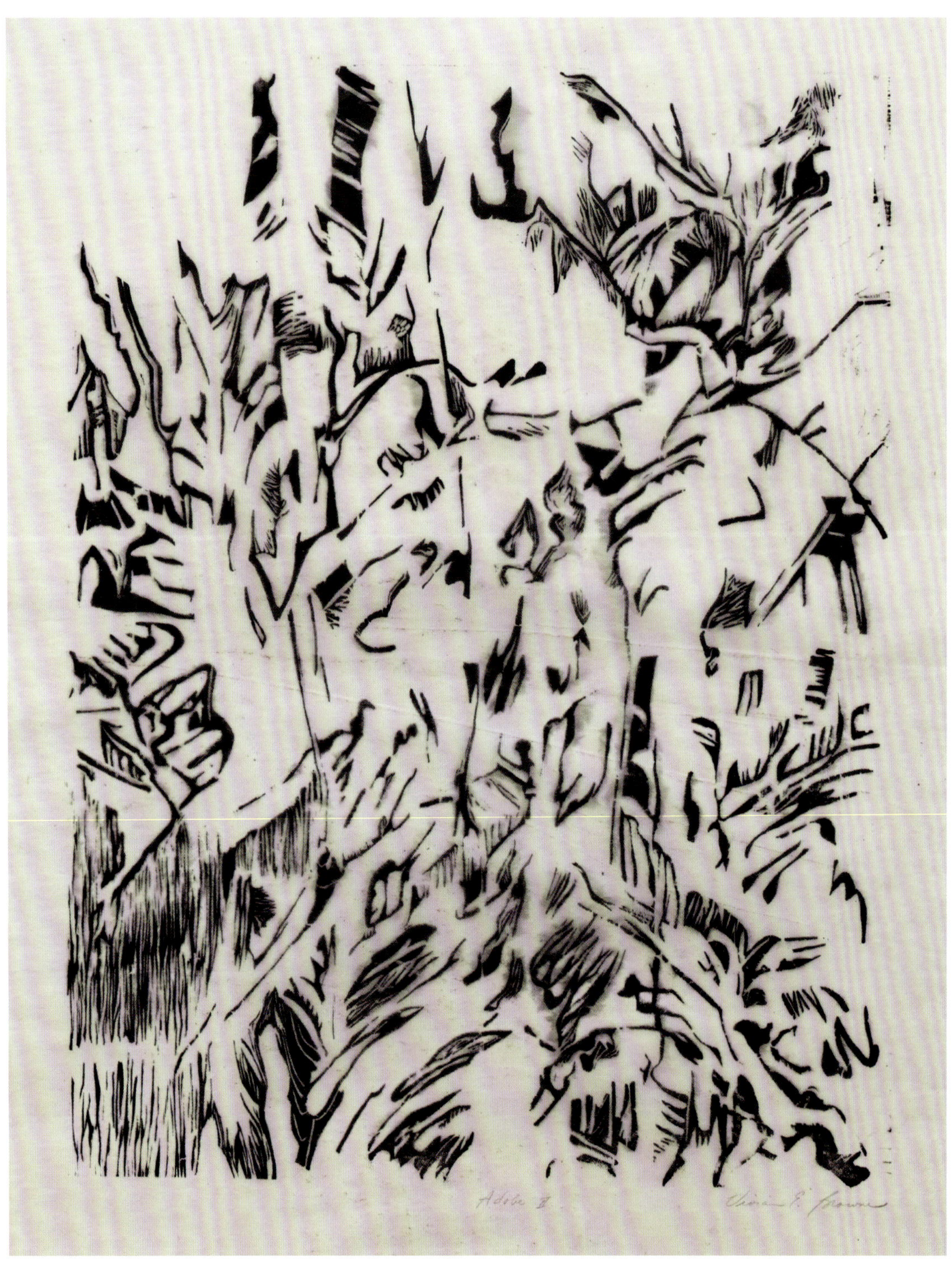

Plate 54
Adobe II, 1987
Woodcut on paper
39 ½ × 26 ½ inches
Adobe Krow Archives, CA
and RYAN LEE Gallery, NY

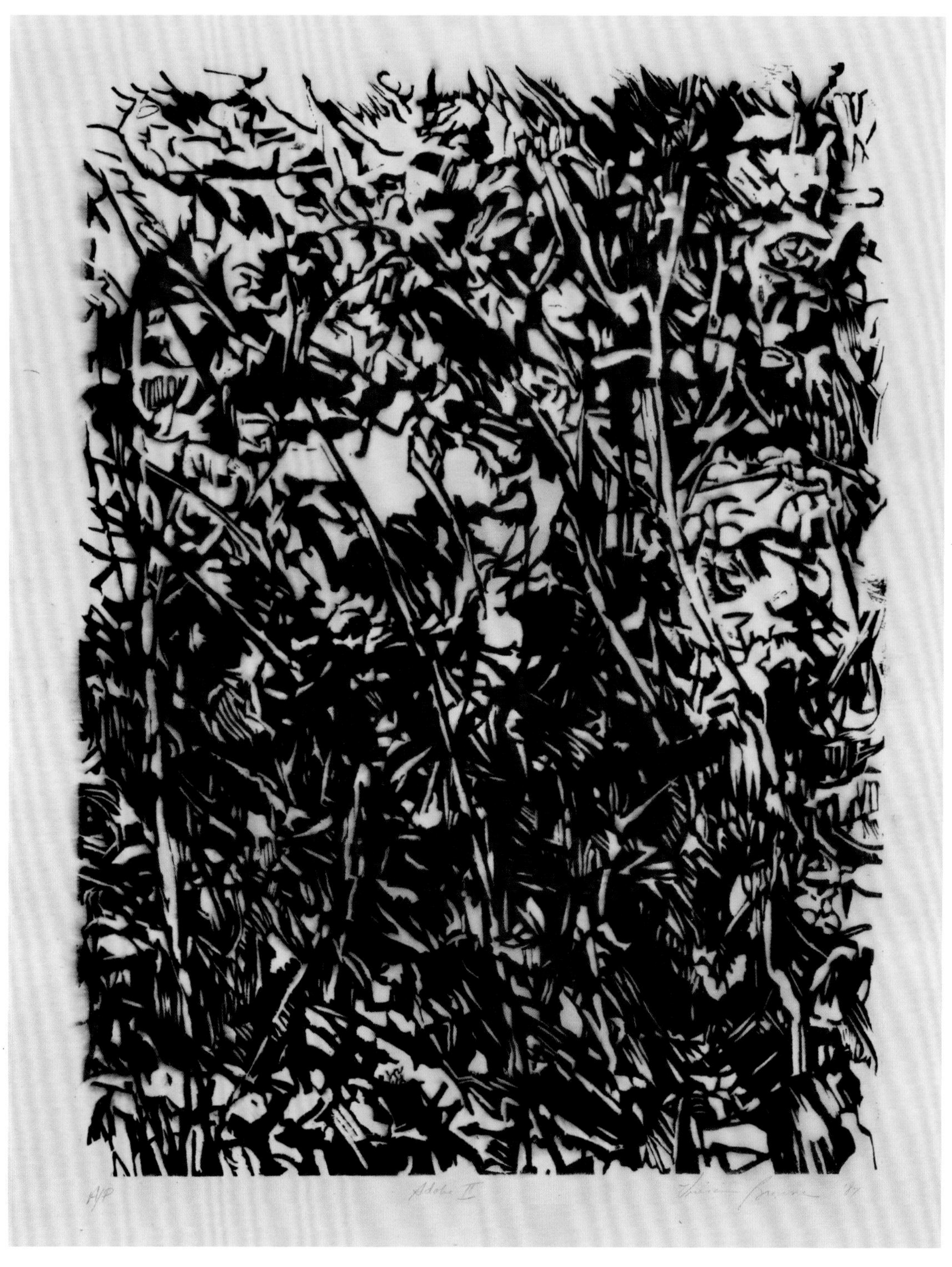

Plate 55
Adobe III, 1987
Woodcut on paper
39 ¼ × 26 ¾ inches
Adobe Krow Archives, CA
and RYAN LEE Gallery, NY

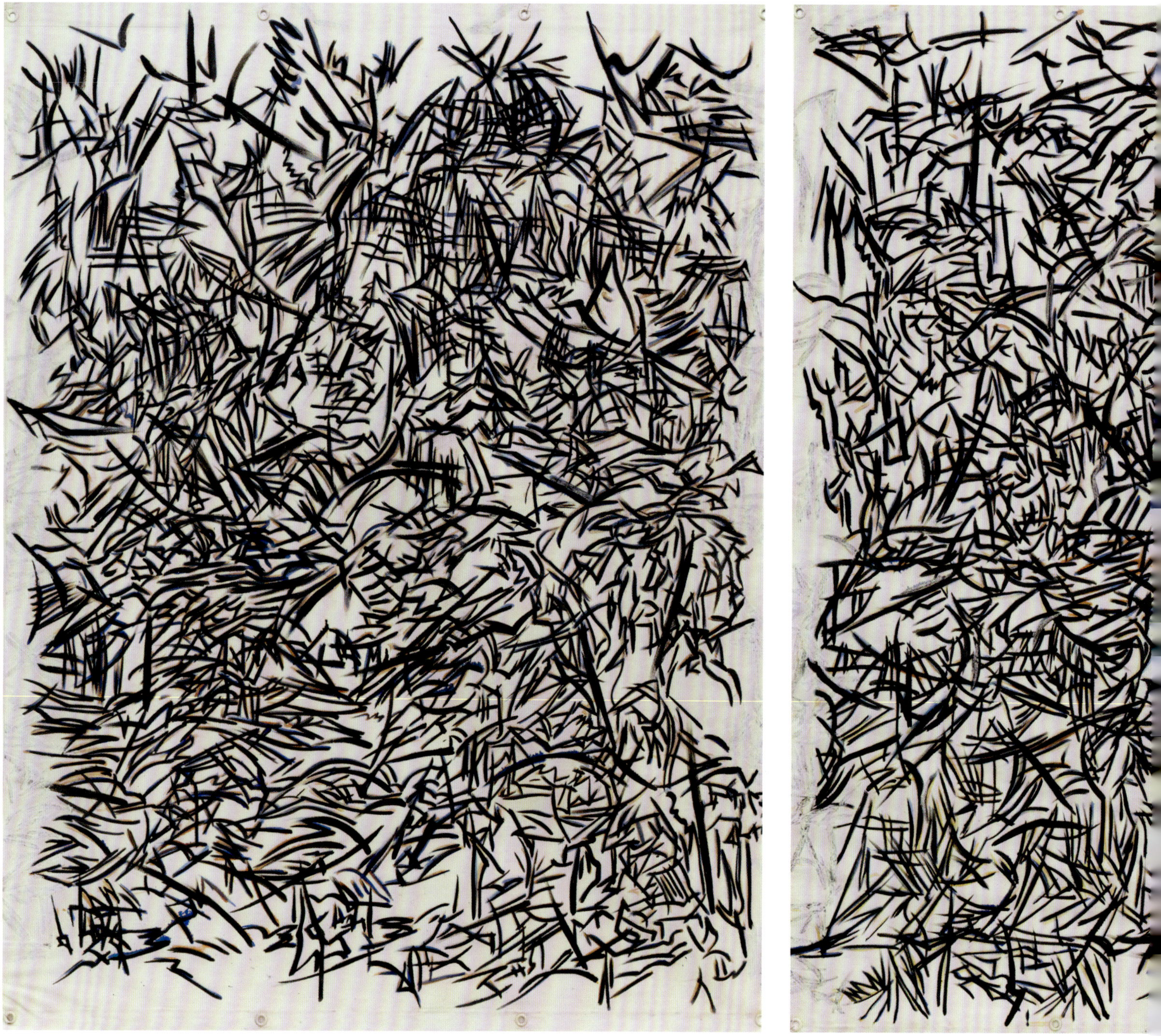

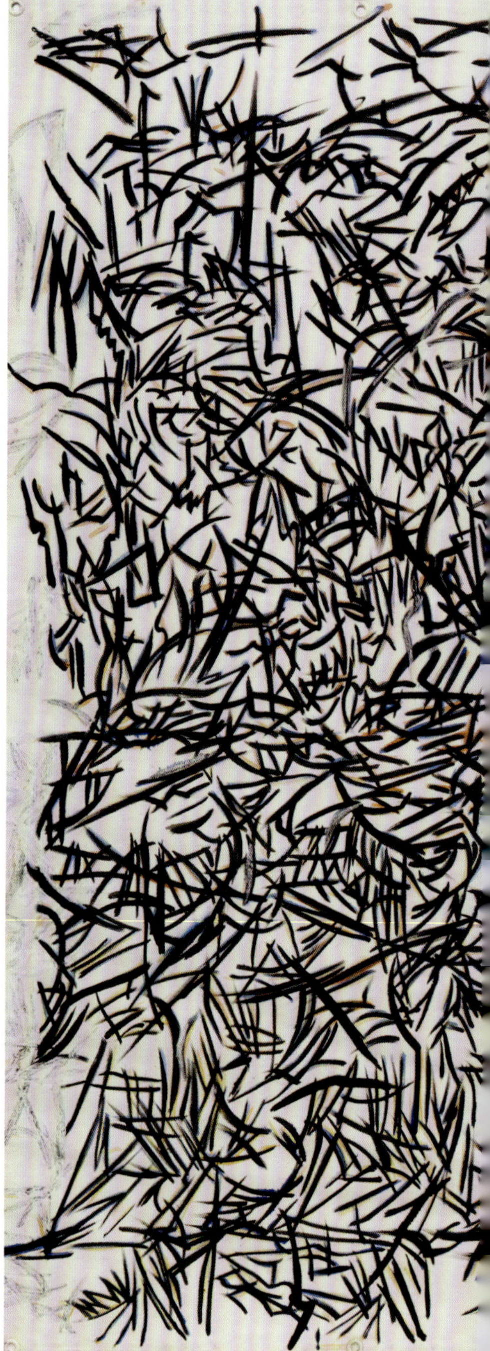

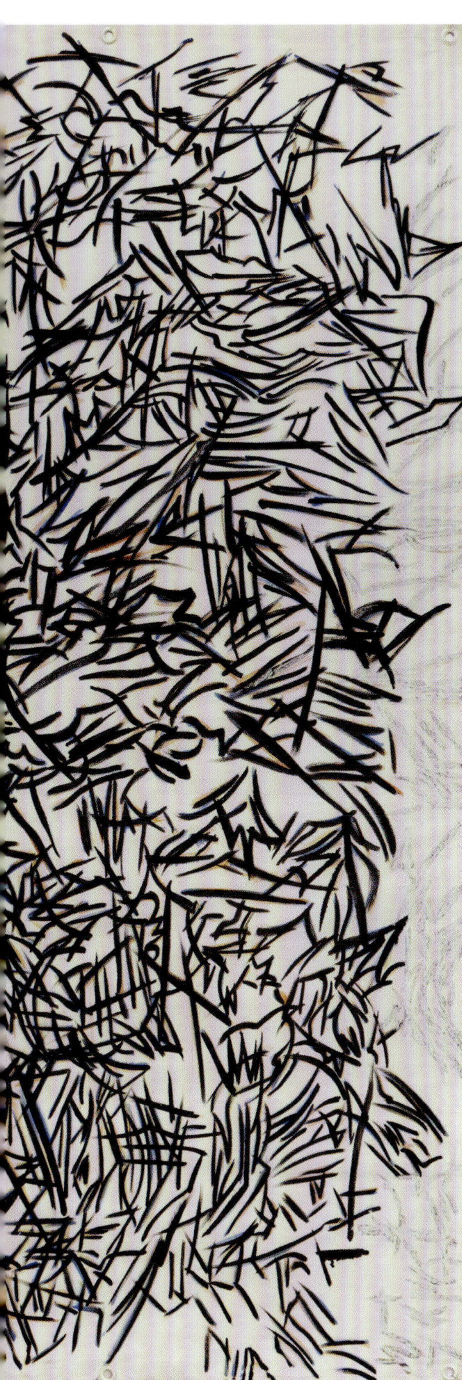

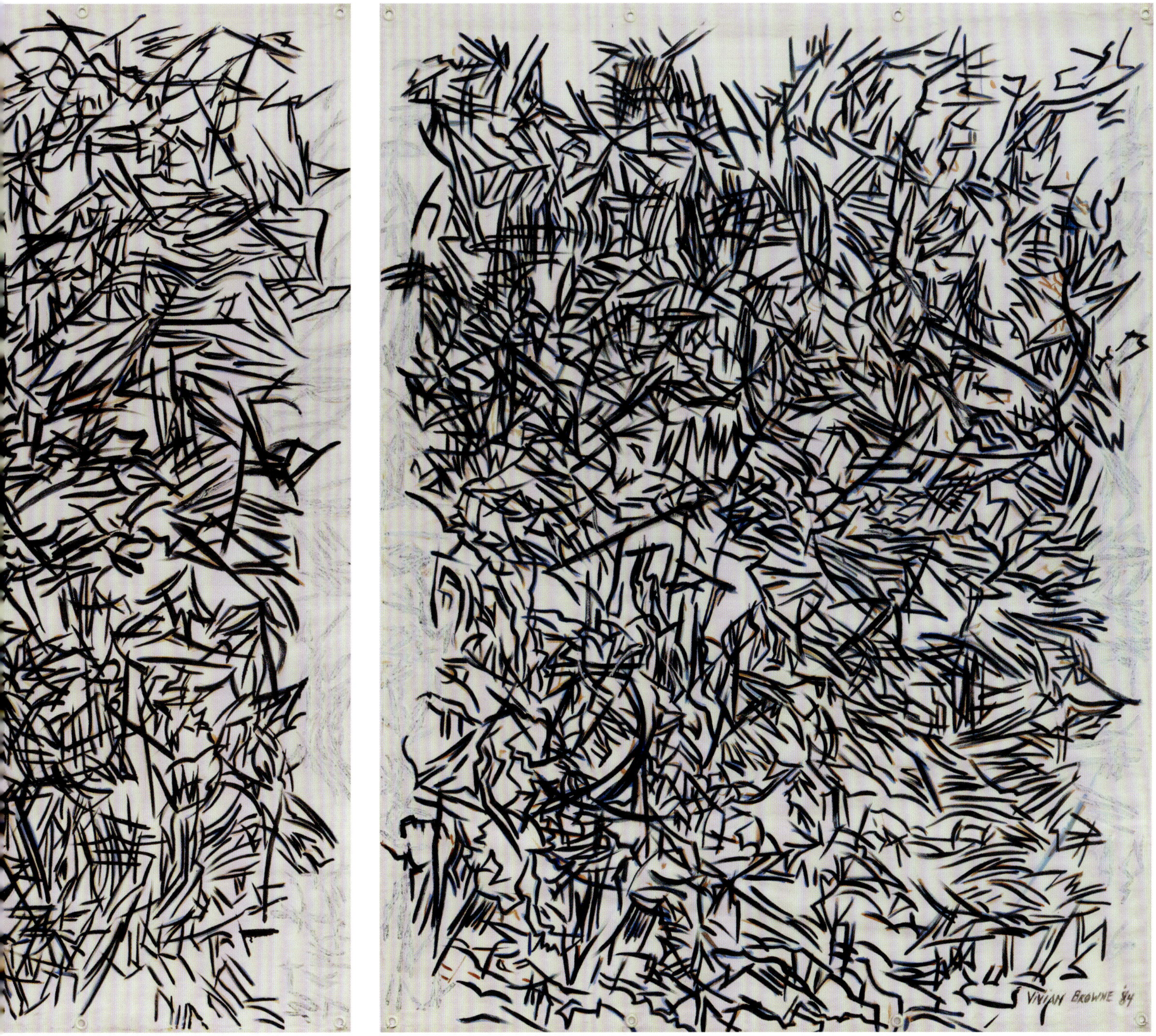

Plate 56
Oaks, 1984
Acrylic on canvas
61 × 126 inches
Adobe Krow Archives, CA
and RYAN LEE Gallery, NY

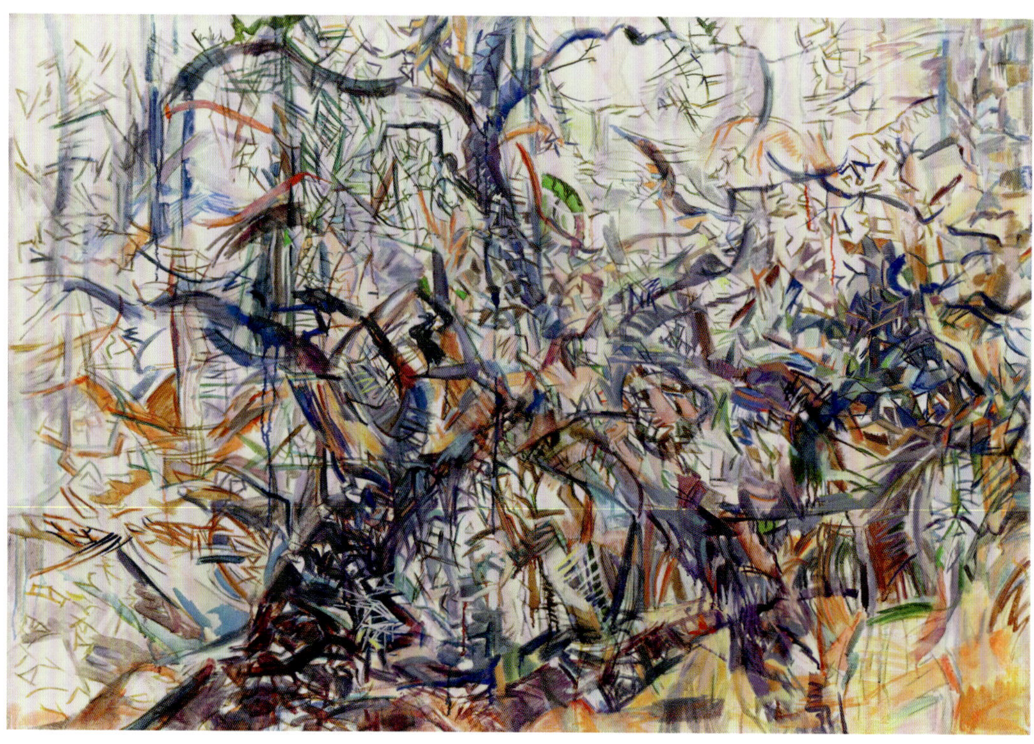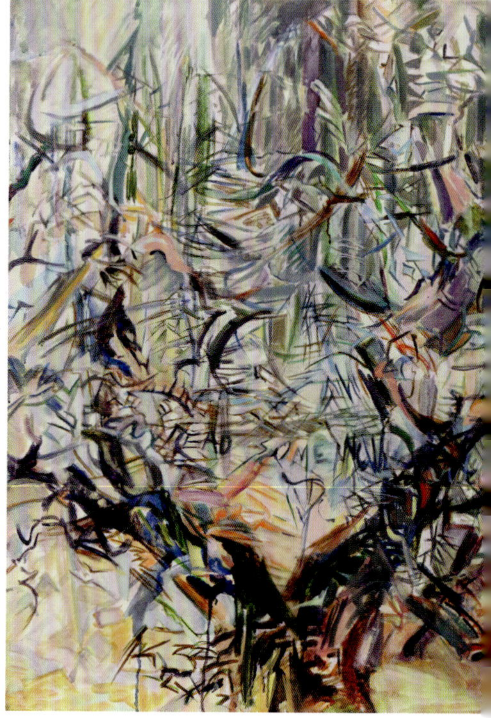

Plate 57
***The Sound Itself is All #59*, 1984**
Oil on canvas
38 ½ × 169 ½ inches
Adobe Krow Archives, CA
and RYAN LEE Gallery, NY

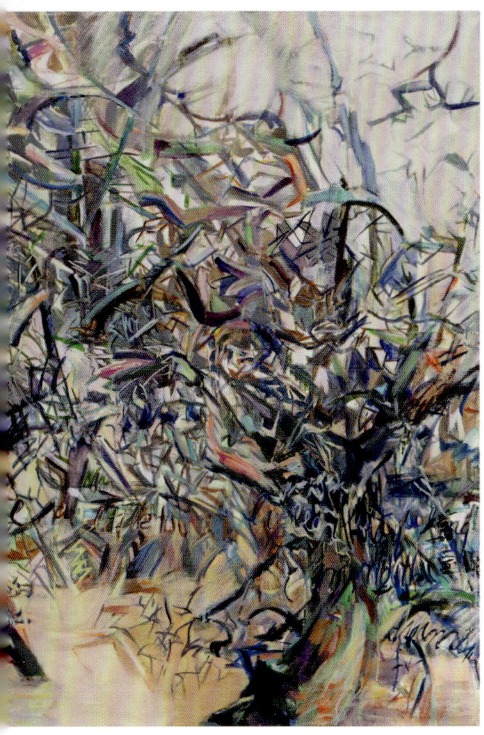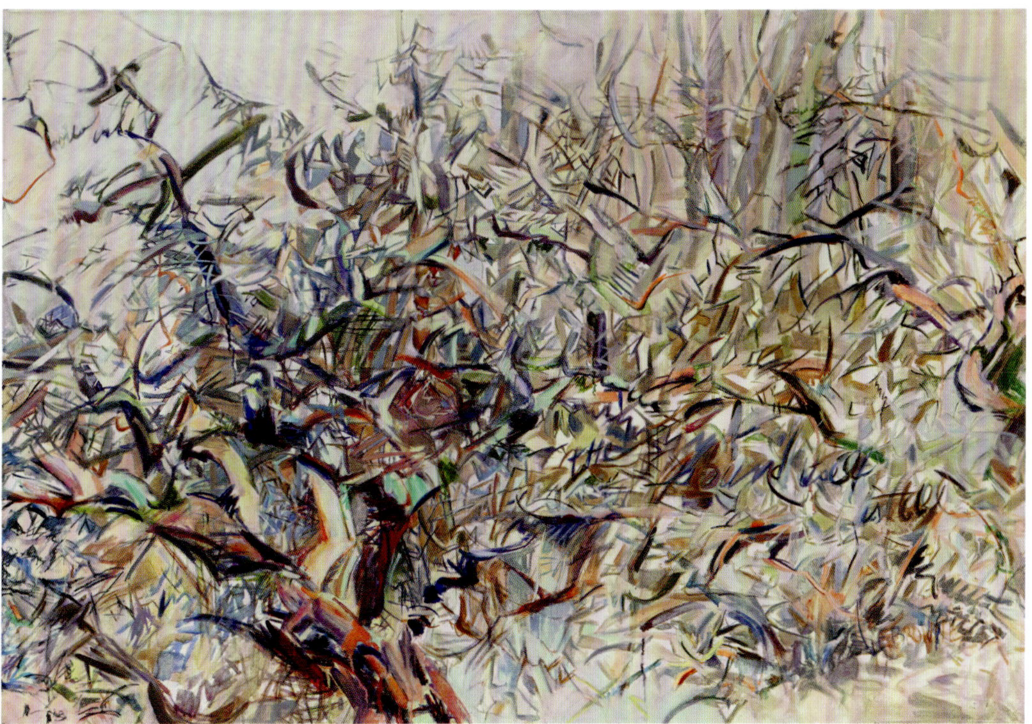

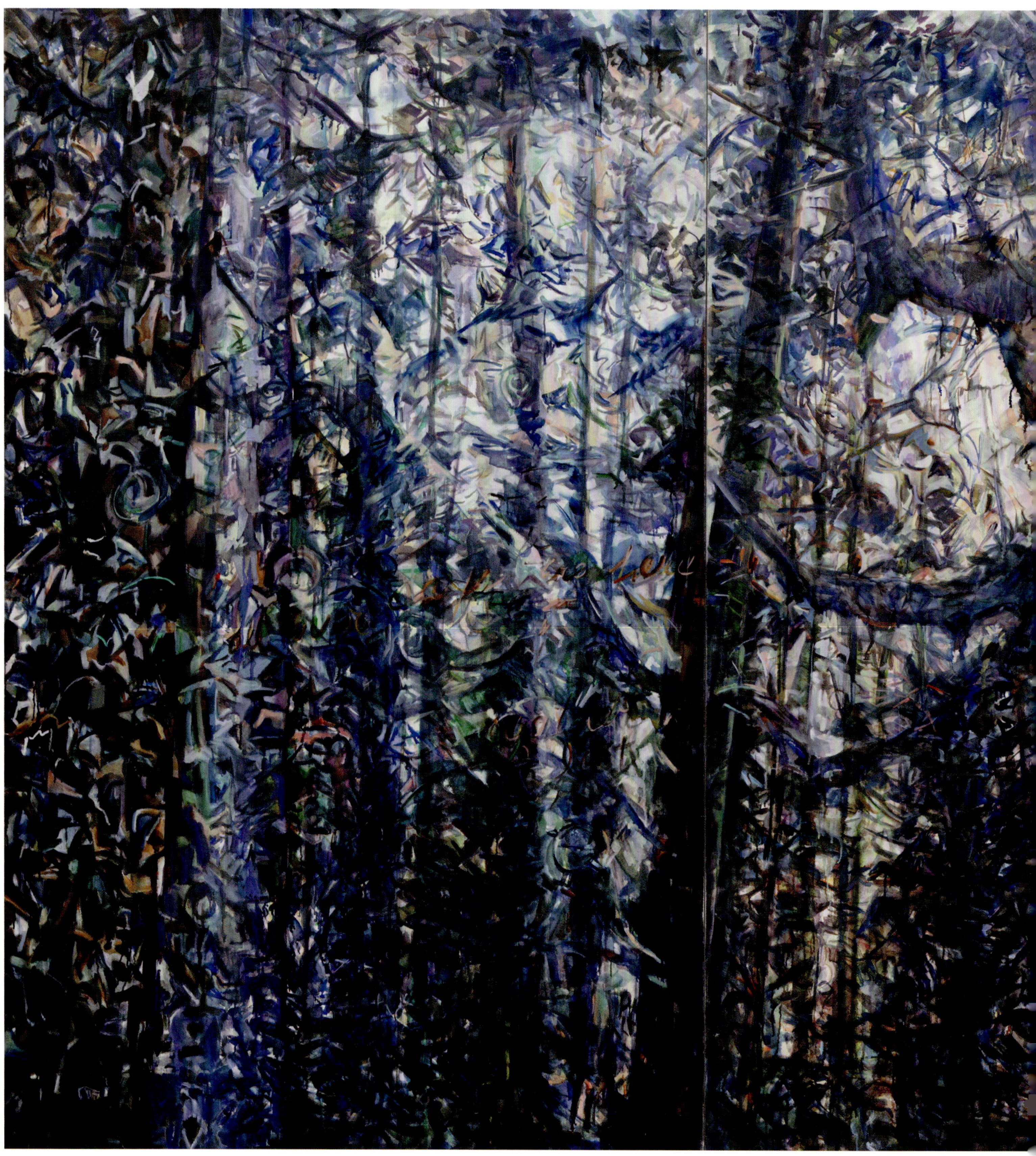

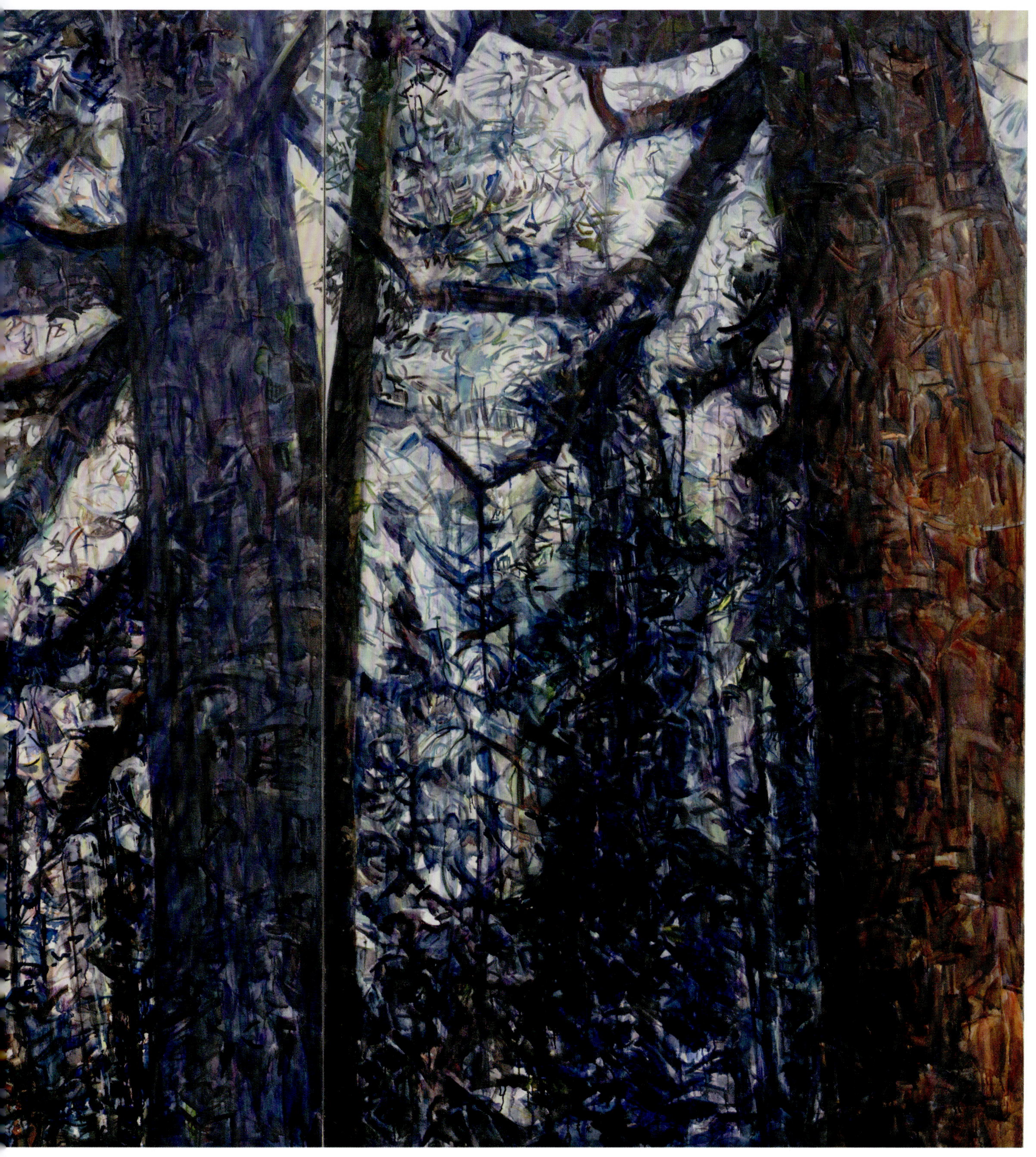

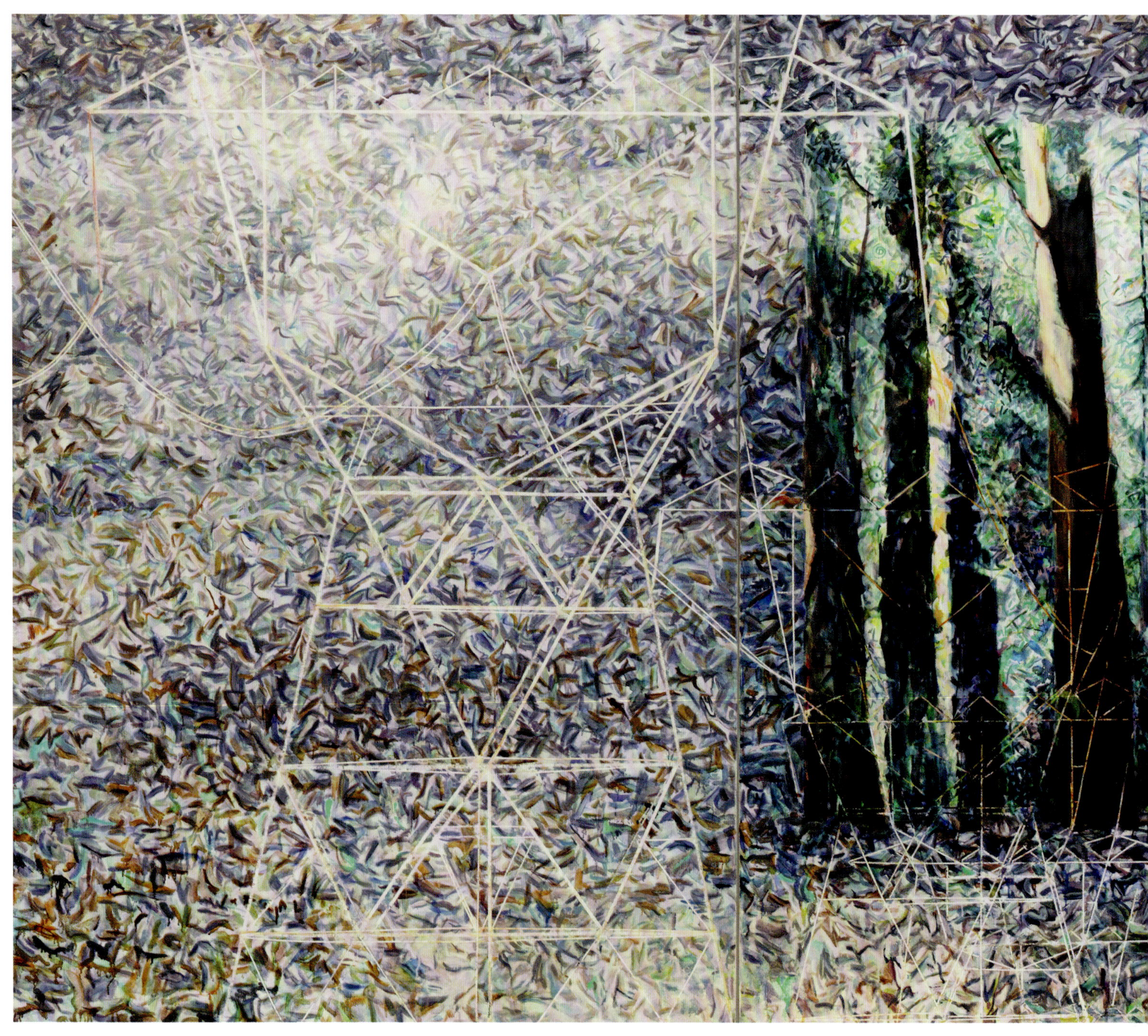

Plate 58 (previous spread)
Metasequoia #13, 1987
Oil on canvas
70 × 148 inches
Adobe Krow Archives, CA
and RYAN LEE Gallery, NY

Plate 59
Semper Virens, 1989
Oil on canvas
68 × 160 ½ inches
Adobe Krow Archives, CA
and RYAN LEE Gallery, NY

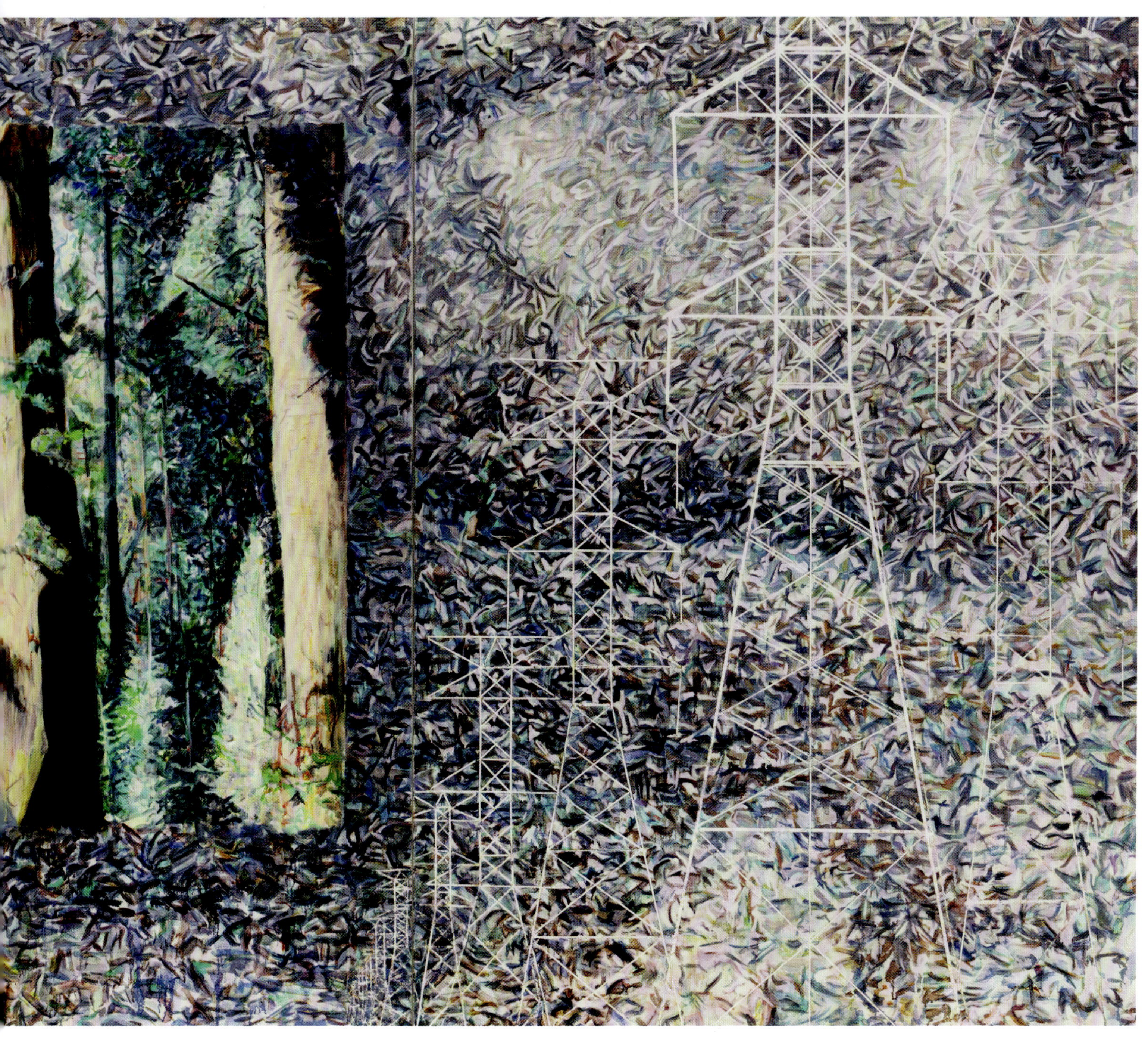

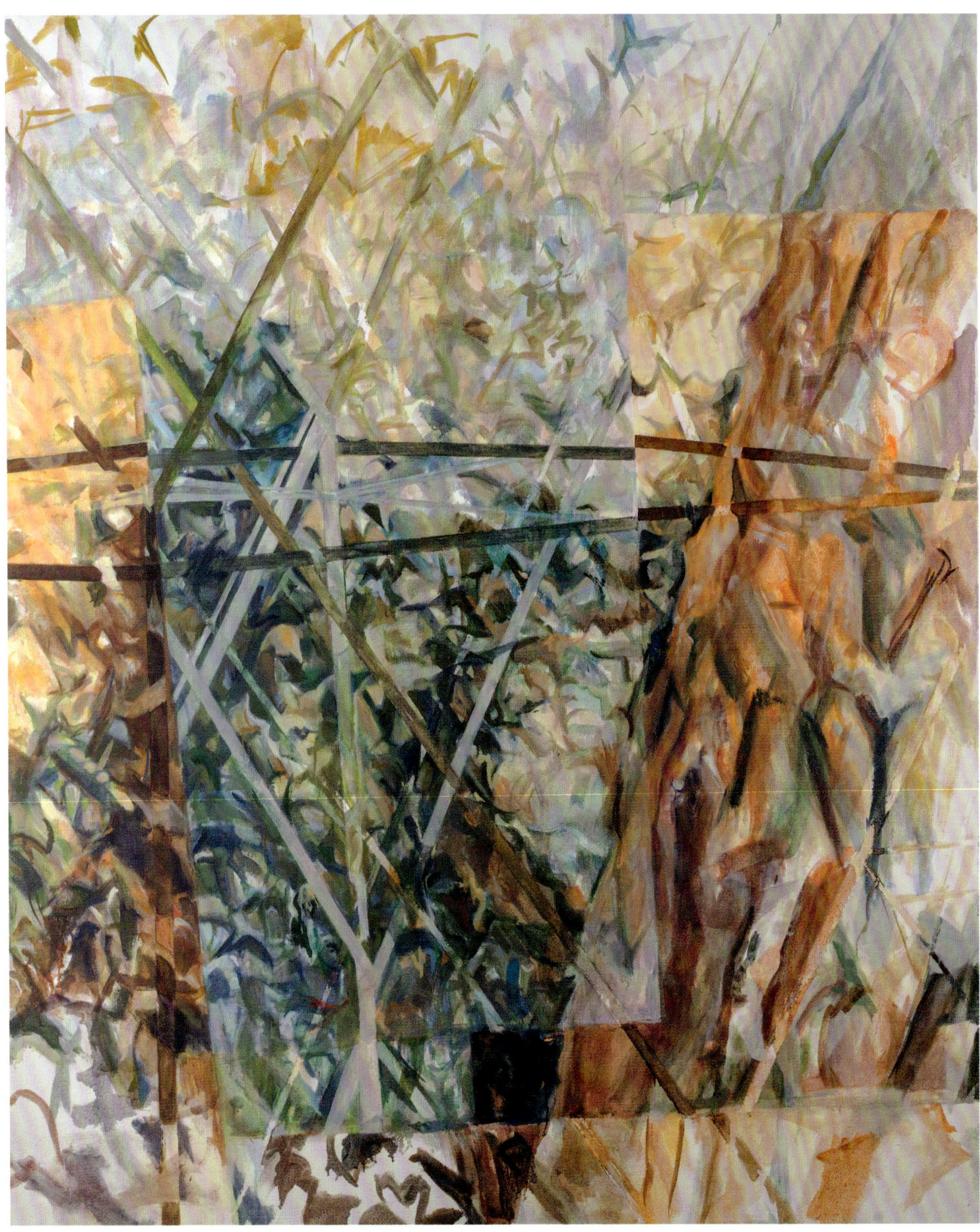

Plate 60
San Joaquin/Diaresis, 1992
Oil on canvas
80 × 68 inches
Wadsworth Atheneum Museum of Art, Hartford, CT.
The Ella Gallup Sumner and Mary Catlin Sumner Collection

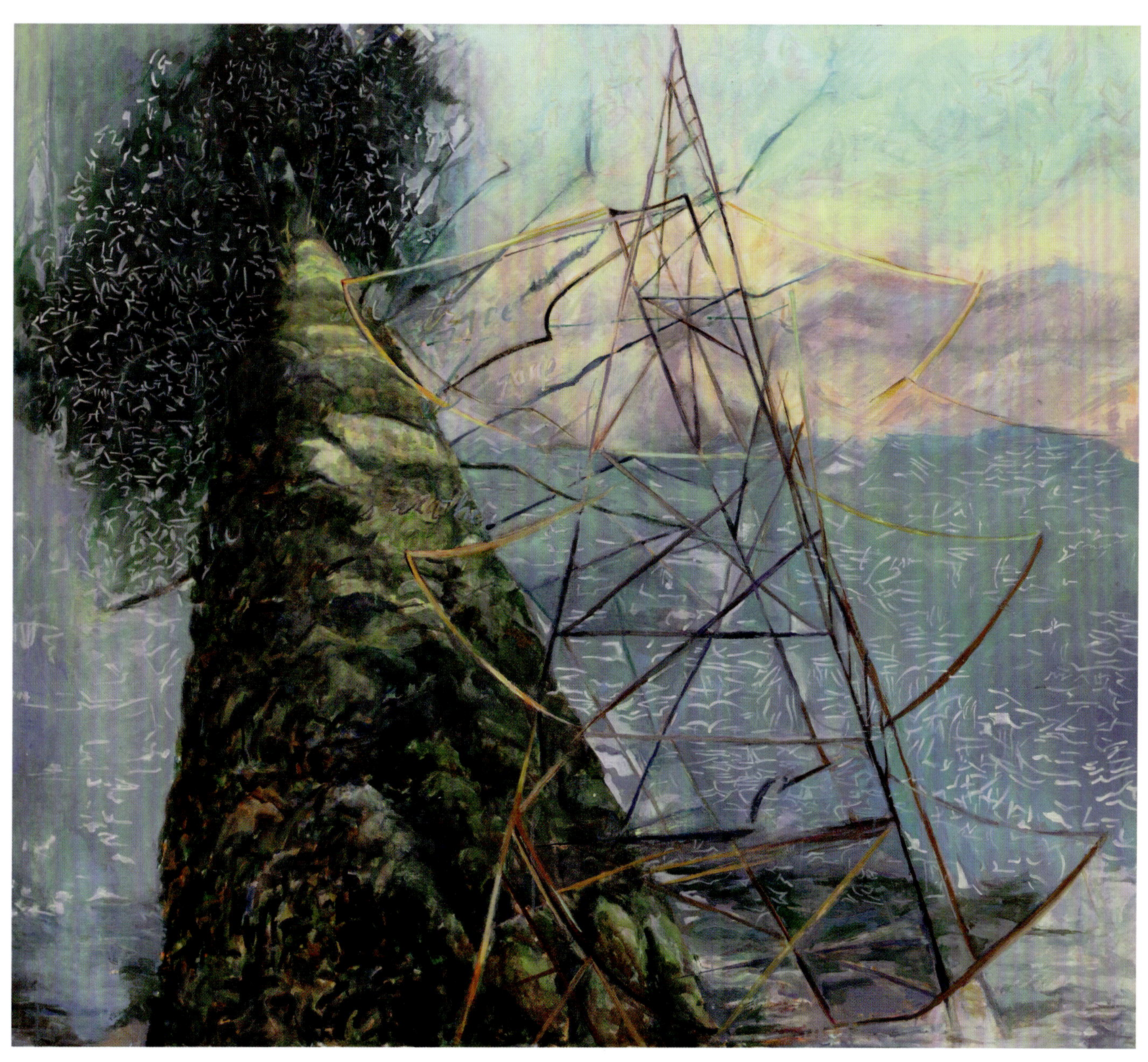

Plate 61
All Trace, c. 1985
Oil on canvas
42 × 48 inches
Adobe Krow Archives, CA
and RYAN LEE Gallery, NY

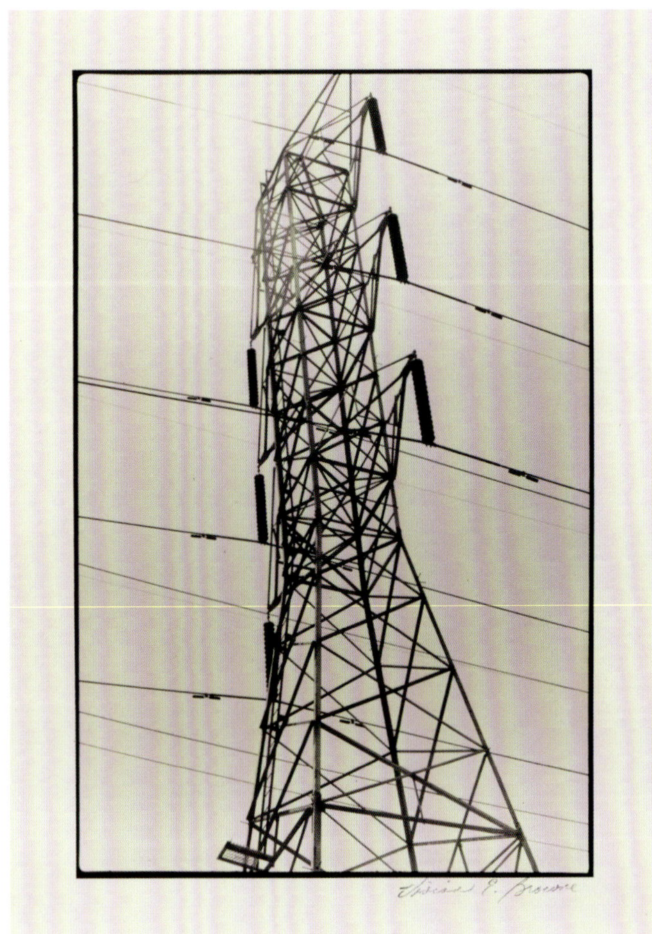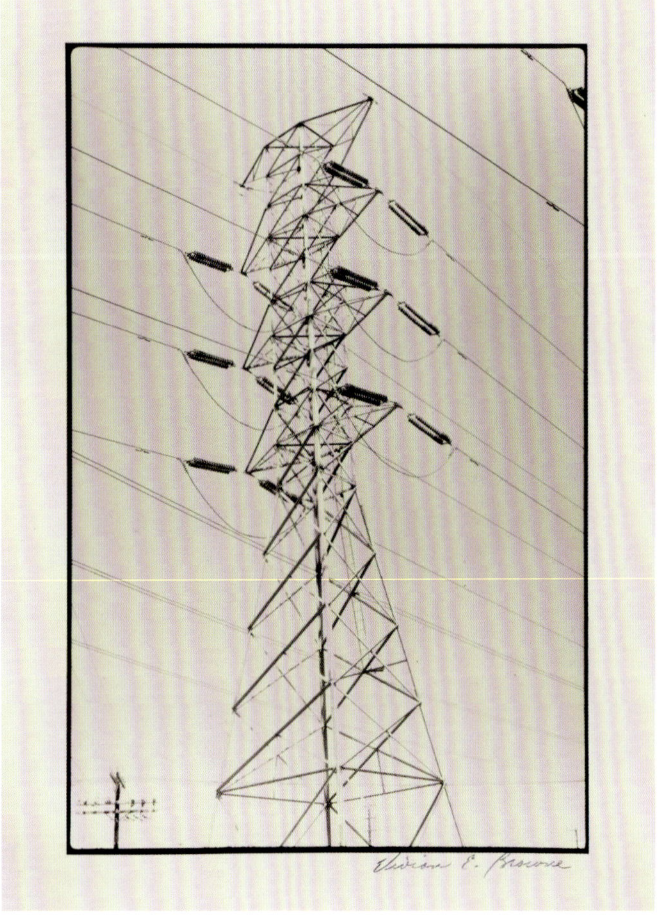

Plate 62
Untitled, c. 1990
Black and white photographs
14 × 11 inches
Adobe Krow Archives, CA
and RYAN LEE Gallery, NY

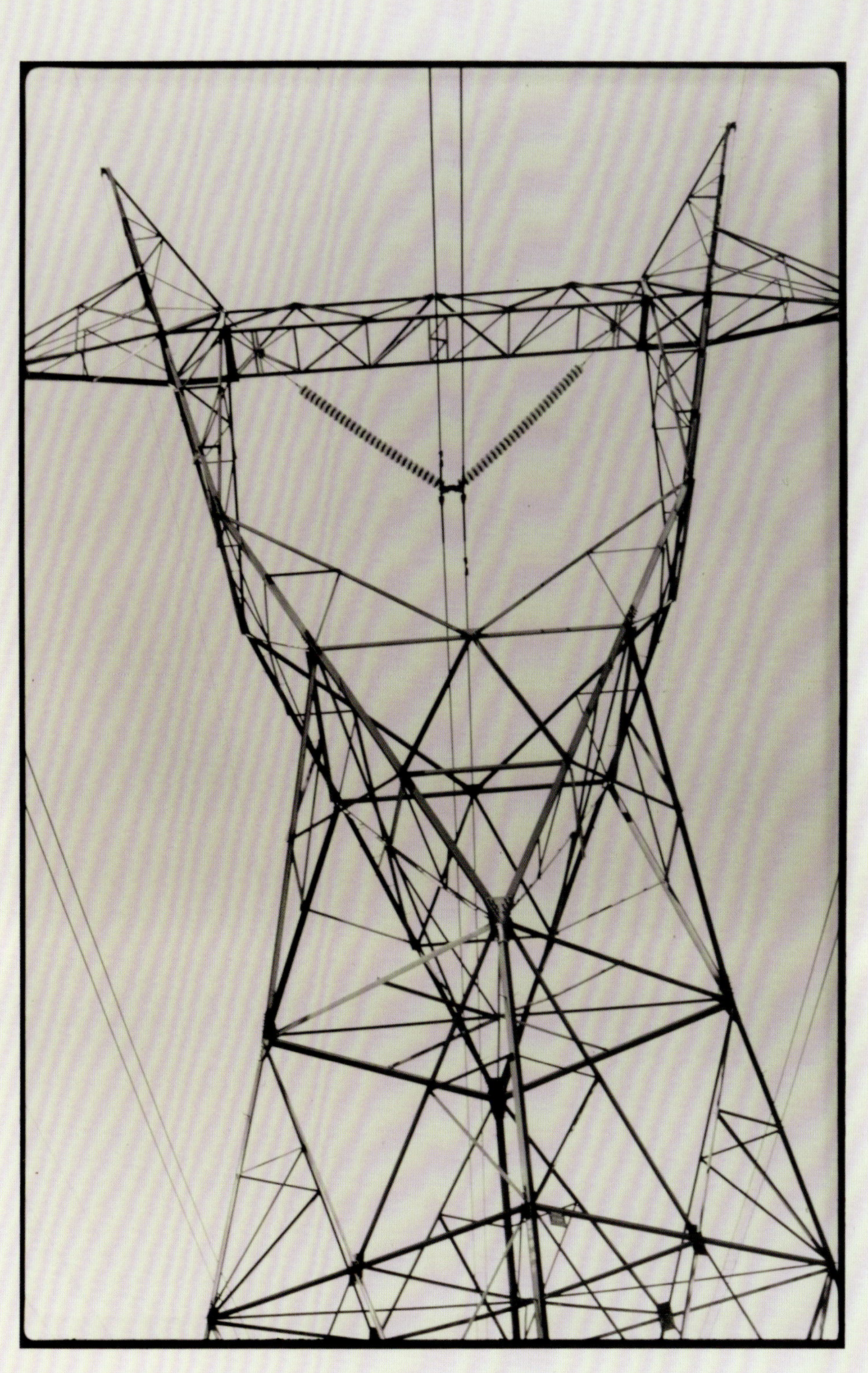

Notes

1   Vivian Browne. Oral history interview by Henri Ghent. July 1, 1968. Archives of American Art, Smithsonian Institution.

2   Lowery S. Sims, "Vivian Browne and William T. Williams," in *Vivian Browne/William T. Williams*, exhibition catalogue, The Jamaica Arts Center, New York, 1988.

3   Vivian Browne. Oral history interview by Henri Ghent. July 1, 1968. Archives of American Art, Smithsonian Institution.

4   Transcript of taped interview between Vivian Browne and James V. Hatch, the prominent academic of Black theater, and the husband of Camille Billops, in Browne's New York studio, 1972. Hatch-Billops Oral History of Black Culture series.

5   Ibid.

6   Archives of American Art Oral History, Vivian Browne, 1968.

7   Black Emergency Cultural Coalition statement, c. 1972.

8   Transcript taped interview, Browne and Hatch, 1972.

9   Mel Tapley, "1 to One art exhibition brings two different artists together," *Amsterdam News*, September 9, 1972.

10 May Stevens, "Vivian Browne: The Trees Speak," *Women Artists News* 12, no. 2 (June 1987): 28.

11 Emma Amos, interview with bell hooks, *Artists and Influence* 14 (1994): 33–57.

12 Quoted by May Stevens in Memorial Lecture, 1994.

13 Vivian Browne. Oral history interview by Henri Ghent. July 1, 1968. Archives of American Art, Smithsonian Institution.

14 The founding of the BECC is often cited with the protest that centered around the opening of the Metropolitan Museum's exhibition *Harlem on My Mind: Cultural Capital of Black America, 1900-1968* on January 16, 1969. This event was an important touchstone for the group, but the earlier exhibition galvanized many of the participating artists several months prior.

15 Transcript of taped interview between Vivian Browne and James V. Hatch in her New York studio, 1972. Hatch-Billops Oral History of Black Culture series.

16 See Grace Glueck, "Art Notes," *The New York Times*, January 31, 1971, Section D, p. 25.

17 See Grace Glueck, "15 of 75 Black Artists Leave As Whitney Exhibition Opens," *The New York Times*, April 6, 1971, p. 50.

18 For a more exhaustive detailing of this history, see Howard Singerman and Sarah Watson (eds.), *Acts of Art and Rebuttal in 1971*, exhibition catalogue, Hunter College Art Galleries, and Bertha and Karl Leubsdorf Art Gallery, New York, 2018.

19 Transcript taped interview, Browne and Hatch, 1972.

20 Vivian Browne. Oral history interview by Henri Ghent. July 1, 1968. Archives of American Art, Smithsonian Institution.

21 Lucy R. Lippard, in *Tradition and Conflict: Images of a Turbulent Decade 1963-1973*, curated by Dr. Mary Schmidt Campbell, exhibition catalogue, Studio Museum in Harlem, New York, 1985, p. 80.

22 *Black Artists in America*: A film produced by Oakley Holmes, Part 4, Interview with Vivian Browne, 1975.

23 Archives of American Art Oral History, Vivian Browne, 1968.

24 Transcript taped interview, Browne and Hatch, 1972.

25 Henri Ghent, *Afro-American Artists: Since 1950: An Exhibition of Paintings, Sculpture and Drawings*, exhibition catalogue, Brooklyn College, New York, 1969.

26 Doty was preparing for the exhibition *Black Artists in America* (1971), which was organized as a concession to the BECC in response to one of their demands that the Whitney have a show of Black artists.

27 "Vivian Browne, Painter, Printmaker, March 10, 1985, Interview between Vivian Browne and Emma Amos," *Artist and Influence*, eds Leo Hamalian and James V. Hatch (New York: Hatch-Billops Collection, 1986), p. 6.

28 The former included *Black Art Exhibition*, Wilson College, Chambersburg, PA (1968), and *Afro-American Artists: Since 1950* at Brooklyn College, both organized by Henri Ghent (1969); she received an invitation to participate in *Harlem:*

69 at the Studio Museum (1969) but did not end up submitting an artwork. The exhibition *USA…? 1971-72* at the Carnegie Institute in Pittsburgh, and *Blacks:USA:1973* at the New York Cultural Center were both organized by Benny Andrews.

29 Archives of American Art Oral History, Faith Ringgold, 1972.

30 Ibid.

31 Ibid.

32 Where We At manifesto, 1977.

33 Heresies Collective statement, 1977.

34 Ibid.

35 The magazine also featured Browne's own contribution of a visual essay recounting acts of racism and micro-aggressions experienced by the artist during her travels in Europe and elsewhere, as well as illustrations of Black women writers and activists for an essay by Michelle Cliff.

36 "Vivian Browne, Painter, Printmaker, March 10, 1985," p. 2.

37 See Sabra Moore, *Openings: A Memoir from the Women's Art Movement, New York City 1970-1992* (New York: New Village Press, 2016).

38 Vivian Browne artist statement, April 20, 1986.

39 "Vivian Browne, Painter, Printmaker, March 10, 1985," p. 9.

40 "Vivian Browne, Painter, Printmaker, March 10, 1985," p. 8.

41 Transcript of taped interview between Vivian Browne and James V. Hatch in her New York studio, 1972. Hatch-Billops Oral History of Black Culture series.

42 In her visual essay "Siftings," published in the 1982 edition of *Heresies* titled "Racism is the Issue," Browne chronicles some of the racist encounters she experienced while traveling in Europe, Cuba, Israel, and Maryland (p. 53).

43 See Larry Neal, "The Black Arts Movement," *The Drama Review* 12, no. 4 (Summer 1968): 29.

44 Barbara Jones Hogu [sic], "Inaugurating AfriCOBRA: History Philosophy, and Aesthetics," *Nka: Journal of Contemporary African Art* 30, no. 1 (Spring 2012): 93.

45 Transcript taped interview, Browne and Hatch, 1972.

46 Ibid.

47 Ibid.

48 Ibid.

49 See Chika Okeke-Agulu, "The Art Society and the Making of Postcolonial Modernism in Nigeria," *South Atlantic Quarterly* 109, no. 3 (Summer 2010): 520.

50 Ibid.: 523–25.

51 Unfortunately, in the information the present author has seen to date, Browne does not mention her interactions with the creative community in Ibadan or other sites in Nigeria and Ghana.

52 Transcript taped interview, Browne and Hatch, 1972.

53 Ibid.

54 "Vivian Browne, Painter, Printmaker, March 10, 1985," p. 8.

55 LeRoi Jones (Amiri Imamu Baraka), *Black Music* (New York: Da Capo Press, 1998), p. 181.

56 *Jus' Jass: Correlations of Painting and Afro-American Classical Music*, exhibition catalogue, Kenkeleba Gallery, New York, 1983.

57 Jones Hogu [sic]: 94–95.

58 "Vivian Browne, Painter, Printmaker, March 10, 1985," p. 9.

59 Browne 1973 television interview, regarding the opening of *African Memories*, by reporter Frank Graham of Channel 6, Providence, Rhode Island. Adobe Krow Archives, Los Angeles.

60 See Theophus "Thee" Smith, "Globalization of Africana Aesthetics," in *Ashé: Ritual Poetics in African Diasporic Expression*, ed. Paul Carter Harrison, Michael D. Harris, and Pellom McDaniels III (Oxford: Taylor & Francis Group, 2022). ProQuest Ebook Central, accessed May 5, 2024.

61 Vivian Browne artist statement, undated, Adobe Krow Archives, Los Angeles, California.

62 Vivian Browne. Oral history interview by Henri Ghent. July 1, 1968. Archives of American Art, Smithsonian Institution.

63 Artist statement, undated.

64 Archives of American Art Oral History, Vivian Browne, 1968.

65 Ibid.

66 "Vivian Browne, Painter, Printmaker, March 10, 1985," p. 9.

67 See Wilfred R. Bion, *Four Discussions with W.R. Bion*, ed. Meg Harris Williams (London: Harris Meltzer Trust, 1978), p. 89.

68 Archives of American Art Oral History, Vivian Browne, 1968.

69 Ibid.

70 Ibid.

71 Ibid.

72 Vivian Browne, interview by Cecilia Davis, *Analogue*, NBC, 1969.

73 Archives of American Art Oral History, Vivian Browne, 1968.

74 See Bion, *Four Discussions*, p. 32.

75 "Vivian Browne, Painter, Printmaker, March 10, 1985," p. 9.

76 Archives of American Art Oral History, Vivian Browne, 1968.

77 "Vivian Browne, Painter, Printmaker, March 10, 1985," p. 9.

78 Archives of American Art Oral History, Vivian Browne, 1968.

79 Browne to Camille Billops, quoted in Billops, "Joe Overstreet, Painter Playwright," January 16, 1976, p. 10.

Sims:

2 Mary Robinson in *Women Artists Series, Douglass [C]ollege 1982–1983*, State University of New Jersey, Rutgers Campus at New Brunswick, p. 9.

3 Elenore Welles, "Exploring the Forest's Strengths," *Artweek* (September 21, 1985), p. 4.

4 Collen Fink, "Browne Exhibits Tenth Solo," *The Daily Targum* (March 4, 1987).

5 I evoke here the alternative feminist designation coined by the premier black writer, Alice Walker.

Image Credits

Pages with uncaptioned images:

p. 4 *The Sound Itself is All #59*, 1984 (Adobe Krow Archives, CA and RYAN LEE Gallery, NY; detail of plate 57)

p. 6 *Little Men #4*, c. 1967 (Collection of James Keith Brown and Eric G. Diefenbach; detail of plate 22)

p. 8 *Diversities*, 1973 (From the collection of Kenny and Elena Marks, courtesy RYAN LEE Gallery; detail of plate 36)

p. 36 *New Yorkers No. 27*, 1967 (Adobe Krow Archives, CA and RYAN LEE Gallery, NY; detail of plate 12)

p. 62 *Bini Apron*, 1973 (The Phillips Collection; detail of plate 35)

p. 92 *Candy Memoriam*, 1980 (Adobe Krow Archives, CA and RYAN LEE Gallery, NY; detail of plate 51)

p. 97 *San Joaquin/Diaresis*, 1992 (Wadsworth Atheneum Museum of Art; detail of plate 60)

p. 109 *Metasequoia #13*, 1987 (Adobe Krow Archives, CA and RYAN LEE Gallery, NY; detail of plate 58)

p. 129 *Untitled (Man in Mountain)*, c. 1974 (Adobe Krow Archives, CA and RYAN LEE Gallery, NY; detail of plate 47)

p. 130 *New Yorkers No. 11*, 1966 (Adobe Krow Archives, CA and RYAN LEE Gallery, NY; detail of plate 10)

p. 133 *Ibeji II*, 1972 (Detroit Institute of Arts; detail of plate 31)

p. 135 *Shango Kingdom*, 1972 (Adobe Krow Archives, CA and RYAN LEE Gallery, NY; detail of plate 29)

All artworks are © Vivian Browne, courtesy of Adobe Krow Archives, CA and RYAN LEE Gallery, NY unless otherwise noted. Archival images are courtesy of Adobe Krow Archives, CA and RYAN LEE Gallery, NY unless otherwise noted. Photographer is noted when known.

Photo by Mary Ellen Andrews. Courtesy of the Hatch-Billops Collection, NY and RYAN LEE Gallery, NY.
p. 14 (right)

Photo by Mary Ellen Andrews. Courtesy of the May Stevens and Rudolf Baranik Foundation, NY and RYAN LEE Gallery, NY.
p. 16 (bottom right)

Photo likely by Mary Ellen Andrews. Courtesy of the May Stevens and Rudolf Baranik Foundation, NY and RYAN LEE Gallery, NY.
p. 15 (right)

© 2024 Artists Rights Society (ARS), New York
p. 41 (left)

Photo by Camille Billops. Courtesy of the Hatch-Billops Collection, NY and RYAN LEE Gallery, NY.
pp. 14 (top left), 14 (bottom left), 19 (bottom right), 27

Photo by Camille Billops
p. 43

Photo by Jeanie Black
pp. 16 (left column, top right), 42

© Courtesy of the Hatch-Billops Collection, NY and RYAN LEE Gallery, NY
pp. 17 (left), 17 (right), 18 (top left), 18 (right), 19 (top right)

Estate of Barbara Jones-Hogu. Courtesy of Lusenhop Fine Art.
p. 66

© The Museum of Modern Art, New York
pp. 54, 55

© The Phillips Collection
pp. 62, 64 (right), 80, 83

© Allen Phillips/Wadsworth Atheneum
p. 122

© Courtesy of Richland Library, Columbia, SC
p. 12 (left)

© 2021 Faith Ringgold / ARS member, photo courtesy ACA Galleries, New York
p. 39 (right)

Courtesy of RYAN LEE Gallery, NY
pp. 21, 46, 48, 62, 80

© Art & Artifacts Division, Schomburg Center for Research in Black Culture, The New York Public Library, New York
pp. 69, 77

© May Stevens; courtesy of the May Stevens and Rudolf Baranik Foundation and RYAN LEE Gallery, NY
p. 40

© Photo by Jan van Raay
pp. 38, 39 (left)

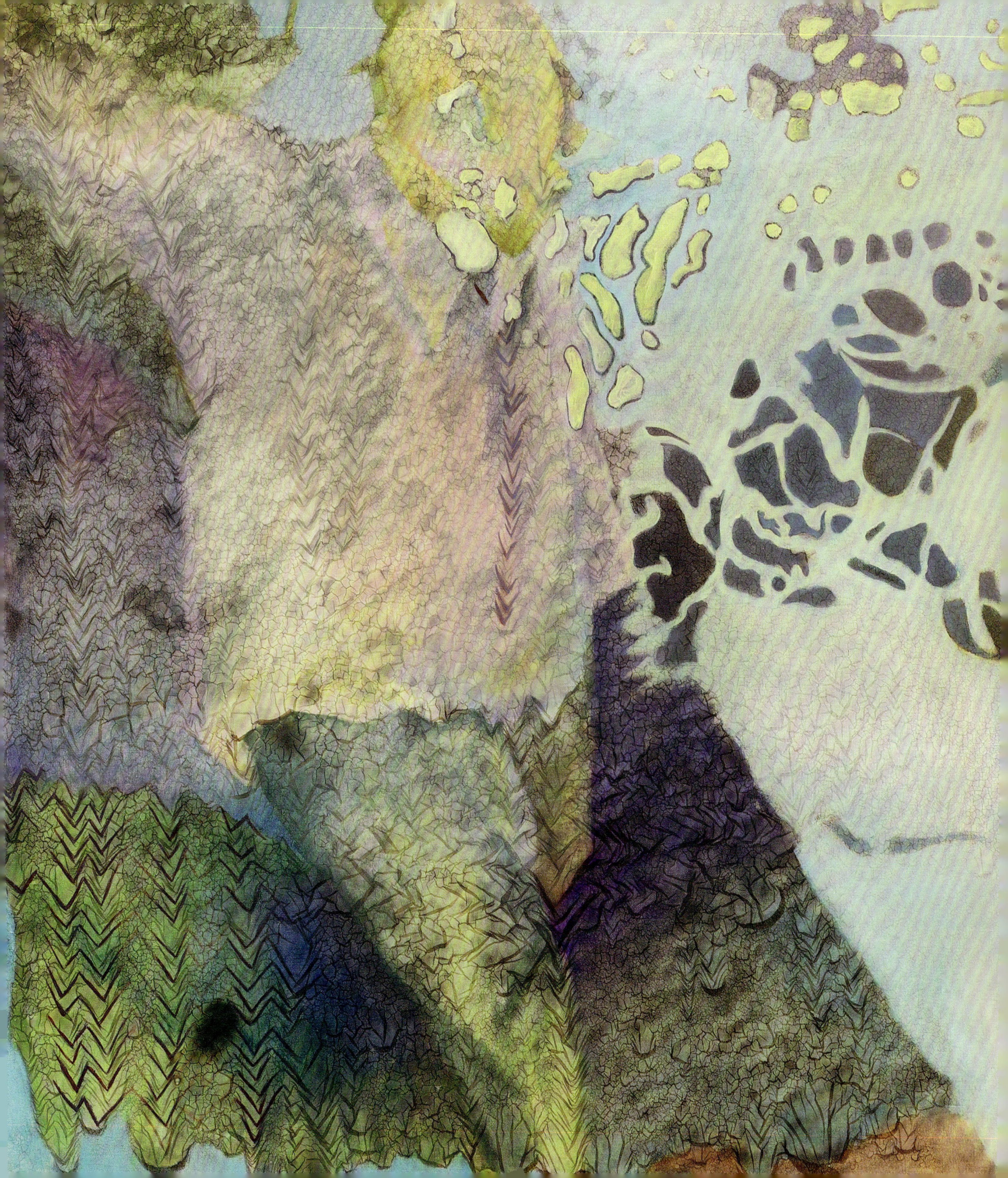

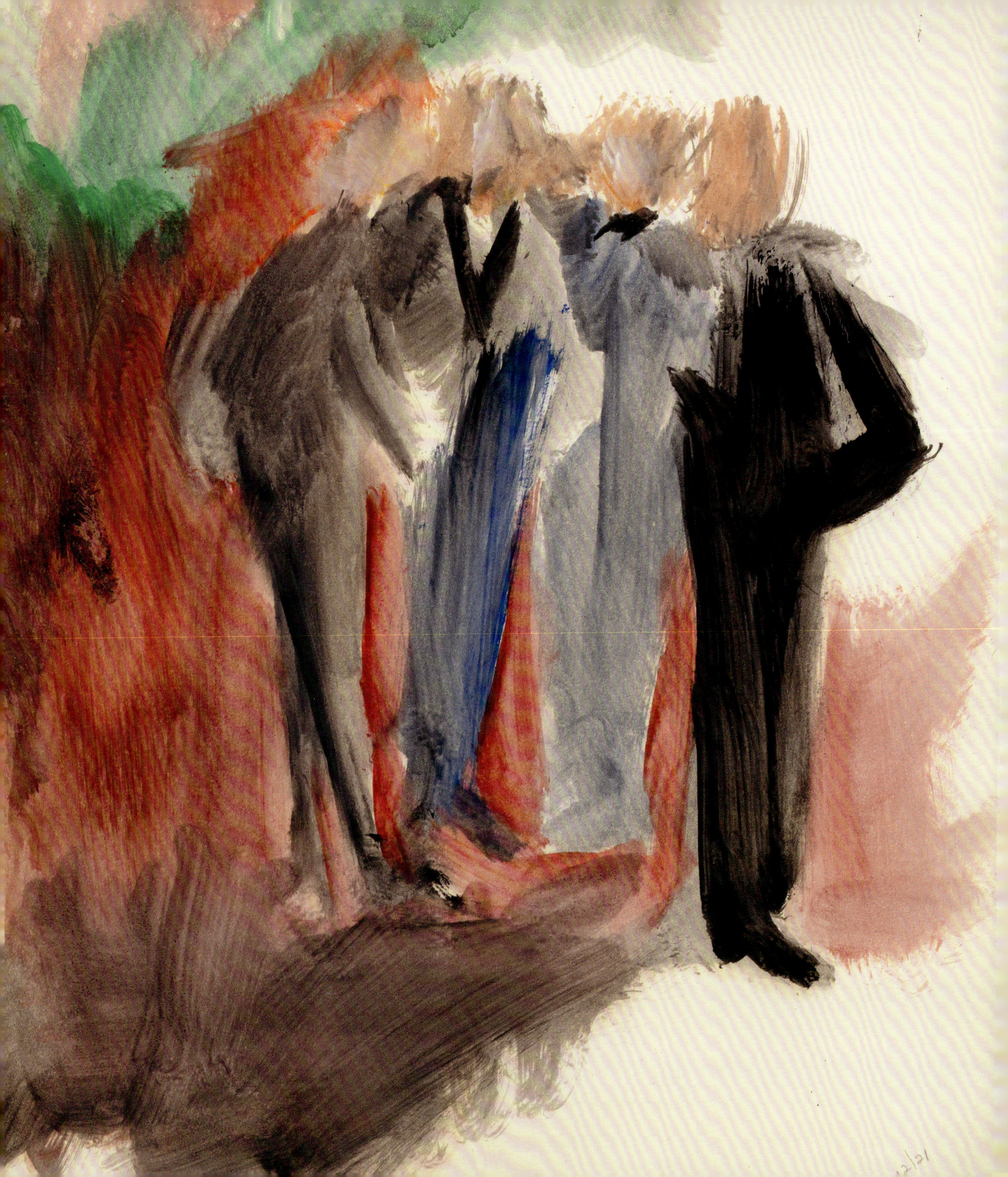

List of Works

All works are Courtesy of Adobe Krow Archives, CA and RYAN LEE Gallery, NY unless otherwise noted

Works of art in the exhibition are subject to change

Mother, 1961
Oil on canvas
42 ½ × 36 ¾ inches
Plate 1

Vivian (Self-portrait), 1965
Oil on canvas
31 ½ × 25 3/8 inches
Private Collector, Delaware,
courtesy RYAN LEE Gallery
Plate 2

Nathan Barrett Playwright, c. 1960
Pastel on paper
20 × 26 ¾ inches
The Larry D. and Brenda A. Thompson Collection
of African American Art
Plate 3

Nude, c. 1960
Pastel on paper
31 × 37 inches
The Larry D. and Brenda A. Thompson Collection
of African American Art
Plate 4

Camille Billops, 1965
Oil on canvas
50 × 44 inches
Plate 5

New Yorkers No. 12, c. 1965
Oil on paper
24 × 17 ¾ inches
Plate 6

New Yorkers No. 42, 1965
Oil on paper
24 ¾ × 17 ¾ inches
Plate 7

New Yorkers No. 34, c. 1965
Oil on paper
23 ¾ × 17 ½ inches
Plate 8

New Yorkers No. 14, c. 1966
Oil on paper
24 × 17 ¾ inches
Plate 9

New Yorkers No. 11, 1966
Oil on paper
24 × 17 ¾ inches
Plate 10

New Yorkers No. 57, 1966
Oil on paper
24 × 17 5/8 inches
Plate 11

New Yorkers No. 27, 1967
Oil on paper
23 ¾ × 17 1/8 inches
Plate 12

New Yorkers No. 22, c. 1967
Oil on paper
23 ¾ × 17 1/8 inches
Plate 13

Seven Deadly Sins, c. 1968
Oil on canvas
59 × 112 inches
Plate 14

**Untitled (Little Man
with Arms Crossed),** c. 1967
Oil on canvas
36 × 20 inches
Baz Family Collection, Colorado,
courtesy RYAN LEE Gallery
Plate 15

Wall Street Dancer, 1968
Oil on canvas
54 × 48 inches
Collection of Beth Rudin DeWoody
Plate 16

Two Men, 1969
Oil on canvas
61 × 48 inches
Baz Family Collection, Colorado,
courtesy RYAN LEE Gallery
Plate 17

Wall Street Jump, 1969
Oil on canvas
59 ¾ × 46 inches
Plate 18

Little Men #12, c. 1967
Oil on paper
23 ¾ × 17 ¾ inches
Plate 19

Little Men #3, c. 1967
Oil on paper
23 ¾ × 17 ¾ inches
Plate 20

Little Men #77, 1967
Oil on paper
23 ¾ × 17 1/8 inches
Plate 21

Little Men #4, c. 1967
Oil on paper
23 ¾ × 17 ¾ inches
Collection of James Keith Brown and Eric G.
Diefenbach, courtesy RYAN LEE Gallery
Plate 22

Little Men #7, 1967
Oil on paper
23 ¾ × 17 1/8 inches
The Museum of Modern Art, New York. Acquired
through the generosity of Marie-Josée and Henry
R. Kravis, 2020
Plate 23

Little Men #86, 1967
Oil on paper
23 ¾ × 17 1/8 inches
The Museum of Modern Art, New York. Acquired
through the generosity of Marie-Josée and Henry
R. Kravis, 2020
Plate 24

Little Men #30 / I Had a Dream,
1967
Oil on paper
17 1/8 × 24 inches
Plate 25

Little Men #102, c. 1967
Oil on paper
23 ¾ × 17 1/8 inches
Private Collection; Promised gift on long-term
loan to the Minneapolis Institute of Art
Plate 26

Little Men #78, c. 1967
Oil on paper
23 ¾ × 17 ¾ inches
Plate 27

Warning, c. 1970
Etching
20 ¾ × 27 ½ inches
Plate 28

Shango Kingdom, 1972
Acrylic on canvas
17 ½ × 48 ¾ inches
Plate 29

Umbrella Plant, 1971
Oil on canvas
48 ¾ × 40 ¾ inches
Plate 30

Ibeji II, 1972
Acrylic on canvas
48 ¾ × 48 ¾ inches
Detroit Institute of Arts, Museum Purchase, Ernest
and Rosemarie Kanzler Foundation Fund, 2024.7
Plate 31

The Chief's Attendant, c. 1972
Acrylic on canvas
60 ¾ × 50 ¾ inches
Plate 32

Benin Equestrian, 1973
Oil on canvas
61 × 51 inches
Art & Artifacts Division, Schomburg Center for
Research in Black Culture, The New York Public
Library, Astor, Lenox and Tilden Foundations
Plate 33

The Gathering, 1973
Acrylic on canvas
55 × 65 inches
Collection of William O. Perkins, III and Lara Perkins,
courtesy RYAN LEE Gallery
Plate 34

Bini Apron, 1973
Acrylic on canvas
48 ¾ × 50 ¾ inches
The Phillips Collection; Gift of Adobe Krow
Archives for Vivian Browne, Los Angeles, 2024
Plate 35

Diversities, 1973
Acrylic on canvas
54 ¾ × 54 ¾ inches
From the collection of Kenny and Elena Marks,
courtesy RYAN LEE Gallery
Plate 36

Tribes Woman, 1971
Watercolor and ink on paper
19 ¾ × 14 inches
Collection of Ruth E. Pachman and Donald T. Fallati,
courtesy RYAN LEE Gallery
Plate 37

Untitled #100, c. 1971
Ink and wash on paper
20 ½ × 13 ¾ inches
The Phillips Collection, Gift of Brenda A.
and Larry D. Thompson, 2024
Plate 38

Africa Sketch #1, 1971
Watercolor and ink on paper
18 ¾ × 24 ¾ inches
Plate 39

Africa Sketch #2, 1971
Watercolor and ink on paper
18 ¾ × 24 ¾ inches
Plate 40

The Bathers, 1971
Gouache, ink, and pastel on paper
19 ¾ × 28 inches
Plate 41

*Nigeria (Self-portrait with Floyd
Coleman)*, 1971
Watercolor and ink on paper
17 ¾ × 24 inches
Plate 42

Egypt 71, 1971
Watercolor, pastel, and ink on paper
20 ½ × 27 ¼ inches
Plate 43

Equestrian, 1971
Etching and aquatint
22 3/8 × 14 15/16 inches
Plate 44

The Prisoner, 1972
Acrylic on canvas
45 ½ × 42 inches
Plate 45

For You, 1974
Oil on canvas
46 ¾ × 50 ¾ inches
Plate 46

Untitled (Man in Mountain), c. 1974
Oil on canvas
40 ¾ × 34 ¾ inches
Plate 47

Sea Forms Abstract, c. 1978
Oil on canvas
25 × 27 inches
Plate 48

Ocean Forms I, 1978
Pastel on paper
40 7/8 × 58 5/8 inches
Plate 49

Shanghai Morning, 1980
Oil on silk and canvas
56 × 40 inches
Plate 50

Candy Memoriam, 1980
Oil on silk and canvas
56 ½ × 38 ¼ inches
Plate 51

Clear Particles Floating Free, 1982
Acrylic on silk and pastel on paper
60 × 132 inches
Plate 52

Adobe I, 1987
Woodcut on paper
40 × 27 inches
Plate 53

Adobe II, 1987
Woodcut on paper
39 ½ × 26 ½ inches
Plate 54

Adobe III, 1987
Woodcut on paper
39 ¼ × 26 ¾ inches
Plate 55

Oaks, 1984
Acrylic on canvas
61 × 126 inches
Plate 56

The Sound Itself is All #59, 1984
Oil on canvas
38 ½ × 169 ½ inches
Plate 57

Metasequoia #13, 1987
Oil on canvas
70 × 148 inches
Plate 58

Semper Virens, 1989
Oil on canvas
68 × 160 ½ inches
Plate 59

San Joaquin/Diaresis, 1992
Oil on canvas
80 × 68 inches
Wadsworth Atheneum Museum of Art, Hartford,
CT. The Ella Gallup Sumner and Mary Catlin
Sumner Collection
Plate 60

All Trace, c. 1985
Oil on canvas
42 × 48 inches
Plate 61

Untitled, c. 1990
Black and white photographs
(mounted under glass, unframed)
14 × 11 inches each
Plate 62

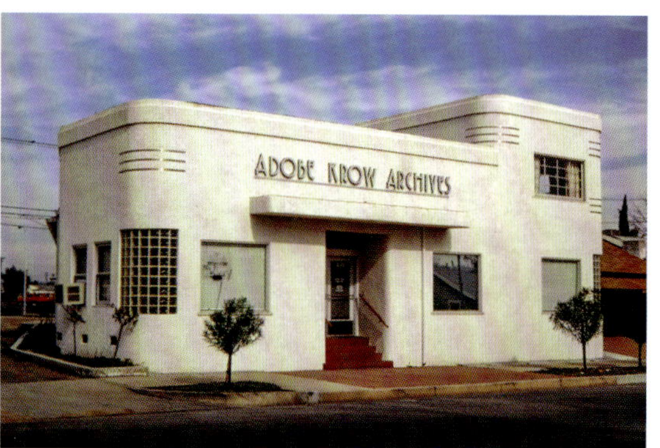

Exterior view of Adobe Krow Archives,
Bakersfield, California, 1997

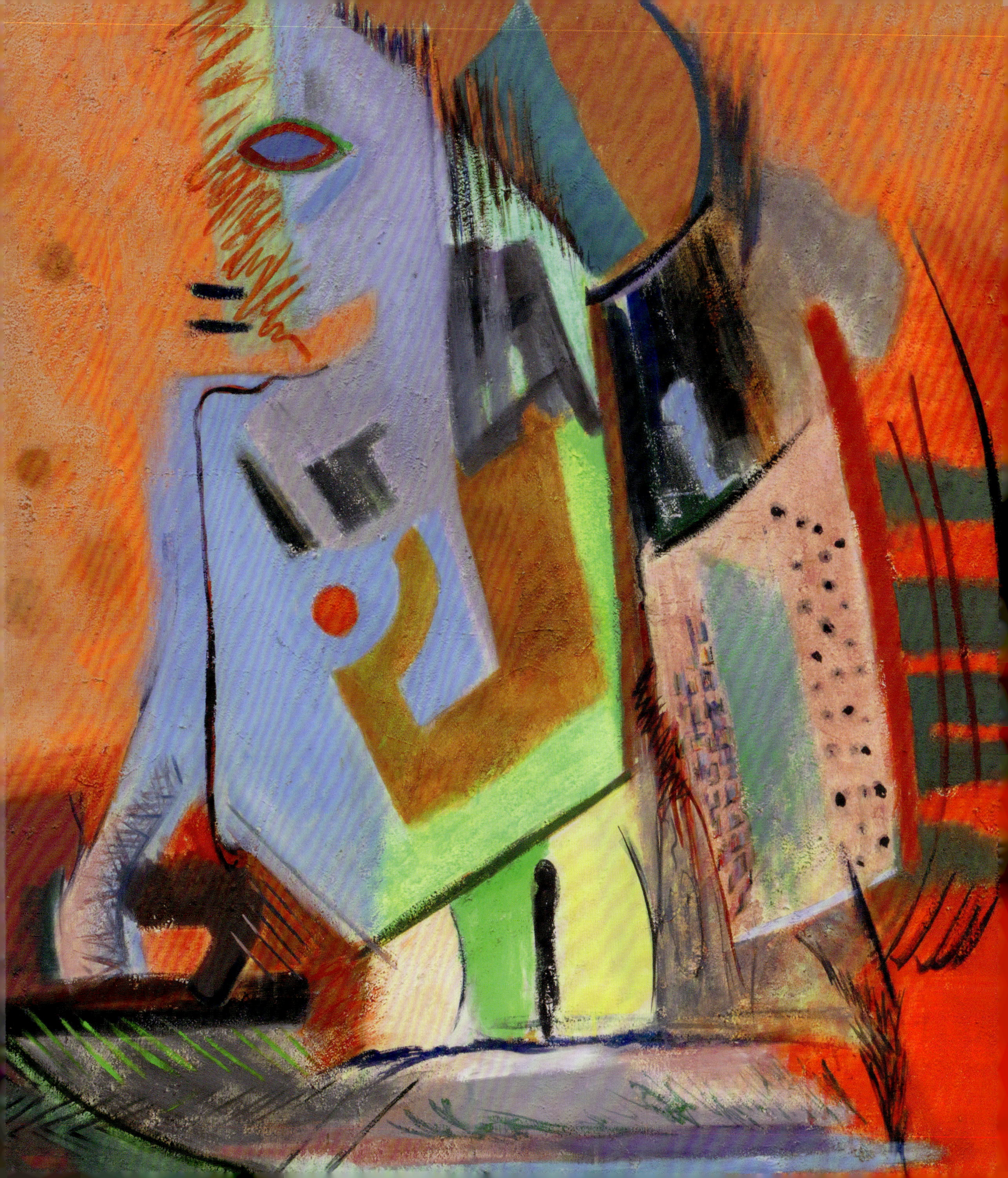

List of Lenders

Adobe Krow Archives, Los Angeles, CA
Collection of Beth Rudin DeWoody
Collection of James Keith Brown and Eric G. Diefenbach
Collection of Kenny and Elena Marks
Collection of Ruth E. Pachman and Donald T. Fallati
Collection of William O. Perkins, III and Lara Perkins
Colleen and Javier Baz
Detroit Institute of Arts
Private Collection, Minneapolis, MN
RYAN LEE Gallery, New York, NY
Schomburg Center for Research in Black Culture, The New York Public Library, New York, NY
The Larry D. and Brenda A. Thompson Collection of African American Art
The Museum of Modern Art, New York
Wadsworth Atheneum Museum of Art

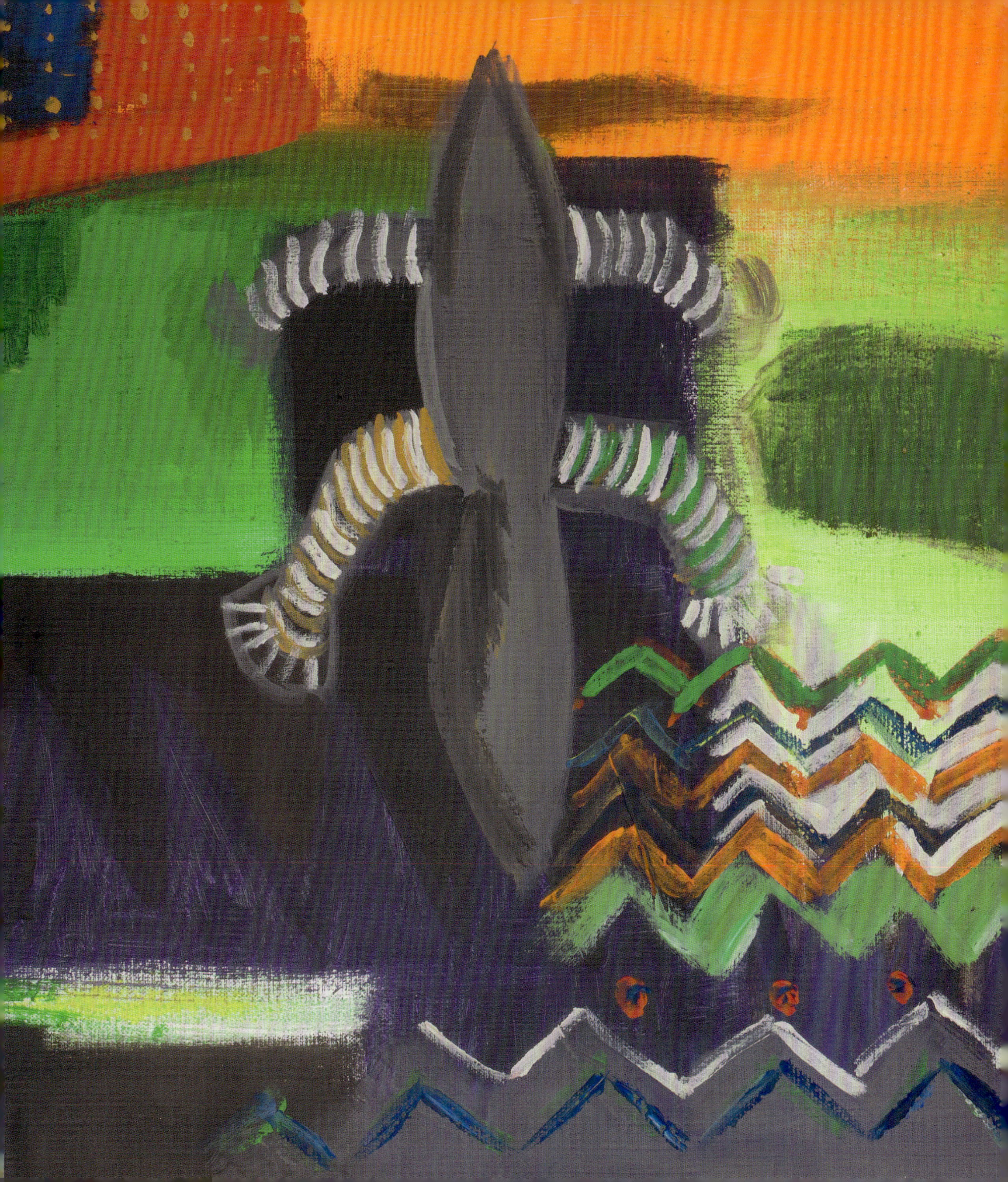

The catalog accompanies the exhibition *Vivian Browne: My Kind of Protest* on display at the Contemporary Arts Center, Cincinnati, OH from January 31–May 25, 2025 and at The Phillips Collection, Washington DC from June 28–September 28, 2025

The exhibition was co-organized by The Phillips Collection and the Contemporary Arts Center curated by Adrienne L. Childs and Amara Antilla

First published in 2025 by
The Phillips Collection
1600 21st Street, NW
Washington DC, 20009
phillipscollection.org

in association with GILES
An imprint of D Giles Limited
66 High Street
Lewes, BN7 1XG, UK
gilesltd.com

ISBN 978-1-913875-86-2 [hardcover edition only]

Dimensions are given in inches. Height precedes width.

For The Phillips Collection:
Jonathan P. Binstock, Vradenburg Director & CEO

Grace McCormick, Curatorial Assistant

For the Contemporary Arts Center:
Christina Vassallo, Alice & Harris Weston Director
Rebecca Roman-Sutton, Director of Exhibitions

For D Giles Ltd:
Copy-edited and proofread by Jenny Wilson
Designed by Ocky Murray
Printed and bound in China

All images are courtesy of Adobe Krow Archives, CA and RYAN LEE Gallery, NY unless otherwise noted.

LCCN 2024914604

Front cover *For You*, 1974 (Adobe Krow Archives, CA and RYAN LEE Gallery, NY; detail of plate 46)

Back cover Vivian Browne in her studio, 1974 (Adobe Krow Archives, CA and RYAN LEE Gallery, NY; detail of p. 27)

p. 2 Vivian Browne in her studio with *Little Men and Africa Series* (Adobe Krow Archives, CA and RYAN LEE Gallery, NY; detail), 1974

Major support for this exhibition tour and associated programs has been provided by the Mellon Foundation, the National Endowment for the Arts, Terra Foundation for American Art, and the Andy Warhol Foundation for the Visual Arts.

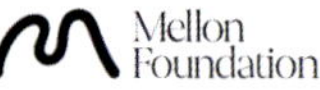

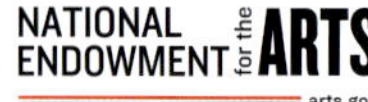

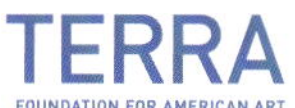

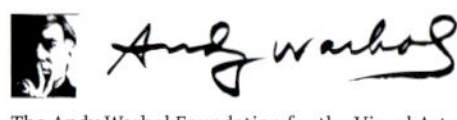

The presentation of *Vivian Browne: My Kind of Protest* at the Contemporary Arts Center is supported by the Greater Cincinnati Foundation and research for this exhibition was supported by the Emily Hall Tremaine Foundation.

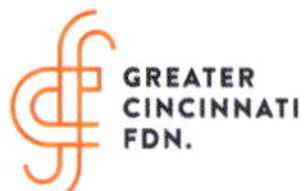

The presentation of *Vivian Browne: My Kind of Protest* at The Phillips Collection is generously supported by Reid Walker.